The Premise and the Promise: Free Trade in the Americas

THE PREMISE AND THE PROMISE: FREE TRADE IN THE AMERICAS

Sylvia Saborio and contributors:

Peter Morici
José Manuel Salazar –Xirinachs
Eduardo Lizano
Richard G. Lipsey
Refik Erzan
Alexander Yeats
Craig VanGrasstek
Gustavo Vega
Andrea Butelmann
Alicia Frohmann
DeLisle Worrell
Alberto Pascó –Font
Roberto Bouzas

Transaction Publishers
New Brunswick (USA) and Oxford (UK)

ISBN: 1-56000-060-0 (cloth)
ISBN: 1-56000-619-6 (paper)
Printed in the United States of America

Library of Congress Cataloging-in-Publication Data

Saborio, Sylvia.
    The Premise and the Promise: Free Trade in the Americas/Sylvia Saborio and contributors.

(U.S.-Third World Policy Perspectives: No. 18)
    1. Free trade—United States. 2. Free trade—Latin America. 3. United States—Commerce—Latin America. 4. Latin America—Commerce—United States. I. Saborio Alvarado, Sylvia. II. Morici, Peter. III. Series: U.S.-Third World Policy Perspectives, No. 18

HF1756.P7   1992   382'.097308—dc20   92-25195

ISBN: 1-56000-060-0 (cloth)
ISBN: 1-56000-619-6 (paper)

Director of Publications: Christine E. Contee
Publications Editor: Jacqueline Edlund-Braun
Edited by Kathleen A. Lynch
Cover and book design by Tim Kenney Design, Inc.

Contents

Foreword   ix

I.   Overview
     The Long and Winding Road from Anchorage to Patagonia
     Sylvia Saborio   3

II. Summaries of Chapter Recommendations   35

III. A Western Hemisphere Free Trade Area

     1. Free Trade in the Americas: A U.S. Perspective
         Peter Morici   53

             The Enterprise for the Americas Initiative   53
             U.S. Commercial Relations with Latin America   56
             Obstacles to Lifting Trade Barriers   61
             GATT, Regionalism, and U.S. Policy   63
             Regionalism and U.S. National Interest   66
             Policy Recommendations   69

     2. Free Trade in the Americas: A Latin American
         Perspective
         José Manuel Salazar-Xirinachs with Eduardo Lizano . . .   75

             Costs and Benefits of Free Trade   76
             Latin American Negotiating Objectives   79
             Macroeconomic Implications of Trade Liberalization . .   84
             Relative Reciprocity and Transitional Measures   87
             Conclusions   90

     3. Getting There: The Path to a Western Hemisphere Free
         Trade Area and Its Structure
         Richard G. Lipsey   95

             Is it a Pipe Dream?   95
             Do We Really Want a WHFTA?   96
             Preconditions for a WHFTA   104
             The Institutional Structure   105
             Conclusions   114

4. **U.S.-Latin American Free Trade Areas:**
    Some Empirical Evidence
    Refik Erzan and Alexander Yeats 117

    Introduction 117
    Characteristics of Intra-American Trade 117
    Likely Effects of FTAs on Latin American Exports .. 120
    Simulation Results for U.S.-Latin America FTAs..... 122
    Potential Effects on Raw Material Processing 124
    Trade Barriers Facing the United States in
        Latin America................................. 126
    Summary and Conclusions 128
    Annex: Dismantling Protection in Sensitive Sectors .. 146

IV. **Subregional Free Trade Agreements**

5. **The North American Free Trade Agreement:**
    A Regional Model?
    Craig VanGrasstek and Gustavo Vega................ 157

    U.S. and Mexican Perspectives on the NAFTA 158
    Traditional Issues: Trade in Goods 160
    New Issues 164
    Consultations and Dispute Settlement 167
    Environmental and Labor Issues................... 170
    Accession to the NAFTA 172
    Conclusions and Recommendations 175

6. **U.S.-Chile Free Trade**
    Andrea Butelmann and Alicia Frohmann 179

    Trends in Chilean Trade Policy 180
    Patterns of Trade with Prospective NAFTA Members. 183
    Issues for U.S.-Chilean Negotiation 188
    Conclusions 191

7. **U.S.-Central America Free Trade**
    Sylvia Saborio 195

    Central America's Trade Profile 196
    The Challenge of Trade Liberalization 202
    Free Trade with the United States? 210
    Conclusions and Recommendations 214

8. **U.S.-Caricom Free Trade**
    DeLisle Worrell 217

    External Economic Relations of Caricom 218
    A Free Trade Area and Caribbean Economic
        Development 222
    The Desirability of the Free Trade Area 224
    Issues for Negotiation 225
    Caribbean Prospects Inside a North American
        Free Trade Area 227
    Conclusions and Recommedations 229

9. **U.S.-Andean Pact Free Trade**
    Alberto Pascó-Font and Sylvia Saborio 233

    Recent Developments and Outlook 233
    U.S.-Andean Pact Trade Relations 237
    U.S.-Andean Free Trade: A Preliminary Assessment . 241
    Conclusions and Recommendations 245

10. **U.S.-Mercosur Free Trade**
    Roberto Bouzas 249

    Economic Integration in the Southern Cone: Record,
        Challenges, and Prospects 249
    U.S.-Mercosur Trade and Trade-Policy Issues:
        An Overview 253
    Incentives and Implications of a U.S.-Mercosur FTA:
        A Preliminary Assessment 261
    Summary and Recommendations 265

Appendix: Membership of Selected Regional Trade Agreements .. 275

About the Overseas Development Council 277
About the Authors 280

Foreword

The 1990s will be a new era in international politics: the Cold War has ended; Europe and Japan have emerged as challengers to U.S. global economic preeminance. In the developing world, varying rates of development progress have led to growing differentiation among countries. As a result, the old neat divisions between east and west and north and south that characterized most of the post-World War II period have broken down.

It is not yet clear what will replace the Cold War as the organizing principle of U.S. foreign policy, nor is it clear how the United States will seek to exercise leadership in a world in which economic interests demand priority and where it is only first among equals. Yet, even before a new world order has been fully articulated, a rebalancing of old relationships has began to take place.

One thing is clear. The 1990s are not likely to be a period of grand global bargains that leads to a "new" Bretton Woods system or a "new international economic order." It is, however, likely to be marked by a new form of multilateralism focused on particular regions or designed to address important global problems. This new "functional multilateralism" will transcend the traditional boundaries of north and south and seek to involve countries with common interests.

One of the more interesting and surprising developments in this regard is the Western Hemisphere's growing interest in closer economic association. The rapprochement between the United States and the Latin American and Caribbean countries can only be understood as the result of new forces driving a redefinition of U.S. foreign policy interests and Latin America's remarkable rejection of authoritarian governments and statist development models. The shift to open societies and open markets is welcome, but their durability is not guaranteed.

These shifts have led to the imminent creation of a North American Free Trade Area encompassing the United States, Canada, and Mexico and to the broader vision of hemispheric partnership outlined in President Bush's Enterprise for the Americas Initiative. Both proposals imply a major change in inter-American relations from the patterns of the 1960s to a vision that reflects the realities of the twenty-first century. However, they must be seen not only as trade proposals but as a broader developmental response to the shift to free societies and free markets that has swept the hemisphere. Democracy and market-oriented economic systems remain fragile developments; if they are to endure, Latin American governments must have access to markets, particularly in the United States, and must be able to attract sufficient investment capital to restore rates of economic growth and deal with long-standing social inequities.

This eighteenth volume in ODC's *U.S.-Third World Policy Perspectives* series focuses on innovative trade proposals that are at the heart of the Enterprise for the Americas Initiative. It is assumed that the North American Free Trade Area is a reality. The analysis therefore examines the rationale, feasibility, and implications of establishing free trade areas between the United States and various countries and subregional groups in the hemisphere. It also highlights the special issues that arise from the vast disparity in size and stage of development between the United States and prospective regional trade partners, as well as the problems posed by the piecemeal approach to regional integration. Finally, the authors make recommendations regarding the best approach for liberalizing trade in the hemisphere.

The Premise and the Promise: Free Trade in the Americas provides a timely and useful first cut at the broad set of issues posed by the new hemispheric trade agenda. Moreover, it presents a wide range of perspectives on those issues by drawing heavily on the intellectual contribution of scholars and policymakers from throughout the hemisphere. ODC hopes to build on the success of this collaboration to establish an intellectual bridge between Washington and Latin America to analyze and discuss salient issues in the evolving hemispheric agenda.

The director of the project, Sylvia Saborio, has served as a senior policymaker in the Costa Rican government and at the United Nations and has been on the faculty of the University of Costa Rica. Prior to joining ODC, she was Minister-Counselor for Finance at her government's embassy in Washington where she played a key role in Costa Rica's negotiations with the international financial institutions and commercial banks.

This project was made possible by a grant from the Andrew W. Mellon Foundation and The North-South Center of the University of Miami, as well as the support of The Ford Foundation, The Rockefeller Foundation, and The William and Flora Hewlett Foundation for the Council's overall program.

John W. Sewell
President
July 1992

■

Overview
The Long and Winding Road
from Anchorage to Patagonia

The Long and Winding Road from Anchorage to Patagonia

Sylvia Saborio

Not long ago, the notion of a free trade area spanning the entire Western Hemisphere would have been dismissed as an utterly implausible proposition by most trade analysts and even the most quixotic advocates of closer inter-American relations. Today, such an undertaking is the centerpiece of the United States-Latin American and Caribbean (LAC) agenda for the 1990s.

A NEW HEMISPHERIC VISION

A hemispheric system of free trade areas (FTAs) is the cornerstone of President Bush's Enterprise for the Americas Initiative (EAI) announced in June 1990, arguably the single most important U.S. initiative toward Latin America and the Caribbean since the Alliance for Progress. If successful, the EAI would result in the largest market in the world—more than 700 million people and a combined GDP of nearly $7 trillion representing 14 percent of the world's population and 31 percent of global wealth (Figure 1).

Both the launching of the EAI and Latin America's enthusiastic response belie a dramatic shift by both sides regarding the possibility and desirability of closer hemispheric cooperation. The EAI is, at heart, Washington's tough recipe for Latin America's economic revival which, while synergistic, is firmly grounded on the premise that good policies are their own reward. Latin America's readiness to take on Washington's challenge, in turn, reflects the sobering lessons of the 1980s concerning the limits of

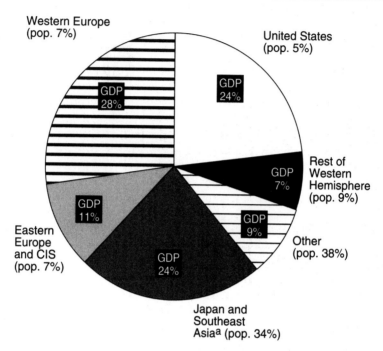

FIGURE 1. THE GLOBAL MARKET
(percent of world GDP and world population)

Western Europe (pop. 7%)
GDP 28%

United States (pop. 5%)
GDP 24%

Rest of Western Hemisphere (pop. 9%)
GDP 7%

Other (pop. 38%)
GDP 9%

Eastern Europe and CIS (pop. 7%)
GDP 11%

Japan and Southeast Asia[a] (pop. 34%)
GDP 24%

Note: Numbers may not add due to rounding.

[a] Includes China.

Sources: United Nations, *U.N. World Economics Survey 1992* (New York: United Nations, 1992); World Bank, *World Bank Atlas 1991* (Washington, DC: World Bank, 1991).

inward-looking development strategies and the failings of pervasive but ineffectual state intervention. The EAI is a bold, yet modest proposal: bold in its vision, modest in its means. It consists of three pillars: trade, debt, and investment.

TRADE. The initiative's overarching concept is the establishment of a hemispheric system of free trade areas based on a premise of reciprocity and mutual gain rather than unilateral concessions. It is this component of the EAI that this volume examines at length.

DEBT. The $12-billion stock of debt owed by Latin America to the U.S. government is to be significantly reduced on a case-by-case basis. Depending on each country's debt profile and reform record, 40 to 80 percent of the outstanding *concessional* claims would be written off, and 10 to 15 percent of the *nonconcessional* claims would be reduced through debt swaps for environmental and developmental purposes.[1] In addition, countries that subscribe to environmental framework agreements with the United States will be able to make interest payments on the residual concessional debt in local currency into a trust fund to support local environmental activities.

Even if fully implemented, the total amount of debt relief provided by these mechanisms will be quite limited, less than 2 percent of the region's total external debt.[2] Moreover, debtors will experience no immediate cash flow relief, since the cutback will be made on the value and tenor of the outstanding claims, rather than on current debt-service charges. The smaller countries in the region stand to gain proportionally more from this provision than their larger neighbors, both because they are likely to be offered the largest write-offs and because a larger share of their total debt is owed to the U.S. government (Table 1).

INVESTMENT. The EAI contains two types of investment provisions. One is the allocation of a growing share of the Inter-American Development Bank's (IDB) existing resources to sectoral loans in support of investment reform and privatization in Latin America.[3] The other is the creation of a $1.5-billion Multilateral Investment Fund (MIF) at the IDB to provide technical assistance for investment reform, human resource development, and small enterprise support.[4]

Investment will be critical to enable Latin America to meet the competitive challenges of trade liberalization and benefit fully from enhanced market opportunities under the EAI. Most countries in the region suffer from supply rigidities and structural bottlenecks, worsened by a decade of economic decline, low investment levels, and massive resource transfers to the rest of the world in the form of debt-service payments and capital flight. Over the last decade, Latin America transferred abroad over $200 billion and will need to continue making sizable transfers in the years ahead.[5] Capital formation in the region is currently $50 billion below what it would have been if 1980 per capita investment levels had been maintained. With so much catching up to do and capital in short supply worldwide, raising investment levels will be a central preoccupa-

TABLE 1. EXTERNAL DEBT OF LATIN AMERICA AND THE CARIBBEAN ($ millions on June 30, 1990)

	Debt to U.S. Government			Total Long-Term External Debt	U.S. Debt as Percent of Total
	Concessional[a]	Noncessional[b]	Total[c]		
Mexico	20	1,705	1,728	80,256	2.2
South America	3,182	2,510	5,893	236,478	2.5
Argentina	36	409	468	53,229	0.9
Bolivia	420	33	481	3,805	12.6
Brazil	1,016	1,228	2,274	90,292	2.5
Chile	367	99	468	13,997	3.3
Colombia	515	528	1,050	15,272	6.9
Ecuador	127	22	205	9,579	2.1
Guyana	102	8	113	987	11.4
Paraguay	35	0	36	2,125	1.7
Peru	525	149	719	14,258	5.0
Uruguay	40	8	50	3,072	1.6
Venezuela	0	26	29	29,862	0.1
Central America	2,202	45	2,429	21,832	11.1
Belize	26	0	30	126	23.8
Costa Rica	458	22	493	3,783	13.0
El Salvador	631	0	724	1,696	42.7
Guatemala	264	0	287	2,199	13.1
Honduras	420	3	437	2,907	15.0
Nicaragua	222	12	252	7,546	3.3
Panama	181	8	205	3,575	5.7
Caribbean	1,413	463	1,941	9,502	20.4
Dominican Republic	531	204	770	3,385	22.7
Grenada	0	0	0	68	0
Haiti	124	9	134	684	19.6
Jamaica	725	100	845	3,636	23.2
St. Vincent	1	0	1	49	2.0
Trinidad and Tobago	0	114	114	1,680	6.8
Total	6,818	4,722	11,991	348,068	3.4

Note: Totals may not add due to certain country exclusions and rounding.

[a]Economic Support Funds, development assistance, and Food for Peace Program (P.L. 480).
[b]Commodity Credit Corporation and U.S. Export-Import Bank.
[c]Total includes foreign military sales, OPIC-Investment Support, Social Progress Trust Fund, and housing and other credit guarantee programs.

Source: U.S. Department of Treasury.

tion for policymakers in the 1990s. The "investment pillar" of the EAI is but a token contribution to this crucial endeavor.

For all its shortcomings of design and implementation[6] to date, the EAI has been a major diplomatic success. It has greatly improved the tenor of U.S.-LAC relations and engaged regional partners in a constructive dialogue that could transform the economic and political landscape of the hemisphere well into the twenty-first century. It is to the premise and the promise of this hemispheric vision that we now turn.

U.S. TRADE POLICY AT A CROSSROADS

The EAI constitutes a departure from the traditional multilateral U.S. trade policy stance but is consistent with the more eclectic approach the United States has followed in recent years.

U.S. Trade Policy in the 1980s

Since the early 1980s, U.S. trade policy has followed a three-track approach: multilateral, bilateral, and unilateral (the latter with both aggressive and defensive tilts). Thus, while continuing to actively pursue its trade agenda at the Uruguay Round of multilateral trade negotiations in the GATT, the United States also entered into bilateral free trade agreements with Israel (1985) and Canada (1989) and is currently engaged in trilateral negotiations with Canada and Mexico toward the creation of a North America Free Trade Area (NAFTA).

At the same time, the United States has stepped up the selective use of unilateral measures for the dual purposes of obtaining import relief and opening up foreign markets to U.S. exports (Table 2). It toughened the rules and intensified the use of trade remedies (countervailing and antidumping actions) in cases where it unilaterally determined that domestic industries were being injured by unfair trade practices. It has

TABLE 2. U.S. TRADE REMEDIES, 1980–1988

	Number of Cases	
	Total	Western Hemisphere
Section 301	43	11
Countervailing	338	96
Antidumping	415	54

Source: Thomas O. Bayard, "Latin America in the Context of U.S. Trade Policy Since 1989," Institute for International Economics, Washington, DC, December 1991, processed.

also devised new legal tools—such as the revamped "Section 301" and the "Super 301" and "Special 301" provisions of the Omnibus Trade and Competitiveness Act of 1988—to threaten or impose sanctions on trading partners that do not conform to particular U.S. trade practices or standards. Finally, frustration over the large, chronic, and seemingly intractable trade deficits with Japan led the United States to push the limits of trade intervention far beyond the conventional confines of trade-remedy actions. The Structural Impediments Initiative aims to get at the root causes of the bilateral trade imbalances by probing into the inner workings of the Japanese (and U.S.) economy, thus blurring the traditional distinction between the realm of trade and domestic policies.

The United States clearly regards these different approaches as compatible and complementary and professes to use them all in the pursuit of freer trade. In fact, policy choice denotes a drift away from liberal multilateralism toward a posture that is not only less multilateral (i.e., more discriminatory) but also less liberal (i.e., more protectionist). It also signals a switch from a largely defensive policy focused on import containment to a more aggressive one focused on export expansion. To some extent, the latter reflects attempts (not always successful) by the administration to use foreign market-opening measures to deflect protectionist and fair trade pressures at home. Finally, in line with the trend toward increased aggressiveness and selectivity, U.S. trade policy has become increasingly politicized. Trade policy formulation has always responded to the concerns of particular domestic constituencies and the economic interests of organized pressure groups, but increasingly, it is used as a vehicle to attain other (noneconomic) policy objectives, from political change (i.e., embargos on Nicaragua and Haiti, sanctions against South Africa) to labor standards and environmental goals.[7] Every major piece of trade legislation in the 1980s contained workers' rights provisions.[8] The hallmark of the 1990s, as the NAFTA negotiations clearly indicate, will be the "greening" of U.S. trade policy. (See Craig VanGrasstek and Gustavo Vega, Chapter 5 in this volume).

Shifting Paradigms

The shift in U.S. trade policy owes much to the burgeoning trade deficits of the early 1980s.[9] Those deficits were largely the result of a mixture of lax fiscal and tight monetary policies that drove up interest rates and induced large inflows of foreign capital and a significant real appreciation of the U.S. dollar. Yet, in the popular mind—and more importantly, in the collective consciousness of the U.S. Congress—those deficits were attributed to the lack of a "level playing field," which allowed foreigners to flood the U.S. market with dumped or subsidized goods, while keeping their own markets heavily protected. A "fair trade doctrine" thus emerged, which inspired the tough trade-remedy provisions and the crowbar approach to pry open foreign markets of the Omnibus Trade and Competitiveness Act of 1988.

At the same time, an alternative interpretation of the deficits arose among those less inclined to blame foreigners for the imbalances: they were attributed to a secular decline in U.S. competitiveness and economic might, principally vis-à-vis Europe and Japan and, to a lesser extent, the Asian newly industrializing countries (NICs).[10] Those fears helped to reinforce the siege mentality about trade matters that persists to this day, even though trade deficits have declined sharply since their peak in 1987, in line with the realignment of the U.S. dollar.

Frustration with the GATT, in both Congress and the administration, also played a role in the drift away from multilateralism. The multilateral process has, indeed, been rendered increasingly unruly by enlarged and diverse GATT membership, by the emergence of middle powers that neither lead nor follow, and by the decline in clout and commitment on the part of the United States itself—heretofore the bulwark of multilateralism. In fairness to the GATT, it must be recognized that the Uruguay Round—now in its sixth year—is the most complex and ambitious set of multilateral trade negotiations ever undertaken, seeking to tackle not just the backlog of unresolved trade issues, but also the extension of GATT disciplines to areas previously outside its purview. It is true, nonetheless, that the Round has been beset by technical and political difficulties from the start, and that, even now, it remains unclear what, or when, its final outcome will be. Even the staunchest multilateralists are beginning to lose heart.

Last, but not least, the gathering strength of regionalism elsewhere may have helped to tip U.S. policy in a regional direction. The consolidation of the single European market by end-1992 is the prime example, but similar, if much less significant, developments are afoot elsewhere in Asia, Africa, and Latin America.[11] Until recently, U.S. bilateral deals were mainly regarded as means of pushing forward the multilateral process. Now they are increasingly viewed as a hedge against a possible failure of the Uruguay Round and a strategic response to the consolidation of regional trade blocs in Europe and possibly even in Asia.

The U.S. conversion to regionalism has fueled an intense debate over the future of the trading system. At issue is whether regionalism will contribute to, or compromise, global free trade. U.S. officials claim that the U.S. commitment to multilateralism and the success of the Uruguay Round remains undiminished and that whatever regional arrangements it might pursue will be fully consistent with its obligations under the GATT.[12] Some analysts fear, nevertheless, that U.S. endorsement of regionalism will inexorably tilt the balance away from multilateralism and lead to the progressive fragmentation of the trading system.[13] Others welcome regional initiatives as a means of delivering at the local level what seems impossible to attain globally in view of the paralysis of the GATT.[14] What everyone seems to agree on is that, for better or for worse, regionalism is here to stay.

U.S. REGIONALISM AND LATIN AMERICA

The U.S. tilt toward regionalism does not, by itself, explain the focus on Latin America. Until recently, most analysts would have expected the likeliest candidates for preferential trade agreements with the United States to be countries in the Pacific Rim—Japan, Taiwan, Korea, Australia—in view of their impressive growth and trade performance. The possibility of a free trade agreement with Mexico—despite the intensity of cross-border links—was considered remote on political grounds, and the rest of Latin America did not even enter the picture.[15] Why then did Latin America become the prime—if not the only—focus of U.S. attention in this regard?

Mexico's decision to seek a free trade agreement with the United States seems to have been the pivotal event. For geopolitical as well as economic reasons, the United States was disinclined to turn down Mexico's request. After all, Mexico is the third largest U.S. trading partner, a country undergoing sweeping economic reforms in which the United States has vast actual and potential interests, and a neighbor with which the United States shares a long and permeable border and an uneasy history. Interpreting—correctly, as it turned out—Mexico's move as the harbinger of a sea change in attitudes in the region at large, President Bush seized the moment to invite other countries in the area to join the movement toward hemispheric free trade. Without Mexico's initial overture, it is doubtful that the EAI would ever have come to pass.[16]

U.S. Interests in Latin America

The EAI's fortuitous origin does not negate its political, economic, even strategic, value. The United States has, of course, a big stake in the stability and prosperity of the region, not least because if these qualities are not achieved, the United States will eventually feel the ripple effects through loan defaults, lower exports, a flood of drugs, or waves of migrants. The United States also has a vital interest in the success of the tide of political reforms and the emergence of democratic regimes in the region. The consolidation of these new democracies requires and deserves strong U.S. support.

Other noneconomic objectives are also at stake. The protection of workers' rights has long been an important dimension of U.S. relations with developing countries, including those in the hemisphere.[17] More recently, environmental standards have assumed increasing salience as an issue of mutual concern to both the United States and Latin America. The traditional U.S. approach to these issues has been almost purely punitive, i.e., denying access to the U.S. market to trading partners that did not conform to the norms. Closer ties between the United States and countries in the region may open up new mechanisms for cooperation to speed up progress in these areas. Closer economic ties will also be instrumental in securing Latin America's cooperation on issues of importance in the U.S. domestic arena such as drug trafficking, money laundering, and migration.

In the economic sphere, the United States has an interest in further encouraging and locking in trade liberalization and market-oriented reforms in Latin America and the Caribbean. In the 1980s, economic decline and financial strangulation in Latin America cost the United States dearly in terms of jobs and income forgone: between 1981 and 1983, U.S. exports to the region dropped by 43 percent and only recouped their 1980 level in 1988. Had previous trends been maintained, some $283 billion in additional sales would have occurred—enough to support some 600,000 additional jobs a year throughout the decade.[18]

Economic reforms and pent-up import demand have made Latin America the fastest growing market for U.S. exports, in recent years accounting for one-sixth of the total increase in U.S. sales abroad. Further liberalization of these still highly protected markets—provided that these countries have the wherewithal to increase foreign purchases—should continue to boost U.S. exports and create U.S. jobs. Similarly, a more hospitable investment climate and better intellectual property protection—two basic conditions of any prospective regional agreement—would also serve U.S. business interests in the region.

Mexico First, Then What?

U.S. economic interests are paramount in the case of Mexico, which accounts for over half of all two-way U.S. trade with Latin America and hosts about one-third of all U.S. manufacturing investment in the region. Even so, the direct impact of a free trade agreement with Mexico on U.S. exports, income, and jobs has been estimated to be positive but only marginal.[19] This is due, in part, to the large disparity between the two economies: Mexican GDP is only 3 percent of the U.S. level, and even though Mexico is the third largest U.S. trading partner, it accounts for only 7.2 percent of all U.S. exports. The small impact is also due to the already high degree of integration of the two economies, so that the marginal contribution of the FTA to this ongoing process is limited, particularly in the short run.

In the longer run, the main benefits of the NAFTA will be the efficiency gains associated with the improvement in the resource mix and the expansion of technological choice within the integrated market. Over time, the fuller incorporation of Mexico into the North American economy can be expected to improve the overall allocation of resources in the enlarged market, increase reciprocal trade and investment flows, enhance the external competitiveness of these economies, and result in higher income growth all around.

The potential of the LAC market (excluding Mexico) is suggested by a population of nearly 350 million and an aggregate GDP approaching $700 billion (Table 3). At present, the rest of LAC combined represents only 6 percent of total U.S. exports—less than Mexico alone. It is, though, next to Mexico, one of the fastest growing U.S. export markets, and one where the United States has a well-established competitive position: nearly 35 cents of each import dollar is spent on U.S. goods.

That said, the economic rationale for pursuing free trade agreements with *individual* countries in the hemisphere is not compelling (Figure 2). Except for Brazil, which has a large market (a population of 150 million and a GDP of $330 billion) that is still heavily protected, the other markets are truly minute by U.S. standards. Moreover, once Mexico is in the free trade zone, the inclusion of additional countries with relatively similar resource endowments (low-cost labor, natural resources) will not contribute nearly as much at the margin to improving the resource pool or expanding technological choice. The benefits of such agreements to the United States would thus be low but so, too, would the costs.

If the economic case for individual FTAs is weak and, judging by the experience with the NAFTA, the political opposition is strong, it is not clear from where the impetus for completing the hemispheric market on a piecemeal basis will come. Washington's incentive to move ahead with the regional plan would presumably depend, to some extent, on events *outside* the hemisphere, in particular the final outcome of the Uruguay Round and the dynamics of bloc formation elsewhere. A collapse of the round would likely precipitate regional movements, both within and outside the Americas. Conversely, a successful outcome of the round would make regional arrangements less attractive but easier to attain.

Washington's decision to move ahead will also depend on how strongly U.S. business supports the process and how strongly the countries of Latin America and the Caribbean argue their case. It would be ironic if after unleashing a torrent of expectations—and courageous reforms—in the region, Washington discovers that it does not really have the resolve to hold *its* end of the bargain. Yet, unless a fairly automatic

TABLE 3. WESTERN HEMISPHERE: BASIC ECONOMIC INDICATORS, 1990

Area/Country	Population (millions)	GDP ($ billions)	GDP per Capita (dollars)	Investment per Capita (dollars)	Trade per GDP (percent)	Inflation (percent)
NORTH AMERICA	276.4	5,999.0	21,706	3,595	23.8	
United States	250.0	5,423.4	21,696	3,486	21.1	4.9
Canada	26.4	575.6	21,803	4,628	50.0	5.7
LATIN AMERICA	431.9	840.5	1,946.0	378	30.7	1,186.3
LAIA	384.0	788.7	2,054	404	28.9	
Mexico	88.6	175.5	1,980	463	38.9	29.9
Chile	13.2	32.3	2,451	550	57.8	27.3
Andean Pact	92.2	154.5	1,677	297	33.3	
Bolivia	7.3	6.4	870	79	28.4	18.0
Colombia	33.0	46.7	1,416	285	30.5	32.0
Ecuador	10.6	13.2	1,249	284	37.8	49.5
Peru	21.6	28.3	1,312	312	28.1	7,657.8
Venezuela	19.7	60.0	3,038	389	37.5	36.5
Mercosur	190.1	426.4	2,244	418	20.9	
Argentina	32.3	84.8	2,623	226	23.1	1,343.9
Brazil	150.4	326.2	2,169	465	19.0	1,585.2
Paraguay	4.3	6.4	1,493	366	55.0	44.1
Uruguay	3.1	9.0	2,921	235	46.8	129.0
CENTRAL AMERICA	26.5	25.5	962	153	51.8	
Costa Rica	3.0	5.1	1,677	402	80.5	27.5
El Salvador	5.3	5.7	1,091	121	45.1	19.3
Guatemala	9.2	8.2	892	114	40.2	59.6
Honduras	5.1	4.5	880	114	47.7	36.4
Nicaragua	3.9	2.0	505	149	54.8	13,490.9
OTHER	21.2	23.8	1,120	189	73.1	
Barbados	0.3	1.5	5,835	1,141	94.2	3.4
Dominican Republic	7.2	5.1	716	157	81.4	100.7
Guyana	0.8	0.4	554	142	146.9	n.a.
Haiti	6.5	2.1	324	35	37.5	26.1
Jamaica	2.5	3.5	1,401	412	108.6	29.7
Panama	2.4	4.7	1,941	55	62.2	1.5
Suriname	0.4	1.3	3,320	518	51.1	n.a.
Trinidad and Tobago	1.2	5.1	4,195	727	58.2	9.5

Note: Numbers may not add due to certain country exclusions and rounding.

Sources: International Monetary Fund, *International Financial Statistics 1991* (Washington, DC: IMF, 1991); Inter-American Development Bank, *Economic and Social Progress in Latin America*, (Washington, DC: IDB, 1991); *Balance Preliminar de la Economía de América Latina y el Caribe, 1991* (Santiago, Chile: CEPAL, December 1991).

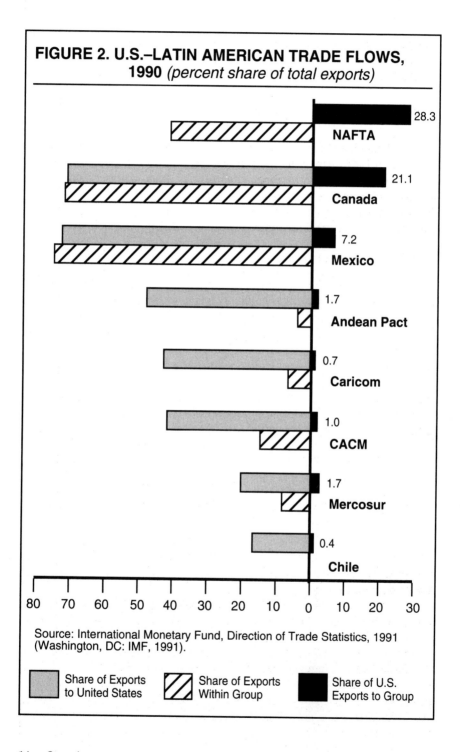

FIGURE 2. U.S.–LATIN AMERICAN TRADE FLOWS, 1990 *(percent share of total exports)*

28.3 NAFTA

21.1 Canada

7.2 Mexico

1.7 Andean Pact

0.7 Caricom

1.0 CACM

1.7 Mercosur

0.4 Chile

80 70 60 50 40 30 20 10 0 10 20 30

Source: International Monetary Fund, Direction of Trade Statistics, 1991 (Washington, DC: IMF, 1991).

Share of Exports to United States

Share of Exports Within Group

Share of U.S. Exports to Group

mechanism for enlarging the NAFTA is put in place that lowers the profile of the political debate each time a new member seeks to join, Washington's interest in further agreements is likely to wane or be diverted elsewhere.

INTEGRATION LATIN STYLE

The idea of free trade areas spanning the Western Hemisphere is not new in Latin America. For the past 30 years, countries in the region have been attempting to forge preferential trade areas among themselves—with relatively little success. What is novel about the EAI is that, instead of opposing such attempts as in the past, the United States now purportedly seeks to steer them, support them, and eventually join them.

Old Style Integration

The initial thrust to regional integration in Latin America occurred in the late 1950s, prompted in part by similar efforts in Europe and by the strategy of import-substitution industrialization championed by the Economic Commission for Latin America and the Caribbean (ECLAC) at the time. Within that framework, preferential trade arrangements were seen essentially as a means to overcome the constraints posed by small domestic markets, by allowing firms to realize the scale economies of the expanded market. High levels of protection from extra-regional imports were deemed necessary, on a temporary basis, while local firms attained enough efficiency to compete not just in their own market but in the world at large. In most cases, the effort also involved a certain amount of industrial planning for the spatial allocation of industrial capacity so as to attain balanced growth.

Four regional arrangements date back to that era (see Appendix for complete listing of regional arrangements):

■ *Latin American Free Trade Association* (LAFTA), established in 1960, comprising Argentina, Bolivia, Brazil, Chile, Colombia, Ecuador, Mexico, Paraguay, Peru, Uruguay, and Venezuela. In 1980, LAFTA was replaced by the *Latin American Integration Association* (LAIA), with the same membership.

■ *Central American Common Market* (CACM), established in 1960, originally comprising Costa Rica, El Salvador, Guatemala, Honduras, and Nicaragua. In 1967 Honduras withdrew from the CACM, establishing instead bilateral agreements with its members; it rejoined the CACM in 1991. Panama is considering joining the CACM.

■ *Caribbean Free Trade Association*, established in 1965 and replaced in 1973 by the *Caribbean Community* (Caricom), comprising Antigua and Barbuda, The Bahamas, Barbados, Belize, Dominica,

Grenada, Guyana, Jamaica, Montserrat, St. Kitts and Nevis, St. Lucia, St. Vincent and the Grenadines, and Trinidad and Tobago.

■ *Andean Pact* (AP), established in 1969, originally comprising Bolivia, Chile, Colombia, Ecuador, and Peru. Venezuela joined the Pact in 1973. Chile withdrew from membership in 1976.

The evolution of these agreements followed roughly the same pattern, albeit with different intensities. For the first decade or so, during the "easy" phase of import substitution, intraregional trade expanded fairly rapidly (particularly in the CACM). The process then lost considerable dynamism until it practically ground to a halt in the early 1980s under the pressure of severe foreign-exchange shortages and the debt crisis. In no case did the regional market become the dominant market: intraregional market shares peaked at 26 percent (1970) in CACM, 14 percent (1975-1980) in LAFTA/LAIA and 4.8 percent (1988) in the AP. Nevertheless, the arrangements did contribute to industrialization and did lead to export diversification into manufactures, especially for the larger members of the free trade zone.

The purpose of these early integration efforts was not trade liberalization as such, but rather protection in an expanded market. They were a crude version of a strategy of "import protection for export promotion" that sought to nurture infant industries until they could successfully compete abroad.[20] However, vested interests in most cases preferred the rents of these highly protected markets to the potentially larger but riskier rewards of exporting.

The agreements ultimately failed because import-substitution activities did not develop the efficiency necessary to propel the process forward. The pattern of industrial protection induced activities that were typically capital- and import-intensive, generating neither the domestic value added nor the foreign exchange necessary to become self-sustaining. Efforts to rationalize the process usually failed because the removal of trade barriers—both intraregional and external—was typically a highly selective, discretionary affair that invariably fell prey to the vested interests of import competing groups. Over time, macroeconomic policy became increasingly hemmed in by inconsistencies in the model—in particular the chronic fiscal and external deficits—until it too imploded, along with the debt crisis in the early 1980s. On top of these intrinsic inconsistencies in the basic model, the regional agreements also lacked adequate institutional mechanisms for settling disputes and remedying enforcement lapses.

New Age Integration

The integrationist revival that began to sweep the region in the late 1980s is an entirely different proposition. As part of the broader agenda of economic reforms, it is outward-oriented rather than inward-looking. It seeks rather than shuns foreign investment as a source of capital, technology, and distribution outlets. It relies primarily on market signals and competitive forces rather than on policy interventions to allocate resources. And, last but not least, it favors across-the-board, automatic measures over selective, piecemeal approaches to minimize backsliding and special interest pressure.

This new spirit inspired the reconstitution of the Andean Pact. In 1989, AP members agreed to establish a free trade area by 1995 and a full-fledged common market by 1997. These deadlines were subsequently moved up to 1992 and 1993, respectively. The process of reciprocal trade liberalization has proceeded even further between the two largest members of the Pact, Venezuela and Colombia. (See Alberto Pascó-Font and Sylvia Saborio, Chapter 9 in this volume). Similarly, in 1990, the countries of Central America agreed to resuscitate the CACM by allowing the free movement of regionally produced goods—including agricultural products—by end-1992, as well as reverting to a common external tariff with a maximum rate of 20 percent by 1994. (See Sylvia Saborio, Chapter 7 in this volume.) Members of the Caribbean Community (Caricom), likewise, agreed in 1990 to step up the process of internal and external liberalization. (See DeLisle Worrell, Chapter 8 in this volume.) Minor lapses and slippages aside, this outward-looking integrationist revival is a remarkable development.

The most recent addition to the new trend is Mercosur, the (future) Southern Cone Common Market, comprising Argentina, Brazil, Paraguay, and Uruguay, established by the Treaty of Asunción in March 1991. Its origin dates back to a series of unremarkable, partial bilateral agreements in the old mold between Argentina and Brazil undertaken in 1986-1987. These partial deals were subsequently replaced by a comprehensive agreement to remove virtually all tariff and nontariff barriers (NTBs) according to a specified schedule. Uruguay and Paraguay joined the process in 1991, and it was agreed then that the scope of the treaty would be broadened to include a common external tariff and macroeconomic policy harmonization. A full-fledged common market is due to come into effect in 1995. (See Roberto Bouzas, Chapter 10 in this volume.)

The New Economic Geography

The movement toward regional integration has turned into a veritable stampede in the wake of Mexico's decision to seek a free trade agreement with the United States and Washington's announcement of the EAI. In a matter of months, a large number of bilateral and plurilateral trade agreements have been hatched, so that by now the region is literally crisscrossed by such arrangements (Table 4).

TABLE 4. REGIONAL TRADE ARRANGEMENTS IN THE WESTERN HEMISPHERE[a]

	Existing Arrangements							Prospective Arrangements					
	United States-Canada	CACM	Caricom[b]	LAIA	Mercosur[c]	Andean Pact[d]	Chile-Mexico	NAFTA	EAI	Mexico-Central America	Chile-Colombia-Venezuela	Colombia-Mexico-Venezuela[e]	Venezuela-Central America
Founded	1968	1961	1973	1960/80	1991	1969	1991						
Objective	FTA	CM	CM	FTA	FTA	FTA	FTA	FTA	FTA	FTA	FTA	FTA	FTA
Canada	•							•					
Mexico	•			•			•	•		•		•	
United States	•							•	•				
Belize			•						•				
Costa Rica		•							•	•			•
El Salvador		•							•	•			•
Guatemala		•							•	•			•
Honduras		•							•	•			•
Nicaragua		•							•	•			•
Panama		(•)							•				•
Antigua and Barbuda			•						•				
The Bahamas			•						•				
Barbados			•						•				
Dominica			•						•				
Grenada			•						•				
Jamaica			•						•				
Montserrat			•						•				
St. Kitts and Nevis			•						•				
St. Lucia			•						•				
St. Vincent			•						•				
Trinidad and Tobago			•						•				

TABLE 4. REGIONAL TRADE ARRANGEMENTS IN THE WESTERN HEMISPHERE[a] (Continued)

	Existing Arrangements						Prospective Arrangements					
	CACM	Caricom[b]	LAIA	Mercosur[c]	Andean Pact[d]	Chile-Mexico	NAFA	EAI(US)	Mexico-Central America[h]	Chile-Colombia-Venezuela	Colombia-Mexico-Venezuela[e]	Venezuela-Central America
United States-Canada												
Argentina			●	●				●				
Bolivia			●		●			●				
Brazil			●	●				●				
Chile			●			●		●		●		
Colombia			●		●			●		●	●	
Ecuador			●		●			●				
Guyana		●						●				
Paraguay			●	●				●				
Peru			●		●			●				
Uruguay			●	●				●				
Venezuela			●		●			●		●	●	●

Notes: FTA = free trade area; CM = common market. Parentheses indicate that Panama is considering joining the arrangement.

[a]Does not include unilateral preferencial arrangements.

[b]Aims to achieve a common external market by 1995.

[c]Currently an FTA, Mercosur aims to establish a common market by 1995.

[d]Efforts are under way to revive AP and create a common market by 1994.

[e]The trade and investment agreement was signed in 1991, and trilateral limited free trade is expected by end-1993.

Source: Adopted from Angusto de la Torre and Margaret Kelly, *Regional Trade Arrangements*, Occasional Paper 93, (Washington, DC: International Monetary Fund, March 1992).

Much of the activity revolves around the United States. Between May 1990 and December 1991, the United States signed 15 Framework Trade and Investment Agreements covering 30 countries, including a joint agreement with the four members of Mercosur and one with Caricom's 13 member states. Such framework agreements do not, in and of themselves, obligate either party to take specific policy action. They are instead consultative mechanisms to identify, discuss, and seek solutions to problems and irritants in the reciprocal commercial relationship. As a matter of course, they are considered precursors to eventual free trade agreements, even though, formally, they carry no such presumption.

In fact, the United States has steadfastly turned down all requests to start free trade negotiations until the NAFTA is completed, although it did promise Chile that it would be the next in line. Washington's rejections have, by default, catapulted Mexico to a position of prominence as the presumed gateway to North America. On that premise, several countries from the region and elsewhere, have approached Mexico with proposals for preferential trade arrangements, which Mexico has been willing to accomodate, even though it can only grant access to its own market.[21]

Mexico itself has initiated some of these trade overtures, e.g., to Central America. Even though the economic interests involved are inconsequential in most cases, the strengthening of trade links with Latin America provides some political cover against domestic opposition to closer ties with the United States. Moreover, these side deals with Mexico serve to divert attention from most LAC countries' real goal: access to the U.S. market. This is important insofar as Mexico's benefits from NAFTA depend in part on exclusivity. The longer Mexico can exploit its "primogeniture" as the one and only Latin American country in the FTA, the greater its benefits are likely to be.

In any event, other countries seeking to enter the North American market through the back door are likely to be sorely disappointed. Negotiators from each of the three countries are taking pains to prevent any of them from being used as a launching platform for the transshipment of goods from nonmember countries to the integrated North American market. Accordingly, the NAFTA agreement will contain strict rules-of-origin and domestic content provisions, carefully crafted to forestall such trade deflection. (See VanGrasstek and Vega, Chapter 5.)

As a result of the U.S. refusal to enter into additional FTAs and Mexico's willingness to do so practically on demand, a curious structure is evolving in North America: a NAFTA plus a Mexico-centered hub of additional accords, with Mexico alone straddling both. This is not the way it was supposed to happen. The hub-and-spoke concept[22] was originally developed to persuade Canada to join the NAFTA talks so as to prevent the United States from becoming the "hub" in a system of overlapping

FTAs. As the hub, the United States would enjoy preferences in the markets of each "spoke" country with which it had bilateral agreements. The spokes, on the other hand, not only would not enjoy preferences in each other's markets but would also have to share among themselves the preferences in the hub market. The hub-and-spoke model, even with the United States as the hub, was deemed suboptimal on equity, efficiency, and political grounds. On all those counts, a Mexico-centered hub would be even less desirable. To correct this aberration, it is of the utmost importance that the NAFTA itelf contain a mechanism for its orderly extension to the rest of the hemisphere. (See Richard G. Lipsey, Chapter 3 in this volume).

CATCHING THE FREE TRADE EXPRESS: ALL ABOARD?

The Economics of FTAs

In theory, the economics of free trade areas are pretty straightforward. The preferential elimination of mutual trade barriers among FTA members generates two types of effects: static and dynamic. In the short-run, the elimination of trade barriers induces a once-and-for-all reallocation of existing resources (static effects). Such effects, are beneficial if they lead to the replacement of inefficient domestic production by low-cost imports (trade creation). They may be welfare-reducing, however, if they result in the displacement of low-cost imports from outside the FTA by less efficient sources of supply within the FTA (trade diversion).[23] To this basic calculus must be added the transitional adjustment costs linked to the reallocation of resources.

Over the longer run, FTAs affect the rate of growth of their members (dynamic effects) by influencing investment decisions and the efficiency with which resources are used, as well as through distributional effects among its members. Although generally less well understood and far more difficult to quantify, those dynamic effects are believed to be far more important than the short-term, static effects of FTAs. Finally, FTAs, especially large ones, also affect nonmembers by diverting trade and investment from them, or conversely, by generating income-induced increases in demand for their exports.

This framework suggests the basic incentives and deterrents that Latin America and the Caribbean face in seeking a FTA with the United States. Their primary objective would be to secure expanded, assured, and preferential access to the U.S. market and, in so doing, enhance their attractiveness as an investment site and, hence, their growth prospects. By the same token, they would also have a strong incentive to avoid the costs of exclusion (in terms of trade and, especially, investment diversion) from a U.S.-centric FTA. In fact, the main allure of the FTA has to do more with investment than with trade. Mexico's decision to seek a FTA hinged largely on that, and Chile's eagerness to follow closely on Mexico's footsteps obeys essentially the same logic. (See Andrea Butelmann and Alicia Frohmann, Chapter 6 in this volume). Indeed, unless countries manage to expand their productive base and raise their competitiveness, market opportunities do not count for much. Increased investment is, therefore, essential. By locking in domestic reforms and guaranteeing access to foreign markets, a FTA could help to raise the level of investment, both domestic (including the return of flight capital) and foreign.

Asymmetric Reciprocity

FTAs are reciprocal arrangements and as such convey costs as well as benefits. LAC countries would need to balance the potential benefits of a FTA against its potential costs. For Latin America, a FTA with the United States would imply much more than the mere removal of border barriers, difficult as that may be. (See José Manuel Salazar-Xirinachs and Eduardo Lizano, Chapter 2 in this volume.) Renouncing the use of trade and exchange controls vis-à-vis a trading partner with the retaliatory power of the United States would impose strict discipline on the conduct of macroeconomic policy. Macroimbalances of either domestic or external origin would need to be swiftly corrected either through exchange-rate adjustments or through changes in the level of domestic activity.

Countries with a propensity to chronic price instability may need to relinquish the use of the exchange rate as an adjustment mechanism and instead peg their currency to the dollar to avoid trade and investment volatility and possibly even claims of unfair pricing practices.[24] Similarly, countries that rely heavily on trade taxes as a source of revenues—such as the small countries of Central America and the Caribbean—would need to undertake a sweeping tax reform prior to the FTA or radically downsize the public sector. Although macroeconomic policy coordination as such would be out of the question, LAC countries would still need to harmonize their policy stance with that of the United States to be able to function properly under the FTA. (See Salazar and Lizano, Chapter 2).

In fact, opting for a FTA with the United States would entail adopting a fairly comprehensive policy package along the lines of the laissez-faire type of capitalism favored by the United States. (See Peter Morici, Chapter 1 in this volume). This implies that constraints might be placed on the use of certain policy instruments (e.g., subsidies) that LAC countries might wish to use to attain particular development objectives, or that these countries will have to adopt certain standards set by the

United States—i.e., in the area of intellectual property rights, labor standards, or environmental norms—which may or may not be appropriate to countries at much lower stages of development. LAC countries would, therefore, need to weigh the implications of being locked into a particular pattern of specialization and economic behavior against the consequences of nonparticipation.

Two additional issues arise from the fundamental asymmetry in the U.S.-LAC relationship. One is the possibility that a FTA among such unequal partners might produce significant polarization effects, concentrating the benefits in some members at the expense of others. (See Lipsey, Chapter 3.) Investment patterns will be the key factor in this regard. Investment is likely to flow to countries that offer a stable and attractive domestic policy climate, a sizable market, and locational advantages in the United States or foreign markets. The smaller, less developed economies in the region, which used to enjoy certain exclusive preferences in the U.S. market under concessional arrangements such as the CBI, may be the biggest losers. They may be relegated to a choice between becoming a periphery of the center or remaining a periphery of the periphery. In the event, they may not even face that choice, since the United States has as little incentive to enter into FTAs with such countries as it does to join arrangements with most other countries in the region.

The second issue raised by the asymmetry is the highly skewed distribution of adjustment burdens posed by the FTA. Because initial levels of protection are higher in Latin America than in the United States, the adjustment required to deliver *free* trade would be that much greater. Moreover, the difference in size and mutual importance as trading partners clearly puts the brunt of the adjustment burden on Latin America. The flip side of this argument is that the countries that experience the greatest adjustment costs are the ones that stand to reap the biggest gains, since adjustment is the process of reallocating resources to more efficient uses.[25] The validity of the argument critically depends on whether or not the countries undergoing the adjustment will have the resources necessary to finance the transition. Unless large amounts of funds become available—either through autonomous capital flows or through compensatory transfers of some sort—trade liberalization would need to proceed slowly, apace with the development of export activities to replace the import-competing industries that succumb to foreign competition. Otherwise, the process might prove unsustainable and lead to policy reversal. (See Salazar and Lizano, Chapter 2).

As it stands, the EAI contains no financial provisions similar to the structural funds employed by the European Community (EC) to help out its less affluent members. The argument often made against such provisions is that, unlike the EC process of deep integration, what the United States is proposing to Latin America is merely a free trade deal. Indeed,

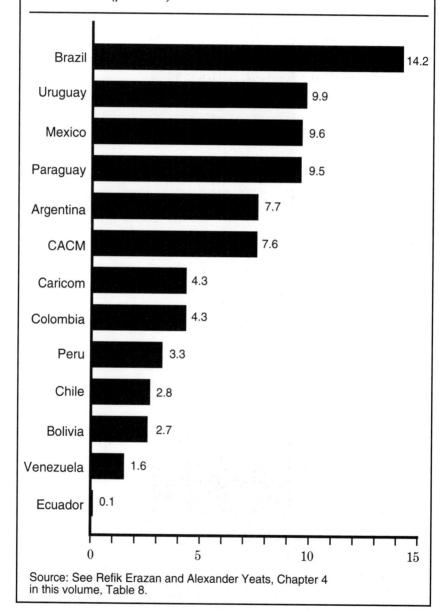

FIGURE 3. PROJECTED LATIN AMERICAN EXPORT
GAINS FROM FREE TRADE AREAS,
EXPORT GROWTH, BY COUNTRY
(percent)

Country	
Brazil	14.2
Uruguay	9.9
Mexico	9.6
Paraguay	9.5
Argentina	7.7
CACM	7.6
Caricom	4.3
Colombia	4.3
Peru	3.3
Chile	2.8
Bolivia	2.7
Venezuela	1.6
Ecuador	0.1

Source: See Refik Erazan and Alexander Yeats, Chapter 4
in this volume, Table 8.

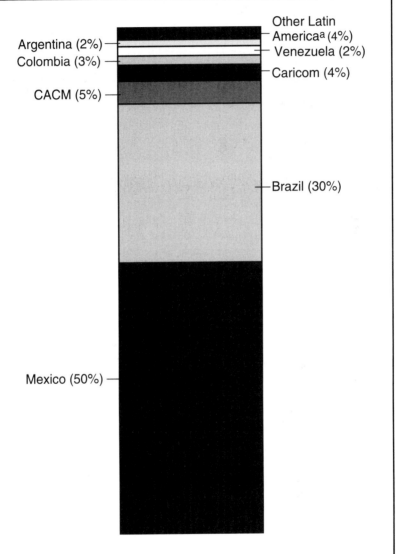

FIGURE 4. SHARE OF TOTAL PROJECTED EXPORT GAINS TO LATIN AMERICA *(percent)*

Argentina (2%)
Colombia (3%)
CACM (5%)
Mexico (50%)

Other Latin America[a] (4%)
Venezuela (2%)
Caricom (4%)
Brazil (30%)

[a]Includes Uruguay (1.5%), Peru (0.8%), Chile (0.7%), Ecuador (0.4%), Bolivia (0.1%), and Paraguay (0.1%).

Source: See Refik Erzan and Alexander Yeats, Chapter 4 in this volume, Table 8.

for the United States that is true, but from a Latin American perspective, the FTA has far more profound implications: it entails the adoption of a brand new development model.

The notion of a North American Development Bank and Adjustment Fund has been proposed by economist Albert Fishlow and others, as an essential complement to support the process of economic integration in North America.[26] A similar facility, perhaps at the IDB, may become necessary if the broader process of regional integration is to succeed.

Sizing Up the Gains: Some Empirical Results

In the short run, the potential (static) trade gains from a preferential removal of U.S. barriers to Latin American exports appear to be relatively small and unevenly distributed. Refik Erzan and Alexander Yeats (Chapter 4 in this volume) estimate a one-time increase in LAC exports to the United States of around 6.6 percent if all U.S. tariffs on LAC exports are preferentially removed. In the event hard core nontariff barriers (i.e., quantitative restrictions and flexible import fees) were simultaneously relaxed as well, the impact would be about a third larger (8.8 percent). Their calculations also indicate that half the gains would accrue to Mexico, an additional third to Brazil, and the remaining 20 percent would be split among the rest (Figures 3 and 4).

The impact is muted by the fact that U.S. tariffs on LAC exports are already relatively low as a result of preferential arrangements—such as the Generalized System of Preferences (GSP) and CBI—and the fact that LAC exports to the United States are concentrated in primary commodities and raw materials, which carry zero or low MFN duties.

The United States does maintain high import duties and NTBs on a number of products of export interest to LAC countries—notably textiles and apparel, footwear and leather goods, steel, and certain agricultural products. The removal of such barriers would have an appreciable impact on export growth in the short run, since installed capacity is not being fully utilized due to the restrictions. More important, the removal of trade barriers on these products would greatly improve *future* export prospects, by enabling LAC countries to diversify their export base and increase the value added of their export bundle. Future export prospects would improve even more if the FTA delivered assurances about future market access—particularly regarding the discretionary use of U.S. trade remedies—and put in place a fair and effective mechanism for settling disputes.

Market opportunities, however, are not enough. To take advantage of expanded access to the U.S. market, LAC countries will need to hone their skills, save more, and invest more. Sound domestic policies and assured access to the U.S. market should enhance their chances in the increasingly competitive global scramble for investment capital. Yet, it is not obvious that as more and more countries strike deals with the United States they will be able to attract large amounts of investment—as Mexico has done and Chile hopes to do—although the converse may well be true, i.e., that those countries that do not have deals will have a harder time attracting investment.

As export platforms to the United States, few countries could compete with Mexico for a wide range of products, given Mexico's proximity to, and degree of integration with, the U.S. market. The margin of substitutability among LAC suppliers to the United States can be inferred from the amount of trade diversion that would occur as a result of a U.S.-Mexico FTA. Erzan and Yeats found that, within the hemisphere, Brazil and Central America would be the most affected, but that the brunt of trade diversion would, in fact, be borne by extraregional suppliers.

Interestingly, the greatest danger of trade diversion within the hemisphere appears to lie elsewhere: in the possible displacement of intra-LAC trade by U.S. exports. For a broad range of products, the United States competes with other Latin American and Caribbean suppliers in regional markets. If, as a result of separate bilateral FTAs, the United States obtained preferential access to those markets, it could easily displace other Latin American suppliers. The specter of being locked out of regional markets by a patchwork of bilateral FTAs should give pause to those pushing the bilateral route willy-nilly.

In fact, if the EAI resulted in a series of bilateral FTAs as opposed to a single expanding FTA, a great opportunity to set the regional economy on a path to prosperity would have been lost. Although unencumbered access to the U.S. market may be the single most important prize, Latin America and Caribbean countries cannot, individually or collectively, make that market their only target of opportunity. The piecemeal approach to free trade poses many dangers, not the least of which is the risk of regional disintegration. In principle, a single plurilateral deal encompassing the entire hemisphere would have been the best way to proceed. This may not have been feasible—although more improbable things have happened lately. The next best course of action may well be a staggered approach, exposing countries to progressively higher levels of competition without discriminating against their natural trading partners. The starting point would be domestic reforms, followed by consolidation of subregional groups, and eventually accession to the NAFTA. The next logical step would be trade liberalization at the multilateral level, since by then these countries would presumably be world class competitors.

CONCLUSIONS AND RECOMMENDATIONS

Compared to a well-functioning, multilateral trading regime, a regional trading arrangement such as the EAI is strictly second best. In an imperfect world, the regional approach has more appeal, for it has the potential of freeing trade further and faster than currently seems feasible at the global level. If regionalism is to be a benign force, however, it must overcome the impulse toward closed, exclusionary arrangements and emulate the best features of the multilateral approach. In other words, regional blocs should be building blocs, not stumbling blocs, to a reconstituted global trading regime.

That overarching objective has important implications for the process under way in the Western Hemisphere. It suggests what type of features FTAs ought to have, how the process of regional integration ought to proceed, and how the regional FTA ought to relate to the world at large.

A "Good Economics" FTA

The objective of FTAs should be to *free* trade, not to *manage* trade to the detriment of either nonmembers or weaker members. They should be comprehensive in scope, including sectors where protection is most entrenched, and cover the whole range of trade restraints, including tariffs, NTBs, and procedural protectionism. At the same time, they should exclude more subtle types of protection exercised through unduly restrictive rules-of-origin and local content provisions. Such exclusionary features against non-FTA suppliers and investors would lock FTA members into inefficient patterns of specialization and deprive them of badly needed sources of external capital.[27]

FTAs must take heed of the vast heterogeneity of the region. They should, therefore, allow for variable, possibly asymmetric phase-in and phase-out periods, especially for less developed members of the FTA. Those countries will also need some time to catch up to the higher standards—food safety, environmental—that they will be required to adopt as members of the FTA. Finally, a mechanism for financial and technical assistance to support structural transformation must be put in place, not necessarily as part of the FTA itself, but as an adjunct to it.

Enlargement of the FTA

The new regional architecture requires an orderly process of expansion. To avoid the inefficiencies of a crazy-quilt pattern of overlapping but inconsistent free trade areas, the NAFTA should become the core of the hemispheric system. The NAFTA agreement should, thus, be crafted in terms that allow for its enlargement, not as a tailor-made deal exclusively for North America. Accordingly, the NAFTA should contain an accession clause, and some type of fast-track mechanism must be put in place to streamline the process of accession.

For the sake of good politics as well as good economics, the process of accession to the regional accord should be as fair, objective, transparent, consistent, and automatic as possible. The accession clause should specify the conditions for eligibility to the FTA as well as the principles, practices, and procedures by which all FTA members must abide. At the time of accession, only the calendar for compliance with the terms of the agreement would need to be negotiated. Clear rules of accession would have three main advantages:

■ They would allow LAC countries to self-select if and when they meet the eligibility criteria and are prepared to accept the basic rights and obligations of the FTA. The United States would not need to decide at every turn who is next in line. Politically and diplomatically, this would be a big advantage.

■ An orderly process of accession without artificial deadlines, while still encouraging reform, would not pressure LAC countries into seeking entry into the FTA before they are ready. As a result, adjustment costs would be lower, and the risk of slippage would be less.

■ The basic agreement would not need to be renegotiated each time a new member joined. Congress would still participate in the process, but since the basic parameters of the FTA would be already agreed upon, Congress would merely have to concur with the proposed calendar for implementation of the agreement.

The inclusion of a well-structured docking clause to the NAFTA and adequate fast-track provisions are crucial. Without a fairly automatic, low-profile mechanism of accession, the process of regional integration may well grind to a halt after Mexico.

Minding the GATT

Both the United States and Latin America have an overriding interest in the well-being of the GATT and the multilateral trading system. The United States is a global trader whose extraregional trading interests dwarf its interests in trade with Latin America and the Caribbean. Latin America also has commercial interests outside the hemisphere that it would not wish to jeopardize. Moreover, as small players in the global arena, LAC countries realize that a strong GATT is the only protection they have against harassment and abuse by larger players, within or outside the hemisphere. Paradoxically, the need for a well-functioning GATT is *stronger*, not weaker, under a regional approach, to ensure that power politics do not pervert due process and that the interests of nonmembers are not unduly hurt. Simply put, regional arrangements require policing. Without such constraints, they could easily degenerate into protectionist blocs. Nobody's interests would be served by that.

Even under the best of circumstances, stitching together a free trade zone from Anchorage to Patagonia will take time and a great deal of determination. And clearly, if the promise behind the premise of free trade as a road to regional prosperity is to materialize, the process must lead to the integration, not balkanization, of the hemisphere.

Notes

[1] To date, only the reduction of a portion of P.L. 480 claims has been authorized by the U.S. Congress, as part of the 1990 Farm Bill. The write-downs done so far have been in the range of 40 percent (Chile) to 80 percent (Bolivia, Jamaica) of the outstanding obligations.

[2] The provision has potentially greater importance, insofar as it sets the precedent of official debt relief for middle-income debtors. If similar action were taken by other official creditors at the Paris Club, the benefits to the region could quadruple.

[3] Up to 25 percent of the Bank's loan portfolio could be allocated to policy-based sectoral loans, according to the provisions of the Seventh Capital Replenishment of the IDB.

[4] The MIF was created on February 12, 1992 with a capital base of $1.3 billion, but it will not be operational until the Congress authorizes and appropriates the U.S. contribution. Initially, the MIF was to be capitalized by $500-million subscriptions from the United States, Japan, and Europe over a five-year period. Refusal by the Europeans to contribute their share prompted 13 Latin American countries to pledge nearly $100 million of their own resources to the fund so as not to jeopardize its creation.

[5] See Richard E. Feinberg, Eduardo Fernández-Arias, and Frank Sader, *Debt Reduction and North-South Resource Transfers to the Year 2000*, Policy Essay No. 3 (Washington, DC: Overseas Development Council, 1992); and John Williamson, "The Prospects for Financial Flows to Latin America," paper presented at a workshop of the Inter-American Dialogue on Integration in the World Economy, Washington, DC, December 18-20, 1991.

[6] The U.S. Congress has failed to pass implementing legislation or budgetary authority on any EAI-related provisions, except for a portion of the P.L. 480 debt included in the 1990 Farm Bill.

[7] The use of trade policy to attain a variety of noneconomic goals parallels trends in aid conditionality. See Joan M. Nelson with Stephanie J. Eglinton, *Encouraging Democracy: What Role for Conditioned Aid?*, Policy Essay No. 4 (Washington DC: Overseas Development Council, 1992). This is the first of a series of ODC studies on political, environmental, military, and poverty conditionality in the 1990s.

[8] Workers' rights provisions were included in the Caribbean Basin Initiative (1983 and 1989), the Generalized System of Preferences (1984), and the Omnibus Trade and Competitiveness Act (1988). Similar provisions were also included in legislation on the Overseas Private Investment Corporation (1985) and U.S. participation in the Multilateral Investment Guarantee Agency affiliated with the World Bank. See *Beyond Subsistence: Labor Standards and Third World Development*, report of the symposium co-convened by the International Labor Affairs of the U.S. Department of Labor and the Overseas Development Council, Washington, DC, August 1989.

[9] For an excellent discussion of the tensions behind the shift in U.S. trade policy, see Thomas O. Bayard, "Latin America in the Context of US Trade Policy Since 1980," paper presented at a Workshop of the Inter-American Dialogue on Integration in the World Economy, Washington, DC, December 18-20, 1991.

[10] For a discussion of this issue see Martin Wolf's "Comments" to a paper by Ronald J. Wonnacott and Mark Lutz in Jeffrey J. Schott, *Free Trade Areas and U.S. Trade Policy* (Washington, DC: Institute for International Economics, 1989), pp. 89-95.

[11] For a survey of recent regional initiatives, see Augusto de la Torre and Margaret R. Kelly, *Regional Trade Arrangements*, Occasional Paper No. 93 (Washington, DC: International Monetary Fund, March 1992), pp. 8-12.

[12] See, for example, Ambassador Julius L. Katz, Testimony Before the Committee on Finance, U.S. Senate, April 24, 1991.

[13] See, for instance, Jagdish Bhagwati, *Regionalism vs. Multilateralism*, World Bank and CEPR Conference on New Dimensions in Regional Integration, Session I, Paper No.1, Washington, DC, April 2-3, 1992.

[14] See, for instance, Paul Krugman, "Is Bilateralism Bad?" in E. Helpman and A. Razin, *International Trade and Trade Policy* (Cambridge, MA: MIT Press, 1991); and "Regional Blocks: The Good, The Bad and The Ugly," *The International Economy*, November/December 1991, pp. 54-56; Lawrence Summers, "Regionalism and the World Trading System," remarks delivered at Federal Reserve Bank of Kansas City, August 1991; R.W. Dornbusch, "Policy Options for Freer Trade: The Case for Bilateralism," in R.Z. Lawrence and C.L. Schultze (ed.), *An American Trade Strategy: Options for the 1990s* (Washington, DC: The Brookings Institution, 1990).

[15] See, for instance, *Free Trade Areas and U.S. Trade Policy*, op. cit.

[16] Interestingly enough, a document entitled "The Bush Administration's Trade Strategy" issued by the White House on May 23, 1990—just 35 days before the announcement of the EAI—makes no mention of a trade initiative toward Latin America.

[17] See preceding note 8.

[18] See, Stuart K. Tucker, "U.S. Exports to Developing Countries: Analysis and Projections," Overseas Development Council, February 1992, mimeo.

[19] See, for instance, Gary C. Hufbauer and Jeffrey J. Schott, *North American Free Trade: Issues and Recommendations* (Washington, DC: International Institute of Economics, 1992), p. 58; and Sydney Weintraub: "NAFTA and Industry," paper presented at the Brookings Institution's conference on NAFTA: An Assessment of the Research, Washington, DC, April 9-10, 1992. See also, U.S. International Trade Commission, *The Likely Impact on the United States of a Free Trade Agreement with Mexico*, Publication 2353, (Washington, DC: USITC, 1991).

[20] Paul Krugman, "Import Protection as Export Promotion: International Competition in the Presence of Oligopoly and Economies of Sale," in H. Kierzkowski (ed.), *Monopolistic Competition and International Trade* (Clarendon Press: Oxford, 1984).

[21] For instance, Mexico recently entered in a bilateral trade agreement with Thailand. See Ken Stier, "Thai-Mexico Pact Aims to Exploit Nafta Advantages," *The Journal of Commerce*, March 12, 1992.

[22] See, Ronald J. Wonnacott: *The Economics of Overlapping Free Trade Areas and the Mexican Challenge* (Toronto: The Canadian-American Committee, 1991); and Ronald J. Wonnacott, "Canada and the U.S.-Mexico Free Trade Negotiations," *C.D. Howe Institute Commentary*, No. 21 (September 1990); and Richard G. Lipsey, "Canada at the U.S.-Mexico Free Trade Dance: Wallflower or Partner?" *C.D. Howe Institute Commentary*, No. 20 (August 1990).

[23] For a discussion of the efficiency implications of trade diversion see Wonnacott and Lutz, op. cit.

[24] For a discussion of the merits of monetary arrangements in North America, see Tamim Bayoumi and Barry Eichengreen, "Monetary and Exchange Rate Arrangements for NAFTA," paper prepared for the Interamerican Seminar on Macroeconomics, Buenos Aires, Argentina, May 7-9, 1992 (mimeo).

[25] I would like to thank Tom Bayard for making this point while reviewing an earlier draft of this chapter.

[26] See Albert Fishlow, Sherman Robinson, and Raul Hinojosa-Ojeda, "Proposal for a North American Regional Development Bank and Adjustment Fund," conference proceedings, sponsored by the Federal Reserve Bank of Dallas, Dallas, Texas, June 14, 1991.

[27] For some concerns about the North American agreements in this regard see John Whalley, *Regional Trade Arrangements in North America: CUSTA and NAFTA*, World Bank and CEPR Conference on New Dimensions in Regional Integration, Paper No.6, Washington, DC, April 2-3, 1992.

■

Part II
Summaries of
Chapter Recommendations

Summary of
Chapter Recommendations

Free Trade in the Americas: A U.S. Perspective
Peter Morici

A Western Hemisphere Free Trade Area (WHFTA) offers the United States important opportunities to expand exports, specialize more in knowledge-intensive activities, and better match the industrial progress of Japan and the European Community. However, if implemented too quickly, a WHFTA could disrupt the U.S. labor market possibly derailing political support for its commitments to maintaining open access to Latin American products. If incorrectly structured, a WHFTA could weaken the General Agreement on Tariffs and Trade (GATT). This chapter explores these issues and makes the following recommendations for U.S. policy.

1) *Good trade policy requires good domestic policy.* The United States should continue initiatives in the GATT but recognize that regional trade agreements can be a complementary alternative for expanding foreign market access to U.S. exports and increasing specialization in high value-added, knowledge-intensive activities.

Domestically, the administration should emphasize that poorly trained workers and mediocre standards in American schools pose the greatest threat to U.S. prosperity and international competitiveness. It should therefore stress that improvements in human resources must accompany liberal trade policies.

2) *Go slow but be persistent.* Specialization in knowledge-intensive pursuits can increase only as rapidly as U.S. workers' skills can be improved. Therefore, a gradual but persistent opening of U.S. markets seems most appropriate. Negotiating with Mexico now, Chile in two or three years, and then other countries is consistent with this plan. However, a go-slow strategy entails risks. Workers and firms in affected industries may remain unconvinced that protection will decline and disappear, engendering even more intense lobbying to sustain protection of low-wage/low-skill activities.

Denying that free trade will impose some adjustments on workers or industries is not useful. Instead, the administration should convey the overarching message that protection of uncompetitive industries will not reverse declining living standards. Only improving the quality of education and training and opening foreign markets to U.S. knowledge-intensive products will allow Americans to again enjoy rising incomes.

A go-slow strategy could also check the momentum for economic reform in Latin America and the Caribbean and create new sources of trade tensions in the hemisphere. The U.S. strategy of engaging Latin American countries on several fronts—for example, providing debt relief, promoting private investment, negotiating framework agreements, and encouraging regional groupings—is most useful. In addition, an accession clause or "docking provision" should be included in the North American Free Trade Agreement (NAFTA) so that countries that meet the eligibility requirements can join the free trade area (FTA) when they are prepared to accept the disciplines of the agreement.

3) *Be firm and realistic.* The administration should remain firm in requiring that economic reforms be fairly well along before commencing free trade negotiations. Unless Latin American legal and economic institutions become broadly compatible with U.S. approaches to industrial policy, prospects are dim for achieving truly integrated markets and ensuring that U.S. firms and workers are protected from industrial predation.

The United States has to be realistic. It should not expect Latin American nations to open their economies fully without substantial reductions in U.S. trade barriers in mature manufacturing, agriculture, and lower-skilled, tradable services. The United States should engage these countries, as it is doing with Mexico, once their reforms are well along, and it should condition complete removal of U.S. trade barriers on completion of reform goals over mutually agreeable transition periods.

4) *Be very ambitious.* In negotiations, the United States should seek to liberalize a broad range of nontariff measures, investment practices, and trade in services. Only this will ensure a substantial two-way opening of commerce.

Moreover, the United States should seek preferences beyond tariffs. Nontariff preferences and two-tier, most-favored-nation (MFN) treatment are exactly what participants in an economic community practice. Unlike members of a simple free trade area, members of an economic community afford one another terms of access that transcend tariff preferences by harmonizing national policies, practices, and regulations to achieve progress on nontariff measures. Such processes are not inconsistent with the GATT, if they strengthen the GATT rights and protection for member countries and broaden the range of practices subject to GATT-like rules within the FTA.

Generally, the Canada-U.S. Free Trade Agreement (CAFTA) meets this basic test, and extending the CAFTA concept to the rest of the hemisphere would do so as well. As a first step, the United States should negotiate a comprehensive agreement with Mexico, patterned on the CAFTA, with precise modalities and timetables for conforming Mexican economic policies and practices to U.S. and Canadian norms and for removing U.S. and Canadian tariffs, quantitative restrictions, and other nontariff measures inhibiting Mexican exports.

Over time, the basic agreement could be expanded thematically and geographically to cover a broad range of practices and disciplines throughout the hemisphere.

Free Trade in the Americas:
A Latin American Perspective
José Manuel Salazar-Xirinachs with Eduardo Lizano

Latin America has enthusiastically embraced the vision and the challenge of hemispheric free trade, but it has done so, quite correctly, with a prudent and strategic vision. Even before the Enterprise for the Americas (EAI) was announced, most countries in the region had unilaterally undertaken trade and financial reforms, cutting tariffs to about 20 percent and removing many nontariff barriers. However, moving beyond this point to the virtual elimination of all trade barriers vis-à-vis a country of the size and competitive muscle of the United States is an entirely different proposition.

A free trade agreement with the United States would entail significant benefits as well as costs for Latin America. The main potential benefits include a possibly substantial increase in exports to the United States, larger investment flows, and productivity gains associated with domestic efforts to enhance external competitiveness. For these benefits to materialize, however, access to the U.S. market must be effectively enlarged and assured through the removal of U.S. tariff and nontariff barriers, discipline in the use of U.S. trade remedies, and nonexclusionary rules of origin. The ability to exploit such trade and investment opportunities is not an automatic by-product of liberalization, however. Complementary support measures and modernization policies will be required to boost supply response. A stable macroeconomic environment and a clear and consistent framework for long-term investment are essential in this regard. In addition, it will be necessary to remove structural rigidities and bottlenecks that could thwart export growth—i.e., inadequate infrastructure, segmented and inefficient capital markets, lack of skills, insufficient managerial and technological capacities, and ineffectual and rigid public sector bureaucracies.

The main costs of the FTA will be those linked to import penetration. Those costs are likely to be much higher for Latin America than for the United States. Yet, Latin America would only be able to sustain import liberalization if the United States also allowed greater penetration of imports from the region. Otherwise, Latin America would experience unsustainable disequilibria in its balance of payments.

For Latin America a free trade agreement with the United States would entail much more than removing cross-border trade barriers. Such an arrangement would have profound effects on the size, role, and prerogatives of the state, macroeconomic management, and the adoption of international standards in a number of areas. In addition, Latin America's productive sectors would be shaped by hemisphere-wide market forces and control over national economies would be further diluted by global investment trends. Hence, broad cultural and social issues are also involved.

The extreme heterogeneity of the region poses a critical challenge to hemispheric free trade. Vast differences between the United States and Latin American countries in terms of size, productivity, level of development, and mutual importance as trading partners imply that a regional FTA cannot be conceived as a reciprocal exchange among equals. Reciprocal trade liberalization among unequal partners may only be feasible if supplemented by additional measures to prevent an unacceptably skewed distribution of gains and by mechanisms to support rapid growth of exports, investment, and competitiveness in the less developed partners. Whether or not those technical and financial support measures are included in the agreement is not essential. What matters is that the importance of these complementary policies to ensure the viability of free trade areas between countries at different stages of development be recognized. Bridging these disparities will be the most challenging aspect of the FTA for all concerned.

Even if the vision of hemispheric free trade takes years to complete—as it probably will—its legacy is already apparent: it has given a new impetus and a new sense of direction to regional integration efforts. Although important differences regarding optimal transition strategies toward freer trade and investment regimes still persist, today few in Latin America question that this is the way to go.

Getting There: The Path to a Western Hemisphere Free Trade Area and Its Structure
Richard G. Lipsey

Enormous structural changes are sweeping the world. Foreign direct investment has become a major instrument of growth and development. To be left outside major flows of international capital is to be marginalized in today's globalizing economy.

Liberalized, outward-looking, market-oriented (but not necessarily market-worshipping) economic policies are key conditions for playing a strong part in the evolving world economy. A Western Hemisphere Free Trade Area could be a key institution in encouraging and enshrining these developments.

A WHFTA would provide increased and more secure access to the U.S. and other regional markets, and in so doing, it would increase the attractiveness of WHFTA members as locales for foreign as well as domestic investment. To realize its full potential, hemispheric trade should evolve toward a single, comprehensive agreement rather than several separate regional arrangements.

Sound economic policy dictates certain prerequisites for membership in the WHFTA: inflation and fiscal deficits must be under control, outward-looking and market-oriented domestic policies must be in place, and exchange rates must be market-based. Countries wishing to join the WHFTA should be full GATT members and must have significantly reduced their trade barriers prior to WHFTA membership.

If it is to be a major force toward hemispheric prosperity, a WHFTA must be a union of equals based on plurilateral regionalism (i.e., agreements between regional groups in which each member has the same privileges and obligations as all of the others), not on a hub-and-spoke model (i.e., bilateral agreements between individual Latin American countries and the United States). It must be outward-looking, which calls for a FTA rather than a customs union. It must have low external tariffs. And it must be open to all serious new applicants.

The organization should be based on a core of nonnegotiable free trade and investment principles, some important transitional arrangements for new members, and a minimum of country-specific exceptions and special arrangements negotiated with new entrants. Whenever possible, long sunset periods rather than exceptions should be used; they are greatly preferable to permanent grandfathering. Finally, clear conditions for accession to the expanding FTA should be established. Under these conditions, a WHFTA could complement, rather than hinder, further multilateral trade liberalization.

U.S.-Latin American Free Trade Areas: Some Empirical Evidence
Refik Erzan and Alexander Yeats

The major conclusion drawn from Refik Erzan and Alexander Yeats' analysis of the first-round trade effects of eliminating U.S. trade barriers on Latin American exports is that the potential for many Latin American countries to expand exports through FTAs with the United States may be far smaller than is often thought. As a result of general U.S. tariff cutting in previous multilateral trade negotiations (MTNs), the extension of Generalized System of Preferences (GSP) and Caribbean Basin Initiative (CBI) preferences to some Latin American countries, and the concentration of Latin America's exports in primary products facing zero or low barriers, only a small share of Latin America's total exports currently faces important tariff and nontariff barriers in the U.S. market. Mexico and Brazil are somewhat exceptional, but even there, the average tariffs they face and the share of their total exports subject to nontariff barriers (NTBs) in the United States are well below those encountered by countries such as Hong Kong, Korea, or Taiwan. In contrast, the potential for a FTA-induced expansion of U.S. exports to Latin America appears considerably greater, because protection levels in most Latin American countries are significantly higher than those in the United States.

The estimates by Erzan and Yeats indicate that the potential trade gains for most Latin American countries from FTA negotiations with the United States are relatively modest: an increase in aggregate Latin American exports on the order of 8.8 percent if tariffs are removed and hard core NTBs in the U.S. market are liberalized; a 6.6-percent export increase if only tariffs are eliminated. Successful completion of the Uruguay Round would further reduce the worth of FTAs to Latin America, as any reduction in MFN tariffs would lower the margin of preference that could be extended to Latin American exporters. The authors' simulations suggest that Uruguay Round tariff cuts in the 30- to 40-percent range would reduce Latin America's FTA-induced U.S.-bound export growth by about one-third from their baseline projections.

In view of the seemingly limited potential of the FTA approach, Latin American countries might do better by assigning relatively greater importance to multilateral liberalization efforts within the GATT. If FTA negotiations do move forward, however, they should do so in as plurilateral a fashion as possible. The hub-and-spoke model would appear to be the least desirable way to proceed, because such arrangements would maximize the risk of intra-Latin American trade displacement by increasing exports from the United States. The danger of such adverse consequences seems so important that the authors strongly recommend that negotiations on hemispheric FTAs proceed on a multilateral basis to ensure that the interests of individual countries are protected.

The analysis also indicates that the way nontariff barriers are handled in free trade negotiations with the United States is an issue of utmost importance to Latin America, particularly in sectors such as sugar, textiles, and clothing. Considering the United States' past reluctance to make concessions in such sensitive sectors, either multilaterally or bilaterally, the question arises whether or not the United States has the political will to liberalize such barriers in the context of hemispheric FTAs. Yet, without major liberalization by the United States in these areas, the trade gains for Latin America would be quite limited.

The North American Free Trade Agreement: A Regional Model?
Craig VanGrasstek and Gustavo Vega

The ratification of the NAFTA agreement is not expected to be a major hurdle in Mexico, but the process may be more turbulent in Canada and the United States. The Canadian ratification debate could revisit the concerns raised in 1988, when a federal election became a national plebiscite on the CAFTA and the parties opposing the agreement narrowly lost the race. In the United States, the key question is whether or not the executive and legislative branches can arrive at a mutually acceptable price for fast-track approval of the agreement. The White House would be well advised to consider increased funding for trade adjustment assistance programs, as well as border environmental projects, when it submits the agreement to Congress. Besides cushioning some of the negative side effects of increased trade with Mexico, these measures could convince fence-sitting Democrats to vote in favor of the accord. Legislators and trade officials should resist bargaining over matters that might alter the negotiated terms of the NAFTA itself.

Congress and the White House should also agree on the institutional arrangements for new negotiations under the EAI. The legislative branch has a legitimate and necessary role to play in developing U.S. negotiating objectives, overseeing the conduct of commercial diplomacy, and making the final decision to accept or reject agreements. The fast track offers an appropriate balance between these requirements and the need to ensure that trade agreements will not be subject to crippling amendments or dilatory maneuvers. The implementing legislation for the NAFTA should provide a new grant of authority under the fast track, for at least three years. The proposed accession clause should be viewed as a useful complement to the fast-track rules. If properly drafted, the docking provision and the fast track will jointly facilitate the entry of other Latin American and Caribbean countries into the free-trade club.

The accession talks need not be limited to the terms agreed in the trilateral accord. The trading partners may want to have the option to negotiate further with one another. Some NAFTA provisions will inevitably fall short of expectations. The agreement might not offer as much access to the Mexican energy sector as the United States seeks, for example, or might not adequately protect Mexican exporters from harassment under the U.S. trade-remedy laws. Whatever these shortcomings might be, the parties might wish to address them in the context of negotiations with other countries. The NAFTA accession clause should be drafted in a way that lets the original contracting parties make additional concessions, in response to requests from one another or from applicant countries.

Finally, the preoccupation with regional trade arrangements should not make countries in the hemisphere lose sight of the fact that their stake in the outcome of the Uruguay Round of multilateral trade negotiations is even greater. A successful round would not only facilitate reaching regional accords but would help ensure that those accords truly lead to freer trade rather than protected trade in an enlarged area.

U.S.-Chile Free Trade
Andrea Butelmann and Alicia Frohmann

A trade agreement with the United States would have direct effects on Chile's trade and investment flows, as well as indirect economic implications for Chile.

In the short run, the trade effects of the FTA are likely to be small. Chilean exports to the United States already face low levels of protection, but Chile stands to benefit from lower tariff escalation in the U.S. tariff schedule and from assurances about future access to the U.S. market. This would enable Chile to develop new product lines with a higher value-added for export to the U.S. market. On the other hand, granting the United States a significant margin of preference in the Chilean market could cause trade diversion. There is also some concern about being flooded by U.S. imports, although the fact that Chilean import duties are low and uniform makes this an unlikely scenario, except in the case of certain agricultural products (wheat, sugar, and oilseeds), which are protected by variable import levies.

The indirect benefits of the FTA are expected to be at least as important for Chile. The agreement would send a positive signal of Chile's commitment to free trade and a market economy, both to the domestic business community and international investors. It would show that democracy is good for business because it offers continuity and stability and legitimizes market liberalization policies.

According to opinion polls, the Chilean public favors a FTA. Chilean workers have already paid the cost of liberalizing the economy, and increased trade and investment would probably bring about more and better jobs. Most business associations also favor a FTA with the United States, even though the main Chilean exporters to the United States think it would be difficult to increase their U.S. market share, with or without a FTA. They fear that the negotiation of a bilateral agreement may raise conflicts that otherwise might not have surfaced, i.e., the poor environmental conditions in public mining operations or opposition from California fruit growers.

Many Chileans think that Chile should seek economic integration with other Latin American countries and not just with the United States. So far, the Aylwin administration has made important strides toward establishing close trade links with other countries in the region but has refrained from joining any of the subregional groups such as the Southern Cone Common Market (Mercosur) or the Andean Pact. The policy has been, instead, to seek special trade relationships with as many countries as possible to enhance Chilean trade prospects, without viewing them as mutually exclusive alternatives.

In fact, Chile's interests would best be served by the establishment of a truly hemispheric FTA. The inclusion of other Latin American countries in the FTA would increase competition for Chilean exports to the United States, but it would also open markets where Chile faces higher barriers than in the United States, without requiring a commitment to a common external tariff, as it would need to make upon joining Mercosur or the Andean Pact.

U.S.-Central America Free Trade
Sylvia Saborio

The countries of Central America might have preferred to remain essentially free riders, enjoying unilateral and exclusive though limited preferences in the U.S. market; however, the entry of Mexico (and possibly others) to the NAFTA leaves them no choice but to seek to join the FTA as well. Given that these countries already enjoy ample access to the U.S. market, their main reasons for joining the FTA would be essentially defensive, i.e., to avoid the costs in terms of trade and investment diversion that would result from exclusion. As nonmembers, Central American countries would not only face a competitive disadvantage in the U.S. market but would also suffer discrimination vis-à-vis the United States in other members' markets. The cost of exclusion from the FTA would be high and would increase with every new entrant to the preferential trade area.

If Central America is to join the FTA, it would be to its advantage to do it sooner rather than later. This would minimize the cost of exclusion and prevent a temporary competitive disadvantage from becoming a permanent investment loss. The threat of investment diversion is imminent—indeed, it is already happening *in anticipation* of a successful NAFTA. Unfortunately, a full-fledged free trade agreement between the United States and Central America to avert such a threat is not likely to happen any time soon. The United States has made it clear that it will not proceed with further agreements until the NAFTA has been completed and its effects evaluated. In any case, objectively, Central America is not yet ready to take on the rigors of full trade liberalization in the context of a reciprocal trade agreement with the United States.

To bridge this time gap, it is proposed that an interim provision be adopted (either as part of the NAFTA or as a separate bill) to extend to the countries of Central America whatever preferences (beyond those already provided by the CBI) are granted to Mexico and others, say through 1995. During this period, Central American countries would not be required to undertake additional reciprocal obligations but would be expected to continue with domestic and trade reforms under agreements with the IMF, World Bank, IDB, GATT, and USAID. Progress in the implementation of such reforms could be monitored in the context of the framework trade and investment agreements already in place with each of these countries. By 1995, both sides would agree to negotiate in good faith toward a full-fledged agreement to expand two-way trade.

Such a provision would temporarily protect these tiny economies from the unintended fallout of Mexico's entry into NAFTA, while providing a mechanism for the transition from unilateralism to some type of reciprocity in U.S. commercial relations with these countries. This is no free ride, considering the obvious asymmetries involved and the enormity of the reforms these countries must undertake to become eligible for a FTA. The cost to the United States would be virtually nil, because the Central American countries account for little more than 1 percent of total U.S. imports, and 80 percent of those imports already enter the United States duty free. Yet, it would give these countries both a strong incentive and a fighting chance to sustain the process of trade liberalization and market-oriented reform on which they have embarked.

U.S.-Caricom Free Trade
DeLisle Worrell

The Caribbean welcomes greater economic interchange with North America that is compatible with the region's export-oriented strategy. Caribbean leaders are naturally apprehensive about a free trade area that requires reciprocal treatment between North America and the Caribbean because of the great disparity in economic development and size between the two regions. The free trade provisions should not be hastily implemented as local producers could be easily overwhelmed by the vastly greater knowledge and resources of their North American competitors. Caribbean economic policy is based on the confidence that the region can develop dynamic, internationally competitive firms based on the region's skill and knowledge base. This development, however, requires time as well as technical and financial assistance to bring Caribbean exporters up to the required standards of international competitiveness.

A central issue in an eventual North American-Caricom Free Trade Area would be the removal of nontariff barriers. The Canada-United States Free Trade Agreement (CAFTA) contains several provisions to counter nontariff barriers. Caricom negotiators will seek similar provisions for any North American-Caricom Free Trade Agreement, with effective mechanisms for their enforcement.

The Caricom would need assurances that there will be no significant exclusions of products of export interest to the Caribbean. A major defect of the CBI is the exclusion of textiles, apparel, and footwear from its provisions. Caricom would also wish to ensure that the rules of origin under a FTA are not less favorable than those currently enforced under the CBI.

Undue injury to the Caribbean economies from trade liberalization should be avoided. Free access to the Caribbean market by U.S. producers would need to be phased in over a sufficient time period to allow Caribbean producers to gain needed knowledge for their full, active participation in the international market.

Caricom's obligations under a FTA would need to be reconciled with its Lomé obligations. The provisions of the Lomé Convention require that the European Community be given at least as favorable trade treatment as any other international trading partner of the African, Caribbean, and Pacific signatories. Caricom would have to provide free trade access to the European Community if it provided similar access to North America. That can be contemplated only after the long-term growth of a diversified Caribbean export sector is deemed to be secure.

In negotiating a free trade agreement with North America, Caricom should make sure that:

- Financial and technical assistance are included in the package to help make Caricom firms more competitive in international markets and to overcome the costs and externalities of reaching that standard.
- Effective mechanisms are established to control the use of non-tariff barriers and other administrative barriers to trade. Such mechanisms must be transparent and provide built-in compensation for the vast inequities in size and political influence between the United States and the Caribbean.
- The timing is appropriate for the implementation of the many provisions that will make up the free trade package. A long gestation period is necessary to ensure that Caribbean firms acquire the maturity that will enable them to be truly competitive and not to be overwhelmed by North American giants.

Finally, Caribbean countries should insist that transitional measures be adopted to ensure that their interests not be unduly jeopardized by the NAFTA, since their participation in a reciprocal free trade arrangement with North America can only be expected to happen a few years hence.

U.S.-Andean Pact Free Trade Agreement
Alberto Pascó-Font and Sylvia Saborio

Despite the evident political will on the part of the Andean Pact countries—Bolivia, Colombia, Ecuador, Peru, and Venezuela—to strengthen relations with the United States, a FTA between the United States and the Andean Pact (AP) as a group is not a foregone conclusion. Tensions within the group make the future of the AP itself somewhat uncertain. Conceivably, the U.S. decision on whether or not to limit FTAs to subregional groups (except for Chile) could have a bearing on whether the AP breaks up or firms up.

The Andean countries have no alternative but to become better integrated into the world economy, but rushing into a FTA with the United States, separately or together, might not be in their best interests. Andean countries should concentrate, first of all, on stabilizing their economies, modernizing their industry, and coping with their social problems. As a corollary, they should undertake unilateral trade liberalization measures. Such measures are a prerequisite for a well-functioning Andean Common Market, as much as for any trade arrangement with the United States.

Once the Andean countries have progressed on these tasks, they should concentrate on the process of regional integration. The consolidation of the Andean Common Market with a reasonably low common external tariff would smooth the transition of these economies into a more competitive environment by letting local firms develop the scale economies of the extended regional market before exposing them to fierce competition from abroad. A separate but related reason for consolidating the regional market first would be to forestall an exchange of bilateral preferences between individual AP members and the United States (or other partners), which might displace a fair amount of intra-AP trade and might also result in a complex (and potentially trade-distorting) set of rules and procedures to administer trade flows according to different places of origin or destination.

Eventually, though, AP countries will want to join a U.S.-centric FTA. The prospect of having their industrial exports placed at a competitive disadvantage in the U.S. market will put pressure on AP members to accelerate the pace of reform so as to join the FTA. This pressure will become stronger over time, as the cost of exclusion from the FTA rises with each new entrant.

This process of accession to the FTA might be expedited by replacing or folding existing bilateral agreements between individual AP members and the United States into a joint framework trade and investment agreement between the Andean Pact and the United States. At the same time, the AP should develop adequate coordinating mechanisms among its members to allow for joint negotiations with the United States.

From the AP perspective, the overarching objective of the negotiations should be to secure enhanced and assured access for Andean exports to the U.S. market under stable and contractually bound conditions. In principle, the negotiations should be as comprehensive as possible, covering all tradables (services as well as goods); all types of restrictions (tariffs, NTBs, and other trade restraints, including trade remedies, i.e., antidumping, countervailing and Section 301 actions), and provisions for the settlement of disputes. In addition, the negotiations should take into account the vast differences in the level of development of the parties involved. In particular, the principle of "relative reciprocity" should prevail in two areas: intellectual property protection, where a balance must be struck between the protection of foreign property rights and the legitimate need for technology transfer under reasonable conditions, and the timetable for phasing out tariff and nontariff barriers.

Finally, to benefit from enhanced access to the U.S. market, the Andean countries will need large additional investments, both to expand their export capacity and to remove supply bottlenecks that may block the export drive. The EAI investment and debt relief provisions should help in this regard. In addition, these countries' efforts on the drug front should be supported. Without outside assistance, it is unlikely that the Andean countries would be able successfully to wage a war on drugs and on poverty and at the same time become world class competitors.

U.S.-Mercosur Free Trade
Roberto Bouzas

A FTA between the United States and Mercosur—the (future) common market made up of Argentina, Brazil, Paraguay, and Uruguay—may be problematic in various respects. A major issue relates to the partners' differences in size and level of development, which will affect the distribution of costs and benefits and might eventually make a negotiation politically unfeasible. For Mercosur, efficiency gains from trade creation under a FTA with the United States would have to be weighed against potentially large welfare losses from trade diversion. In fact, because the United States and Mercosur are not natural trading partners and protection within Mercosur may be considerable, the potential for trade diversion could be large. Similarly, the reallocation of resources stemming from the elimination of trade barriers will be accompanied by high adjustment costs which, given the disparities in size, might pose obstacles to a FTA.

The dynamic gains from a FTA are likely to be more attractive than net static welfare gains. In fact, enhanced investment flows and competition, scale economies, and reduced uncertainty can all boost economic growth in Mercosur. However, potential benefits in terms of export expansion would greatly depend on the removal of NTBs and on curbing the scope of procedural protectionism in the United States, which limits effective access to that market.

The positive effects of a FTA on capital inflows should not be exaggerated, particularly in the case of Mercosur countries, which do not enjoy the locational advantages of Mexico. Furthermore, some of the potential benefits might be preempted by those accrued by the first countries to join a FTA with the United States.

A FTA with the United States would be tantamount to unilateral liberalization (except for trade diversion). Whether or not this is an appropriate policy course is debatable, especially for large, semi-industrialized economies such as Brazil. That some Mercosur countries may be more eager than others for a FTA with the United States will likely play a role in intra-Mercosur negotiations: if progress is too slow, or is in an undesired direction, one or more Mercosur members might find an incentive to break away.

Defensive considerations are likely to carry a good deal of weight in Mercosur's willingness to negotiate a FTA with the United States. Further antagonism between trade blocs and a more aggressive and bilateralist U.S. trade policy stance would strengthen the incentives to ensure against mounting protectionism and marginalization in the world economy. In a scenario of fragmentation, even economies with highly diversified markets would probably do better as members of a "unnatural" trade bloc than as independent participants in a conflictive trade environment. Similarly, the more Latin American countries that enter into FTAs with the United States, the higher the incentives for Mercosur countries to follow suit. Because the potential of the regional market for Mercosur exports is high, the costs of discrimination may be considerable. As economies with diversified markets, Mercosur countries will have to weigh carefully whether other trade partners are likely to retaliate against a FTA with the United States, since retaliation could counteract the benefits of larger exports to the latter.

Finally, FTA negotiations should not be launched under the pressure of short-run policy considerations (such as strengthening finance availability) without paying attention to the long-run and structural implications. In this respect, the present excitement over FTAs with the United States may be premature.

In the short to medium term, Mercosur countries should focus on advancing the subregional integration process and promoting a transparent accession mechanism as part of NAFTA. Progress toward subregional integration could strengthen Mercosur's eventual bargaining stance vis-à-vis the larger and more powerful U.S.-NAFTA partners and, indeed, the rest of the world. In the meantime, trade issues of common interest can be addressed in the context of the U.S.-Mercosur framework trade and investment agreement.

Part III
A Western Hemisphere Free Trade Area

Chapter One

Free Trade in the Americas: A U.S. Perspective

Peter Morici

A Western Hemisphere Free Trade Area (WHFTA), as envisioned in the Enterprise for the Americas Initiative (EAI), offers the United States and Latin America important opportunities for mutual gain.

Comprehensive free trade agreements, eliminating tariffs and liberalizing many nontariff barriers (NTBs), offer Latin America an incentive and an opportunity to successfully complete economic reforms and emulate the development progress of the East Asian newly industrializing countries (NICs). In turn, regional free trade areas (FTAs) offer the United States the opportunity to exchange in a gradual and digestible manner, low-skill/wage jobs for high-skill/wage jobs in knowledge-intensive activities. From a U.S. perspective, achieving these gains will hinge on the scope and structure of trade agreements.

THE ENTERPRISE FOR THE AMERICAS INITIATIVE

Unveiled in June 1990, EAI has three principal components—trade, investment, and debt relief. The trade component has the greatest potential of the three for fundamentally transforming the character and substance of U.S.-Latin American commercial relations and improving Latin American development prospects.

Trade

President Bush has embraced, as a long-term goal, a free trade area from Anchorage to Tierra del Fuego. The administration envisions negotiating FTAs with individual countries. (e.g., Mexico), and with regional groups, such as the Southern Cone Common Market (Mercosur).[1] Formal talks with countries outside North America will not begin until an agreement with Mexico is in place, because "Congress will want to see the positive results of the North American Free Trade Agreement before authorizing. . . new free trade agreements with other trading parties in the region."[2]

The United States has specific expectations for the economic regimes of free-trade partners. According to Ambassador Carla Hills, "Countries must be committed to a stable macroeconomic environment and to market-oriented policies before negotiations begin."[3] "Market-oriented policies" include good standing in the General Agreement on Tariffs and Trade (GATT), a willingness to open the economy to foreign investment and trade in services, and a commitment to enforce "world class" protection of intellectual property.

Recognizing that most Latin American countries do not yet meet these expectations, the United States has negotiated framework trade and investment agreements with Mercosur, the Caribbean Community (Caricom),[4] and most other countries in the region. Similar to the 1987 framework agreement with Mexico, these establish consultative mechanisms for addressing specific trade problems and resolving disputes.

Potential Breadth of Agreements

The Canada-United States Free Trade Agreement (CAFTA) provides a starting point for shaping a North American Free Trade Agreement (NAFTA). The structure of negotiating groups and Hills' statement outlining the basic requirements for EAI trade agreements bear this out.[5]

As in the CAFTA, in subsequent regional arrangements the United States should seek agreements that embody GATT rights and protection, while broadening the range of practices and deepening the disciplines covered. Essentially, such agreements should be GATT consistent; phase out tariffs and nontariff barriers—e.g., quotas, product standards, and discrimination in government procurement; establish comprehensive regimes for services—e.g., banking and finance, insurance, land transportation, and telecommunications; create comprehensive frameworks for foreign investment, including national treatment and prohibitions on performance requirements such as domestic content mandates and exporting goals; guarantee broad protection for intellectual property; provide for dispute settlement; and discipline the use of safeguards, subsidies, state trading, balance-of-payments restrictions, and foreign-exchange controls.

In the case of NAFTA, special provisions regarding natural resources are contemplated, and environmental and workplace safety issues are being discussed in parallel to trade negotiations.

Judging from the experience with Canada, negotiating such broad agreements would be a protracted process. For many nontariff measures, the CAFTA only establishes a standstill and broad goals for follow-on negotiations, which are expected to take many years.

EAI and the Broader U.S. Trade Agenda

U.S. objectives for CAFTA and the EAI closely resemble the agenda for the Uruguay Round, and in breadth if not depth, the European Community (EC) 1992 agenda. In the CAFTA, the United States and Canada essentially sought to establish a single market—an economic community without a common external tariff. Now in the EAI, by pushing its multilateral agenda harder and faster regionally, the United States seeks to extend this single market to first Mexico and then perhaps to Chile and other countries willing to adopt market-oriented trade and industrial policies.

Clearly, the administration is asking a lot of its neighbors. Unlike the Caribbean Basin Initiative (CBI), the United States is offering to lower its trade barriers in exchange for improved access for U.S. exports and investment and systemic reforms that pass U.S. scrutiny. How far is the United States willing to go in reforming its own import regime?

The CBI extends unilateral tariff preferences to exports from Central America and the Caribbean but generally excludes the most import-sensitive U.S. industries—e.g., textiles and apparel, footwear, many leather products (and their vinyl substitutes), and sugar and sugar-containing products. These tend to be commodities for which the United States maintains tariff spikes—most favored nation (MFN) tariffs above 15 percent.

Tariffs aside, the most significant barriers to Latin American exports in the United States are perceived to be: 1) the arbitrary application of subsidy/countervailing and dumping duties and other unilateral actions under U.S. trade law; and 2) management of imports of apparel, steel, and agricultural commodities.

CAFTA Chapters 11, 18, and 19 effectively established a separate U.S.-Canada regime for the application of trade-remedy laws but the agreement did not address the management of trade in declining manufacturing industries and agriculture. Agriculture was not central to U.S.-Canada economic relations but is at the core of U.S. relations with Latin America.

In a NAFTA or WHFTA, it would be technically possible to establish common and more rigorous hemispheric disciplines for subsidy/countervailing and dumping duties and other trade remedies, while maintaining existing approaches toward other countries.

Regarding declining industries and agriculture, the United

States may be able to open its markets to Mexico, while maintaining some measure of protection toward imports from other countries; however, opening access to U.S. markets to many other Latin American countries would end the effectiveness of most U.S. import-management programs.

U.S. COMMERCIAL RELATIONS WITH LATIN AMERICA

In terms of gross domestic product (GDP) and population, a NAFTA would surpass the EC and the market represented by Japan and the East Asian NICs. Adding the rest of Latin America would nearly double the NAFTA market population (Table 1).

Latin America purchases about 14 percent of U.S. exports, a bigger share than either Japan or the East Asian NICs (Table 2).[6] In 1989, machinery and transport equipment accounted for 42 percent of U.S. sales to Latin America. On the import side, petroleum accounted for a quarter of U.S. purchases (Table 3). Led by Mexico, machinery and transportation equipment accounted for another quarter of U.S. imports from Latin America.[7] Other important U.S. purchases included apparel, footwear,

TABLE 1. COMPARISON OF MAJOR REGIONAL MARKETS		
Country/Group	Gross Domestic Product ($ billions)	Population (millions)
North America	6,329	363
United States	5,424	250
Canada	581	25
Mexico	234	88
Other America	598	357
Total, Western Hemisphere	**6,927**	**720**
European Community	4,720	365
Japan and East Asian Newly Industrializing Countries[a]	3,202	199

Note: All data are for 1990 or latest available year.

[a]Includes Hong Kong, Singapore, South Korea, and Taiwan.

Sources: U.S. Department of Commerce "Fact Sheet: Enterprise for the Americas," May 24, 1991, p. 1; and Peter Morici, *Trade Talks with Mexico: A Time for Realism* (Washington, DC: National Planning Association, 1991), Table 2, p. 45.

furniture, plumbing, heating and lighting fixtures, and scientific and controlling instruments.

Latin America is also the host to over $72 billion (19 percent) of all U.S. foreign direct investment—more than Japan and the East Asian NICs combined (Table 4). Seven percent is in petroleum, 33 percent in manufacturing, and 48 percent in banking and other financial services (Table 5).[8]

TABLE 2. U.S. MERCHANDISE TRADE WITH LATIN AMERICA AND OTHER MAJOR PARTNERS ($ millions)

Country/Group	1979	1989	1990
Latin America			
Exports	28,555	48,842	54,272
Imports	30,532	57,502	64,320
Balance	-1,977	-8,660	-10,048
of which Mexico			
Exports	9,931	24,678	28,103
Imports	8,798	27,128	30,495
Balance	1,133	-2,450	-2,392
Canada			
Exports	38,690	80,657	83,572
Imports	39,227	89,934	93,026
Balance	-537	-9,277	-9,454
European Community			
Exports	42,474	84,514	96,276
Imports	33,219	85,508	91,326
Balance	9,255	-994	4,950
Japan			
Exports	17,629	43,863	47,977
Imports	26,260	93,532	89,667
Balance	-8,631	-49,669	-41,690
East Asian Newly Industrializing Countries[a]			
Exports	11,252	37,661	39,882
Imports	15,420	63,960	60,504
Balance	-4,168	-26,299	-20,622
All U.S. Trade			
Exports	184,473	361,451	389,550
Imports	212,009	477,368	497,665
Balance	-27,536	-115,917	-108,115

[a]Includes Hong Kong, Singapore, South Korea, and Taiwan.

Source: *Survey of Current Business*, Vol. 71, No. 6 (June 1991), pp. 50-52.

TABLE 3. COMMODITY DISTRIBUTION OF U.S. TRADE WITH MEXICO AND OTHER LATIN AMERICAN COUNTRIES, 1989 (percent)

Commodity Category	Imports			Exports		
	Total Latin America	Mexico	Other Latin America	Total Latin America	Mexico	Other Latin America
Food and Live Animals	15.4	8.9	20.9	8.3	8.3	8.4
Beverages and Tobacco	0.9	0.9	0.8	0.5	0.1	0.9
Crude Materials, Inedible, Except Minerals	4.1	2.5	5.6	5.1	6.2	3.9
Mineral Fuels, Lubricants, and Related Products	25.0	16.2	32.5	4.3	3.0	5.6
Animal and Vegetable Oils, Fats, Waxes	0.1	0.1	0.2	0.9	0.6	1.1
Chemicals and Related Products, NEC	3.0	2.2	3.6	12.5	9.1	16.0
Manufactured Goods	11.1	10.1	12.0	11.1	12.3	9.9
Machinery and Transport Equipment	24.9	44.5	8.3	41.9	45.0	38.7
Miscellaneous Manufactured Articles	12.6	10.1	14.7	10.5	10.3	10.7
Commodities and Transactions, NEC	2.8	4.5	1.4	4.9	5.1	4.7
Total Trade ($ billions)	**59.7**	**27.4**	**32.3**	**47.3**	**24.0**	**23.3**

Notes: NEC indicates not elsewhere classified (>). Numbers may not add because of rounding.

Source: Organisation for Economic Co-operation and Development, *Foreign Trade by Commodities: Series C* (Paris: OECD Publications, 1990).

TABLE 4. U.S. DIRECT INVESTMENT ABROAD, 1990 ($ millions)

Country/Group	All Industries	Of Which in Manufacturing
Latin America	72,467	23,802
Mexico	9,360	7,314
Central America[a]	1,029	494
South America	24,920	15,242
Other Latin America	37,158	752
Canada	68,431	33,231
European Community	172,940	81,264
Japan	20,994	10,623
East Asian Newly Industrializing Countries[b]	14,877	5,505
Other	71,785	13,795
Total	**421,494**	**168,220**

[a]Includes Belize, Costa Rica, El Salvador, Guatemala, Honduras, and Nicaragua.

[b]Includes Hong Kong, Singapore, South Korea, and Taiwan.

Source: *Survey of Current Business*, Vol. 71, No. 8 (August 1991), p. 88.

Seven rounds of GATT-sponsored multilaterally negotiated tariff cuts, as well as U.S. participation in the Generalized System of Preferences (GSP), the Caribbean Basin Initiative, and the Maquiladora Program for Mexico,[9] have greatly reduced the importance of tariffs in U.S. trade policy. According to the U.S. International Trade Commission (USITC), the trade-weighted average U.S. tariff on manufactured imports from all sources was 3.4 percent in 1989;[10] however, the United States maintains high tariffs on many important products for Latin America (see Erzan and Yeats, Chapter 4 of this volume).

Latin American products also face many quantitative restrictions—for example, voluntary restraints agreements (VRAs) for basic and specialty steel, controls on imports of textiles and apparel under the Multi-Fibre Arrangement (MFA), and controls on imports of sugar and sugar-containing products, cotton and certain basic cotton products, peanuts, meat, and dairy products. The United States also imposes seasonal tariffs and marketing orders on fresh fruits and vegetables, affecting many Latin American exports and potential exports. Further, as noted, the arbitrary application of U.S. trade-remedy laws is as much of a concern for Latin America as for competitors in Europe and Asia. Overall, Erzan and Yeats estimate that 39 percent of Latin American exports face some type of nontariff barrier.

Trade barriers to U.S. exports in Latin America consist of tariffs and tariff surcharges; quotas and import licensing schemes; and assorted practices under discussion in the GATT. These practices include government procurement, discriminatory product standards, subsidies, trade-related intellectual property issues (TRIPs), trade-related investment measures (TRIMs), and regulatory and licensing issues in business and financial services. Broader systemic barriers, the legacy of Latin American development policies before the mid-1980s, are also present.

Erzan and Yeats estimate that the average tariff on U.S. exports to Mexico and South America is about 20 percent, and note that such exports are often subject to considerable surcharges and other types of nontariff barriers.

TABLE 5. U.S. DIRECT INVESTMENT IN THE WESTERN HEMISPHERE, BY INDUSTRY AND MAJOR REGION (percent)

Type of Industry	Total	Latin America			Caribbean	Canada
		Mexico	South America	Central America[a]		
Petroleum	7.3	0.9	8.2	25.4	7.8	15.6
Manufacturing	32.8	78.1	61.2	48.0	2.0	48.6
Food and kindred products	4.3	9.8	7.2	25.3	0.4	3.3
Chemicals and allied products	7.5	17.1	13.1	10.1	1.2	9.4
Primary and fabricated metals	2.4	3.6	5.4	4.5	(S)	4.4
Machinery, except electrical	3.9	3.3	10.0	(A)	(A)	4.0
Electric and electronic equipment	2.1	6.0	3.8	1.9	(A)	3.2
Transportation equipment	4.6	18.7	7.2	(A)	(A)	11.6
Other manufactures	8.1	19.8	15.4	9.9	(S)	12.7
Wholesale Trade	4.0	5.4	3.2	1.4	4.3	6.0
Banking	10.5	0.3	6.9	1.4	15.7	1.5
Other Finance Insurance and Real Estate	37.6	3.4	8.3	2.0	66.9	17.6
Services	2.4	1.7	4.2	5.6	1.2	2.3
Other	5.4	10.3	8.1	16.1	2.1	8.4
Total ($ millions)	**72,467**	**9,360**	**24,920**	**1,030**	**37,157**	**68,431**

Notes: (A) is less than 0.05 percent; (S) is suppressed to avoid disclosure of individual company data. Numbers may not add because of rounding.

[a]Includes Belize, Costa Rica, El Salvador, Guatemala, Honduras, and Nicaragua.

Source: *Survey of Current Business*, Vol. 71, No.8 (August 1991), p. 88.

OBSTACLES TO LIFTING TRADE BARRIERS

Clearly, eliminating tariffs and liberalizing nontariff barriers would open important new market opportunities and long-run economic benefits from increased specialization; yet political and institutional obstacles confront policymakers in both the United States and Latin America.

United States

From a technical and systemic perspective, it would not be difficult to impose meaningful disciplines on U.S. trade-remedy laws, and gradually phase out tariff spikes, the Multi-Fibre Arrangement, the sugar program, and most other U.S. devices for protecting declining industries and farmers. The real obstacles are political, and they lie in the constituent pressures on the Congress and the President. Overcoming these will depend in part on Latin America's willingness to accept long phase-down periods for trade barriers and to open its markets fully to U.S. products.

Elsewhere, I have argued that both the benefits and labor adjustments that may be expected as a consequence of a U.S.-Mexico agreement would be much greater than suggested by the economic studies published to date.[11] Most of the reasons offered generalize to extending a NAFTA to other Latin American nations. Essentially free trade offers the United States many more opportunities to specialize in higher value, technology-intensive products than econometric models can estimate on the basis of historical observations. The resulting movement along the production possibility frontier will displace many blue- and gray-collar workers who will encounter significant difficulties moving into high-skill/wage jobs. Even if aggressive retraining and relocation programs are made available, these workers will be handicapped by inadequacies in their general educational backgrounds. Free trade with Mexico and Latin America would not be the main source of difficulties for industrial workers—i.e., the diminishing numbers of high-paying factory jobs, declining real wages, and the growing disparity between their incomes and those of skilled professionals. However, the incremental adjustments imposed by free trade could easily become the target of opportunistic pundits and politicians. The resulting pressure on the Congress and the President could result in American backsliding on commitments to liberalize trade.

Therefore, agreements establishing a WHFTA must strike an important bargain: Latin American countries would need to accept long phase-down periods for tariffs and quantitative restrictions to satisfy the most affected segments of U.S. industry and agriculture in exchange for ironclad assurances that the United States will widen access in each of these industries every year of the transition period and that all tariffs and quantitative restrictions will be eliminated by the end of the transition period.

This said, the opening of U.S. markets to low- and medium-technology manufactures and agricultural commodities would receive enduring political support in the United States only if a WHFTA delivered on the new opportunities promised for U.S. sales of sophisticated producer durables and services. If Latin American governments did not accept U.S. comparative advantages and sheltered computer and other technology-intensive industries, the exchange of high-skill/wage for low-skill/wage jobs would not materialize for American workers, despite the promises of free trade proponents. Then, the door to the American market would slam shut as quickly as it had opened.

Latin America

From a technical and systemic perspective, opening Latin American markets to U.S. exports poses much more vexing problems than achieving progress among the United States, Canada, and the EC. These problems persist despite earnest intent on the part of Latin American leaders. They are rooted in part in the institutional legacy of past industrial development policies, and the fact that the economies are less developed.

Through the 1980s, the tariffs and other discriminatory practices at the core of Latin American import-substitution development strategies went far beyond fine tuning imports to create reasonable market opportunities for emerging industries. These practices were part of a comprehensive nexus of foreign investment, industrial, technology, labor market, and social policies asserting economic nationalism and independence from American hegemony. These policies were often ideologically driven by flawed notions about how to manage mixed capitalist economies most effectively.

For example, in Mexico before 1985, tariffs averaged 24 percent, and nearly every import required a license. The parastatal sector produced 18 percent of GDP. Foreign ownership was restricted and subject to tough local sourcing and export performance requirements where it was permitted. Many domestic prices were controlled, and strict industrial product standards and service industry regulations favored the use of domestic products. Protection was extremely weak for foreign intellectual property.[12]

Mexico was not unique. But now, throughout Latin America, governments encumbered by debt have stepped beyond macroeconomic remedies in great strides to open their economies to trade, attract foreign investment, liberalize their industrial policies, and move the locus of economic decisionmaking from government ministries to private businesses.

Although the progress to date is impressive, it has yet to prove decisive. Even Mexico, a country with one of the most ambitious reform programs, needs to do much more.[13] The methods of the old regime were not merely a matter of policy, a reflection of the acquisitive instincts of privileged groups, or the problems of underdevelopment; they were deeply rooted in culture and legitimate Latin American concerns about national self-determination and sovereignty.

As both sides seek closer economic links, two critical questions emerge:

■ Will reforms in Latin America go far enough to ensure reasonably free and secure market access for U.S. goods, services, and investments?

■ In what direction will the quest for market-responsive economic regimes take individual Latin American countries? In the long run, will they emulate U.S.-like, neo-laissez-faire policies or will they choose more Japanese/French models of public-private cooperation?

In the short run, the direction is important because of the ideological inclinations of the Bush administration—its laissez-faire aspirations clearly color its perceptions of Latin American readiness for free trade negotiations. In the long run, however, the problem is more fundamental and goes to the core of what is needed for a regional free trade area—the effective interface of Latin American and U.S. and Canadian economic institutions.

GATT, REGIONALISM, AND U.S. POLICY

In the 1980s, Americans witnessed the victories of two of their long-championed ideals—the triumphs of democratic institutions and the increased acceptance, throughout Europe, Latin America, and Asia of the notion that the mandates of markets, not governments, should guide the development of national economies.

Economic reform in Latin America and the EC 1992 program are emblematic of the latter trend, and on the surface, this movement could have been expected to further rapid progress in multilateral trade negotiations (MTNs). After all, the United States has been a prime mover in the GATT, ever the champion of rules promoting market-driven trade and specialization over government management. Yet, the global movement toward more "market-oriented" policies has not translated into much success in multilateral efforts to open commerce among the three major players—the United States, the EC, and Japan. Most progress on the trade front appears to be regional in scope—e.g., the completion of the internal market in the EC, the rapidly expanding web of Japanese trade links with

East and Southeast Asia, the CAFTA, and other U.S. regional gestures such as the CBI and Maquiladora Program.

Motivations Behind Regionalism

Regionalism results largely from three sets of factors that must be recognized to understand the central issues involved in creating a WHFTA.

First, since the Kennedy Round of multilateral trade negotiations (1968-1972), GATT membership has expanded and greatly diversified. Coupled with slower growth in North America and Europe, this has magnified the adjustment costs of genuine multilateral liberalization. By comparison, regional liberalization can provide many benefits of multilateral progress with fewer, better controlled adjustments. For example, by expanding into Spain and Portugal, the EC accessed inexpensive labor and consumer goods but at levels that did not overwhelm EC markets—the combined population of these two countries is only about 10 percent of the entire community.[14] In Asia, Japan could easily be overwhelmed by imports from the East Asian NICs and Southeast Asian nations. Consequently, Japan is careful to manage the growth of imports from its regional trading partners through its *keiretsus*.

Second, progress on many nontariff issues central to the Uruguay Round agenda require considerable harmonization of national practices and regulations, which, though directed toward comparable goals, vary substantially in their basic approaches and rigor. Consider for example, national differences in approval processes for pharmaceuticals. More significantly, national governments sometimes differ in their fundamental public policy goals. Perhaps, the most contentious example has been the protection of intellectual property, which has, at times, put developed and several developing countries at loggerheads. Bridging such differences with more than a hundred players at the GATT table is an extraordinarily difficult task. However, within regional groups, countries often (but not always) share more in terms of their economic and legal institutions. Although the EC 1992 program may have originated in European fears of lost competitive viability, the practical realization of its ambitious initiatives will owe much to this basic calculus.

Third, the global movement toward market-oriented policies does not represent an international conversion to an American vision of market capitalism—one steeped in Smithian notions of laissez-faire—as often espoused by the Bush administration. It is one thing to say that government policies cannot resist market signals—maintain or create industries where a present or potential comparative advantage does not exist—without incurring heavy costs in lost productivity and gross national product (GNP). It is another thing altogether to say that governments have little or no role to play in managing the allocation of resources from declining to emerging activities.

The idea that governments may at once respect the mandates of international markets and help private businesses identify and respond to latent and apparent competitive opportunities may be anathema to the Bush administration, but it remains ingrained in European and Japanese thinking.[15] The resulting ideological tension is at the core of European and Japanese resistance to the American agenda for constraining subsidies and other instruments of industrial policy in the GATT.

In many ways, a new competition of ideas has emerged to replace the old struggle between socialism and capitalism—a competition of paradigms between an American model of *atomistic capitalism* and a Japanese model of *syndicate capitalism*.

In the European and Asian blocs, such ideological conflicts are more manageable or largely suppressed. In Europe, France and Italy are clearly comfortable with pro-market government intervention and have reached accommodations with the other major players—Germany and Great Britain. In Asia, Japan enforces its hegemony by linking investment and technology to market access and exports through its aid policies and the purchasing practices of *keiretsus*.

Implications for a WHFTA

Are these kinds of forces really working in favor of a WHFTA? Probably not.

First, the likely adjustments for the United States from free trade with Mexico alone will have greater consequences for the United States than did Spain and Portugal for the EC. Mexico will account for about 25 percent of the population of the new free trade area. With the addition of several other major economies, the Latin American population could easily be more than 50 percent.

Second, the United States and Canada share much less with Latin America in terms of economic and legal institutions than they do with each other, or the EC for that matter. This makes the harmonization of domestic policies, practices, and regulations to reduce nontariff barriers between the United States, Canada, and Latin America more difficult than reducing barriers to U.S.-Canadian or intra-EC trade.

This whole set of issues could become less vexing, perhaps downright manageable, if Latin American countries achieve continued and rapid progress in reforming their domestic economic institutions and policies and their supporting legal structures. In the end, though, the potential for interface between U.S. and Latin American economic and legal institutions will depend importantly on how closely the emerging Latin American models of market capitalism approximate the U.S. model of atomistic capitalism, on the one hand, or some variant of Japanese syndicate capitalism or French *dirigisme*, on the other hand.

For the time being, Mexico and the rest of Latin America must substantially increase their exports to make their reforms succeed, and intra-Latin American trade, though important, will not suffice by itself. In the current international negotiating environment, these nations find their best opportunities outside Latin America and in the United States. In this context, it is not surprising that the reform process in Mexico and other places in Latin America conforms to the U.S. model.

However, given the long Latin American tradition of government intervention, Americans should not be surprised to see Mexico and other Latin American countries, adopt pro-market industrial policies. This would enable them to exploit market opportunities overlooked or mishandled by past import-substitution regimes, as their economies strengthen and their governments acquire more discretionary resources.

Clearly, people of good will and with good minds can disagree about which model of market capitalism would best serve the United States as the foundation of future progress in the broader multilateral system. However, it is also the case that U.S. industry could become the victim of frequent and substantial industrial predation if 1) the United States forges trade agreements with Latin American countries that preclude U.S. resort to trade-remedy laws; 2) Latin American countries experiment with more *dirigiste* economic development policies; and 3) the U.S. administration continues to embrace a minimalist approach to industrial policy.[16]

REGIONALISM AND U.S. NATIONAL INTEREST

Given the labor adjustment costs and the enormous systemic challenges inherent in integrating the U.S. and Latin American economies, why bother with a NAFTA and a WHFTA? After all, if many American workers lack the skills for new, high-paying jobs, why subject them to competition with $2.00 per hour labor? Even if free trade would raise aggregate incomes, is it good social policy to defray those gains with a much less equal distribution of income?

In other areas of conflict between economic and social policy, the American polity seems willing to accept limited trade-offs between economic efficiency and efforts to assure an equitable distribution of income and achieve other social goals. However, with the United States struggling to keep a place among leading industrial nations—in terms of job quality and worker income—trade policy no longer offers simple, limited trade-offs.

Keeping Up with the Competition

Supporting political and economic reform in Mexico and elsewhere in Latin America serves U.S. political and security interests. As important, seeking further integration with Mexico, and perhaps all of Latin America, serves U.S. domestic and global economic interests. In the end, Americans must recognize the link between good trade policy and good domestic policy. Open markets to low-technology imports and improving the quality of public education are complementary policies.

In Asia, Japan is systematically increasing imports of low-technology products and creating a market for its high-technology goods and services through the investments of its *keiretsus* and tied foreign aid. The most important elements of Tokyo's highly successful industrial strategy and superior growth record are its willingness to accept and manage the labor-market adjustments and increase the proportion of young workers with the general educational attainments and necessary training in technology to make a high-skill economy work.

The United States and the EC can pursue similar strategies by accelerating the growth of their trade with Latin America and Eastern Europe and improving educational opportunities for their workers. Protection against low-wage labor will work against improving domestic employment opportunities by decreasing the incentives to become a more knowledge-intensive economy and exporter of technology-intensive products. The United States and the EC would fall behind Japan in wages and industrial profits, and Japan would be better positioned to finance research and development and further improvements in education and training. Some trends in this direction are already apparent, for instance, the decline in U.S. real wages over the last 15 years, the decline in U.S. research and development budgets relative to Japan for many generic precompetitive technologies, and the increase in Japanese financing of American research and development.

Japan, the United States, and the EC could transform their industrial and labor structures through multilateral trade liberalization. Progress along this route, however, appeals less to politicians than does regionalism. With Japan moving aggressively in Asia and political events pushing the EC toward Eastern Europe, the United States must engage Mexico and much of Latin America to keep up with Japan and the EC, and it must begin the process now.

The Back Door Problem

For the United States, the best market opportunities in Latin America lie in locating low- and medium-technology manufacturing activities in the region and in selling them the producer durables and business services they need to modernize. The basic logic is that U.S. multinational corporations (MNCs) will invest in Latin America; these firms and indigenous entrepreneurs will ship more low- and medium-technology products to the United States; and the United States will export more sophisticated components, machinery, equipment, and knowledge-intensive services to Latin America.

Some critics have made much of the fact that many Asian MNCs are better positioned than U.S. companies to invest in Latin America—comparing, for example, the cash positions of General Motors and Chrysler, and Nissan and Toyota.[17] With the advent of regional free trade, Japanese MNCs, for example, could invest in Latin America to service U.S. markets, and Latin American purchases of knowledge-intensive goods and services, which are now decidedly oriented toward the United States, could migrate toward Japan. The purchasing practices of the *keiretsus* could amplify such a trend.

Conventional rules of origin would do little to discourage such a realignment of trade. U.S. tariffs are generally low[18] and have no affect on the purchases of capital goods and services.[19] U.S. suppliers would initially receive some advantages from tariff-free access in Latin America, but minimal advantages in Mexico. A WHFTA would reduce preferences elsewhere in Latin America to Mexican levels.[20]

If a NAFTA and subsequent trade agreements with other Latin American countries increase U.S. imports more than exports, the increment to the aggregate U.S. trade deficit would be eliminated by other market adjustments—e.g., depreciation of the dollar and a fall in the wages earned by workers making tradable products relative to their counterparts abroad and in other domestic industries.[21] This would exacerbate adjustment pressures on industrial workers. Although economists can argue that adjustments go with the fortunes of fair competition, they must also be recognized as a potential source of constituent pressures on Congress and the President to slow the process of hemispheric economic integration.

In a NAFTA or a WHFTA, the United States may need to seek preferential access in areas besides tariffs to avoid backlash and achieve a balance of new market opportunities with its Latin American partners.[22] However, such exchanges of preferential access would further undermine U.S. adherence to the most favored nation principle. This central element of the GATT has already been weakened by the implementation of the Tokyo Round Codes, the EC 1992 program, and certain provisions of the CAFTA.[23]

A regional trading bloc in North America or the Western Hemisphere need not pose a threat to the broader GATT system, if based on a core agreement like the CAFTA, which broadens and deepens GATT benefits and protection for its members without preempting generalization of the additional benefits to all GATT members. However, any regional framework or series of bilateral agreements (a hub-and-spoke system, perhaps with multiple hubs) outside a central, GATT-consistent discipline would likely result in a web of entangling preferences and conflicting benefits that would eventually choke off further progress on trade liberalization, both in the Western Hemisphere and the GATT.

POLICY RECOMMENDATIONS

In many ways, the United States is on the horns of a dilemma. If it doesn't open its markets to Latin America, it risks stagnation. If it does, it risks major labor market disruptions and jeopardizes long-term progress in the GATT.

For years, the United States has been prodding, urging, and cajoling Latin America to open up, rely on markets, exploit comparative advantages, and welcome foreign investment. Now, with Latin American governments earnestly moving in this direction, the United States is being challenged to take its own advice. This challenge comes at a bad moment for the United States, economically and politically. Burdened by lagging investments in capital and technology and the mediocre performance of U.S. public education, the United States faces wrenching adjustments. Most of them have nothing to do with Latin America, but regional free trade would make adjustment more difficult.

A NAFTA or WHFTA poses additional dangers to U.S. leadership in the GATT, if it entails exchanges of preferences that are inconsistent with GATT principles or future progress in MTNs. The differential progress of reform in Latin America necessitates differential timing for U.S. negotiations with individual countries and groups. But serial negotiations greatly increase the prospects that a multiple hub-and-spoke system will emerge without any GATT-consistent regional discipline.

Facing this conundrum, President Bush's Enterprise for the Americas Initiative and his negotiating stance in the talks with Mexico are generally consistent with the broad elements of an optimum U.S. policy. However, some important details of U.S. policy not yet adequately articulated create some cause for concern. An effective American policy should contain the following four elements.

■ *Good Trade Policy Is Good Domestic Policy.* Multilaterally, the United States should continue initiatives in the GATT but recognize that regional trade agreements are a complementary approach for fostering increased U.S. market access abroad and the necessary adjustments at home to increase specialization in high income-generating, knowledge-intensive activities.

Domestically, the administration should continue to emphasize that the greatest threat to U.S. competitiveness and prosperity is an inadequately trained labor force and mediocre standards in American schools.[24] Going a step further, the administration should state that trade-policy liberalization must be linked to improvements in human resources.

■ *Go Slow But Be Persistent.* The U.S. economy can be reoriented toward more knowledge-intensive pursuits only as fast as U.S. workers can obtain the education and technical training for high-skill/wage pursuits. Therefore, a gradual but persistent approach to opening U.S. markets over a period of 10 to 20 years seems appropriate. Initial administration statements regarding goals for negotiations with Mexico[25] and its sequencing of EAI trade negotiations—Mexico now, perhaps Chile in two or three years, other countries after that—are broadly consistent with such an approach.

A go-slow strategy entails two important sets of risks. First, workers and firms in affected industries and agriculture may not become convinced that protection will continuously decline and eventually end—gradualism could engender intense political lobbying to sustain protection. Second, a gradual opening of U.S. markets and a long wait for Latin American countries could discourage their reform efforts and encourage their leaders to turn to Japanese/French-style industrial development strategies, creating new sources of trade tensions.

With regard to adjustments, administration denials to the U.S. Congress that free trade will impose adjustments of any consequence are not useful.[26] Instead, the administration must continue to convey the message to U.S. firms and workers in import-sensitive industries and to the American polity: protection of declining and uncompetitive industries will not reverse the decline in U.S. living standards; only improving the quality of education and training as a precondition for industrial renewal and opening foreign markets to U.S. knowledge-intensive products will allow Americans to enjoy rising real incomes.

With regard to market opening, the U.S. strategy of engaging Latin American countries on several fronts is most useful (e.g., debt relief, promoting new private investment, negotiating framework agreements, and encouraging regional groupings in Latin America). However, to keep the reform momentum going, the administration should go a step further and include in the NAFTA agreement a "docking provision," so that countries that meet eligibility requirements and are prepared to accept the disciplines of the FTA may join.

■ *Be Firm and Realistic.* The administration must remain firm on its standards for beginning free trade negotiations with Latin American countries. Unless reforms are fairly well along, as in Mexico, the potential is limited for achieving substantial new market access for U.S.

products. Unless Latin America's legal and economic institutions become broadly compatible with U.S. approaches to industrial policy, the prospects are jeopardized for harmonizing U.S. and Latin American policies, practices, and regulations; for achieving truly integrated and open markets; and for ensuring that U.S. firms and workers do not fall prey to industrial predation.

At the same time, the United States has to be realistic. Latin American countries cannot be expected to open their economies fully without substantial liberalization by the United States in mature manufacturing, agriculture, and lower-skilled, tradable services. For its part, the United States should condition full and free access to U.S. markets on completion of reform goals over transition periods that parallel the U.S. removal of trade barriers in import-sensitive sectors.

■ *Be Ambitious.* In negotiations, the United States should look beyond a simple free trade area and seek to liberalize nontariff barriers and measures affecting investment and trade in services. Only this will ensure a substantial two-way opening of commerce. To its credit, the administration has articulated agendas for negotiations with Mexico and other Latin American countries as broad as the ones pursued with Canada in the CAFTA and by the EC in its 1992 program.

Moreover, the United States should seek preferences that go beyond tariffs, first in negotiating a NAFTA, and then when reaching agreements with other Latin American countries. This would harm the GATT only if it is mishandled. Unlike participants in a simple free trade area, nontariff preferences and two-tier MFN are exactly what members of an economic community afford one another. Specifically, the processes of harmonizing national policies, practices, and regulations to achieve progress on nontariff measures (such as the one articulated in the EC 1992 program and by the U.S. administration for negotiations with Canada, Mexico, and other Latin American nations) create preferences beyond mere tariff preferences.

Such processes are not GATT inconsistent if they strengthen GATT member countries' rights and protection in their regional commerce by tightening the disciplines imposed by existing GATT rules as they affect regional commerce and if they broaden the range of practices subject to GATT-like rules to the extent they affect regional commerce. If such regional liberalization does not preclude or impede future progress in the GATT, it may anticipate or encourage future multilateral progress much as the regional elimination of tariffs in Europe preceded and encouraged aggressive multilateral tariff cuts in the Kennedy Round.

Generally, the U.S.-Canadian mutual preferences through the CAFTA meet this test. Extending the CAFTA concept to the rest of the hemisphere could do the same. In the end, the United States is leaning less toward GATT-inconsistent actions than toward creating an economic community in North America (though without a common external tariff regime), and then inviting other countries in the hemisphere to join.

As a first step, the United States should seek a NAFTA patterned on the CAFTA, with fairly precise modalities and timetables for conforming Mexican economic policies and practices to U.S. and Canadian norms, and with suitable transition and safeguard provisions for vulnerable industries in all three countries. As essential, the United States must be prepared to accept precise modalities and timetables for removing its own tariffs and quantitative restrictions and liberalizing other nontariff measures that may inhibit Mexican exports.[27]

The overall objective should be to shape an agreement, that becomes more and more stringent over time until it supersedes the CAFTA by addressing a wider scope of practices. Such an agreement should also contain accession provisions that permit other Latin American countries to enter the community on similar terms and conditions as Mexico.

By following these recommendations, the United States could open substantial new markets in Mexico and elsewhere in Latin America and facilitate the transition to a more knowledge-intensive, higher-wage economy. The challenges of combining good trade policy with sound domestic policies, maintaining credibility with domestic interest groups and foreign leaders, and crafting agreements that serve the best interests of the United States and other countries in the region will be formidable. These, however, are the challenges U.S. policymakers must accept if the United States is to continue to be at the forefront of industrial progress, to offer its citizens prospects for rising income, to maintain its leadership position in the GATT, and to enjoy the wealth necessary to continue to meet its wider global responsibilities.

Notes

[1] The Southern Cone Common Market (Mercosur) is a newly created free trade area (prospective common market), which includes Argentina, Brazil, Uruguay, and Paraguay.

[2] Carla A. Hills, Address by the U.S. Trade Representative at the U.S.-Central American Conference on Trade and Investment, San José, Costa Rica, August 12, 1991.

[3] Ibid.

[4] The Caribbean Community (Caricom) includes Antigua and Barbuda, The Bahamas, Barbados, Belize, Dominica, Grenada, Guyana, Jamaica, Montserrat, St. Kitts and Nevis, St. Lucia, St. Vincent and the Grenadines, and Trinidad and Tobago.

[5] See Carla A. Hills, op. cit.

[6] *Survey of Current Business*, Vol. 71, No. 7 (June 1991).

[7] Organisation for Economic Co-operation and Development, *Foreign Trade by Commodities: Series C, 1989* (Paris: OECD Publications, 1990).

[8] *Survey of Current Business*, Vol. 71, No. 8 (August 1991), pp. 88-89.

[9] Similar benefits are available to other Latin American nations, but with the exception of Mexico and to a lesser extent Argentina and Chile, their participation is negligible.

[10] U.S. International Trade Commission, *The Likely Impacts on the United States of a Free Trade Agreement with Mexico*, USITC Publication 2353 (Washington, DC: February 1991), p. 2-2.

[11] See Peter Morici, *Trade Talks with Mexico: A Time for Realism* (Washington, DC: National Planning Association, 1991), pp. 52-58.

[12] Ibid., pp. 15-35.

[13] This can be seen in the hurdles Mexico must still clear to participate in a trilateral agreement extending many of the CAFTA benefits to Mexico. Such an agreement would raise U.S.-Canada-Mexico trade and investment relations to the same plane as U.S.-Canadian or U.S.-EC relations. See Morici, op. cit. , pp. 66-77.

[14] The EC further cushioned this process by using its regional investment programs to help finance its new members' economic development, thus helping to raise living standards.

[15] Also noteworthy, this view is gaining support among Democrats and some traditionally Republican business leaders outside the Bush administration.

[16] Of course, Latin American nations, like other U.S. trading partners, are concerned about the sincerity of the U.S. commitment, in practice, to laissez-faire principles.

[17] For example, see Morici, op. cit.; and Clyde V. Prestowitz and Robert B. Cohen, *The New North American Order: A Win-Win Strategy for U.S.-Mexican Trade* (Washington, DC: Economic Strategies Institute, 1991).

[18] Many analysts have argued that strict rules of origin would be adequate to minimize such problems. For example, a North American content of 50 or 60 percent could be required. However, the bite of such rules would be directly related to the height of U.S. and Canadian most favored nation (MFN) tariffs. Except for a few products, these tariffs are now so low that they are no longer principal impediments to Latin American exports to the United States.

[19] Rules of origin have no affect on purchases of capital equipment, because the value added created by imported (and domestically produced) capital equipment is treated as domestic content in final product valuations.

[20] In Mexico, tariffs are no longer high enough to make a big difference in the purchasing preferences of Japanese and EC multinational corporations, which like their U.S. brethren often prefer traditional suppliers. The other major Latin American economies do have higher MFN tariffs than Mexico, and these could offer substantially greater margins of preference to U.S. suppliers. However, in a WHFTA, Latin American governments would be under persistent pressure to lower their MFN tariffs on Asian and European capital goods and components to Mexican levels by their need to compete effectively with Mexico for foreign investment. They would be under similar pressure to make their indigenous businesses competitive with Mexican-based enterprises. Overall, competitive pressures may be expected to push MFN tariffs on capital goods and components to the lowest common denominator among major Latin members of a WHFTA.

[21] The overall size of the U.S. trade deficit is determined by savings and investment imbalances between the United States and its principal trading partners. High Japanese savings rates, low U.S. savings rates, and high U.S. federal budget deficits are major variables in this equation.

[22] For example, the United States could seek more liberal terms of access, explicitly or implicitly, with regard to procurement or investment performance requirements.

[23] Preferential treatment for the United States under Mexico's foreign investment regime would run counter to established U.S. policy and generate loud protests from Japan and the EC. However, in the CAFTA, the United States and Canada agreed to preferential treatment, or came close to it, in Chapters 6 (Industrial Product Standards and Testing), 7 (Agricultural Standards and Regulations, Meat and Sugar Quotas), 10 (Automotive Products), 11 (Safeguards), 13 (Government Procurement), 14 and 17 (Business and Financial Services), and 19 (Dumping and Subsidies). Such an approach to Mexico in a NAFTA would amount to U.S. acceptance of a two-tier, regional-GATT application of MFN.

[24] See U.S. Department of Education, *America 2000: An Educational Strategy* (Washington, DC: 1991); and The Secretary's Commission on Achieving Necessary Skills, *What Work Requires of Schools: A SCANS Report for America 2000* (Washington, DC: U.S. Department of Labor, June 1991).

[25] President of the United States, George Bush, *Response of the Administration to Issues Raised in Connection with the Negotiations of A North American Free Trade Agreement* (Washington, DC: Office of the U.S. Trade Representative, 1991), p. 1.

[26] Ibid., p. 3-5.

[27] The United States should seek an agreement with Mexico as broad, but in the short run, not as deep as the CAFTA. It should be broader than the CAFTA in the sense that it should include issues such as intellectual property issues that were left out of the CAFTA. It should be less deep in the short run in that the United States, Canada, and Mexico will need longer phase-in or transition periods than did the United States and Canada in the CAFTA. Mexico faces tough industrial and labor-market adjustments as it completes its economic reforms and eliminates barriers to imports from the United States and Canada at the same time.

Chapter Two

Free Trade in the Americas: A Latin American Perspective

José Manuel Salazar-Xirinachs with Eduardo Lizano

Should Latin America embrace the vision and the challenge of hemispheric free trade or should it pursue alternative strategies? What do individual countries stand to gain by entering into free trade agreements (FTAs) with the United States? Could trade and development objectives be better achieved through nondiscriminatory liberalization instead of preferential arrangements with the United States? Or, why not reject both indiscriminate openness to the world and free trade with North America, and continue instead with Latin American integration efforts, at least temporarily?

The costs and benefits of entering into a FTA with the United States from the point of view of individual Latin American countries or regions is heavily influenced not only by economic factors but also by social and political realities and perceptions. Moreover, the decision on whether or not to enter into a FTA with the United States cannot be based exclusively on the perceived distribution of costs and benefits from the FTA. It must be made by comparing the expected results of joining the FTA with other present or future options these countries may have.

Latin American countries face the following basic options:

■ *Stay the course.* Maintaining protectionist policies, large and interventionist public sectors, and widespread price distortions is clearly not a viable option. The model of industrialization and growth based on import substitution, accomplished important tasks, but its dynamic possibilities are all but exhausted.

■ *Nondiscriminatory insertion into the world economy.* Most countries in Latin America have embarked on major structural reforms that include different degrees of unilateral trade and financial market liberalization. These policies could be continued without entering into discriminatory trade and investment arrangements with selected trading partners. Speed is the main advantage of unilateral liberalization over a negotiated or coordinated process. Its main drawback is that it would not provide preferential access to the U.S. market, thereby reducing the attractiveness of the economy as an investment site.

■ *Further integration with other Latin American countries.* Some observers argue that most Latin American countries are not yet capable of entering into a mutually beneficial free trade relationship with a country of the size and the competitive muscle of the United States, nor are they willing to liberalize unilaterally beyond a certain point. Therefore, given the imperative need of access to larger markets, they should emphasize integrating with other Latin American countries at similar stages of development, as a transitional strategy leading to a full-fledged FTA with the United States or a North American Free Trade Agreement (NAFTA). Such a strategy would entail a less drastic adjustment process than integrating with more developed competitive economies, but consumers would also benefit less. On the other hand, costs might be high if the integrated market is still small, if the countries are not natural trading partners, and if trade barriers vis-à-vis the rest of the world are not sufficiently reduced. Moreover, investment flows into member countries would not be as large in a FTA that did not include large markets such as the United States or NAFTA.

■ *Integration with the United States or NAFTA.* The main advantage of this option over the others would be to attain preferential and assured access to one of the largest markets in the world. This in turn might attract significant flows of investment and technology transfer.

COSTS AND BENEFITS OF FREE TRADE

Economic theory recognizes two types of economic effects from the creation of a FTA: those derived from a more efficient allocation of existing resources as a result of the elimination of trade barriers (*static effects*), and those related to the way in which economic integration affects the growth rate of participating countries (*dynamic effects*).

Static Effects

When a FTA is formed, two things happen: 1) cheaper imports from the FTA partner replace expensive domestic production (*trade creation*);

2) more expensive supplies from the new FTA partners replace previously cheaper imports from the outside world (*trade diversion*). Trade creation is beneficial insofar as it improves productive efficiency, while trade diversion implies global welfare losses. The relative strength of these two effects determines the economic value of the formation of a FTA.

The benefits of a FTA are usually greater: 1) the higher the barriers to trade before the formation of the FTA; 2) the lower the barriers vis-à-vis the rest of the world after its formation; 3) the higher the trade flows prior to the formation of a FTA; 4) the larger the integrated market after the formation of the FTA; and 5) the closer the geographical proximity of the FTA members. The intensity of these trade effects also depends on the extent to which tariff reductions translate into lower offer prices, and the responsiveness of supply and demand to price changes in both markets.

Adjustment costs are not included in this basic calculus. In reality, of course, attaining welfare benefits through resource reallocation invariably entails adjustment costs. Their magnitude and distribution depends on the particulars of each case.

Within this framework, the net welfare gains or losses from entering into a FTA with the United States would depend on the following simple arithmetic: the benefits associated with the increased exports to the United States *plus* the benefit to the consumer from lower priced goods and services from the United States, *minus* the adjustment cost from the displacement of local producers. Thus, consumers and exporters win; producers and workers in displaced activities would lose.

This analysis also suggests that the countries with the greatest incentives to enter a FTA with the United States are those that face the highest entry barriers to the U.S. market and those for which the United States is already a large export market. Conversely, the highest import penetration would be suffered by countries that already obtain a large share of their imports from the United States.[1] Finally, this analysis predicts that a FTA would improve the U.S. trade balance vis-à-vis Latin America, at least in the short term, given the higher initial level of protection in the region and the greater flexibility of supply in the United States.

Dynamic Effects

The main dynamic effects of a FTA with the United States depend on the expansion of effective access to the U.S. market under the agreement and the effective exploitation of trade and investment opportunities offered by improved access. The ability to attract investments, in turn, depends on how successfully reforms reduce uncertainty, provide a stable macroeconomic environment, and establish clear and consistent rules for long-term investment. Costs and benefits would also be influenced by the evolution of the world trading system and by the response of other Latin American countries to the Enterprise for the Americas Initiative (EAI).

EFFECTIVE ACCESS. Effective access entails the removal of tariff and nontariff barriers on virtually all products, including those in which Latin America has or could develop competitive advantages. It also entails discipline in the use of U.S. trade remedies and trade sanctions for supposed violation of environmental and other standards not covered by international covenants. Lack of transparency in this regard would create uncertainty about future access and discourage investment. Finally, for the full benefits from investment to materialize, rules of origin and national content provisions should not discriminate against non-American investors.[2]

EFFECTIVE EXPLOITATION OF MARKET OPPORTUNITIES. The effective exploitation of enhanced trade and investment opportunities requires a degree of international competitiveness that is not an automatic by-product of liberalization. The ability of Latin America to seize market opportunities can be hindered by supply constraints, i.e. inadequate infrastructure, segmented and inefficient capital markets, lack of skills, insufficient managerial and technological expertise, and other institutional shortcomings. Thus, without complementary support measures and productive modernization policies, the dynamic benefits from enhanced market access are unlikely to materialize for these countries.

ADJUSTMENT COSTS. The dynamic costs of free trade with the United States are likely to be steep. Import penetration from the United States could not only destroy existing local production but also hinder the development of activities whose initial costs are high but where competitive advantages could be developed in the medium term. Countries with weak productive structures have two basic options: 1) stretch out the timetable for trade liberalization as much as possible to dilute adjustment costs over time, or 2) accelerate the transformation process by opening up rapidly to maximize the flow of new investment in export activities.

As trade liberalization proceeds, new patterns of specialization and investment will transform the productive structures of both the United States and Latin America. As a result, significant shifts will occur in income distribution within and among countries. Adjustment costs will be higher in Latin America than in the United States because of Latin America's initially higher trade barriers; more distorted price structures; more segmented product, financial, and labor markets; and higher levels of open and disguised unemployment. Conversely, these factors suggest that the opportunities opened to Latin America to improve resource allocation and utilization and speed up gross domestic product (GDP) growth will also be greater than in the United States. For Latin America to be able to adjust without unsustainable balance-of-payments disequilibria, however, the United States must also be willing to undergo some structural adjustment and allow greater penetration of imports from Latin America.

The Piecemeal Approach

Two additional factors can be expected to affect the costs and benefits of joining a FTA with the United States: the basic approach used to expand free trade in the hemisphere and the sequence of accession to a U.S.-centric FTA.

Hemispheric free trade could be attained through the enlargement of a bilateral FTA into a plurilateral arrangement where all members could trade freely among themselves. Alternaltively, a system of overlapping free trade areas could develop with the United States at the center. In such a hub-and-spoke structure, the United States, as the hub, would enjoy preferences in all spoke country markets, whereas the spokes would all share preferences in the U.S. market but would not have preferential access to each others' markets. In terms of the costs and benefits for the hemisphere as a whole, the hub-and-spoke model is clearly inferior to an expanding FTA.[3]

The sequence of accession to a U.S.-centric FTA will also have a bearing on the costs and benefits of joining the FTA. Early joiners will enjoy advantages in terms of both export expansion and investment attraction. Latecomers will be disadvantaged not only by the postponement of benefits but also by possible investment diversion toward the early joiners. The costs of exclusion will rise with time and expanding membership. Countries that stay out of the FTA or join the process late face a double jeopardy: loss of export and investment opportunities in the U.S. market, and competitive disadvantages in the markets of the early joiners.

LATIN AMERICAN NEGOTIATING OBJECTIVES

The establishment of a free trade area between the United States and Latin America will entail much more than lowering tariffs and non-tariff barriers to trade in goods and services. For Latin America, such an arrangement would have profound implications regarding the size, role, and prerogatives of the state; macroeconomic management; and the adoption of international standards in a number of areas. Accordingly, it would be in the interest of these countries to broaden the scope of the agreements beyond mere trade measures to include various forms of economic and financial cooperation and technical assistance in exchange for market access.

Clearly, the contractual arrangements under the EAI will have a major influence on economic development and transformation in the region. In addition, hemisphere-wide market forces will help restructure Latin America's productive sectors, while the globalization of investment and capital will dilute control over national economies. Hence, broad cultural and social issues are also involved, but those lie beyond the scope of this chapter.

The text of the framework agreements (FAs) signed to date between the United States and individual (or groups of) countries in the region provides an approximation of the likely content of future FTAs (Table 1). All FAs include explicit commitments to the General Agreement on Tariffs and Trade (GATT) and a successful completion of the Uruguay Round, and most contain principles regarding investment, services, and intellectual property rights. Three FAs with Mexico, Guatemala, and the Caribbean Community (Caricom) explicitly recognize the vast differences in the level of economic development between the parties. Two regional FAs signed to date—Caricom and the Southern Cone Common Market (Mercosur)[4]—also allude to the contribution of intra-Latin American regional integration to trade and investment liberalization in the hemisphere.

From a Latin American perspective, a prospective FTA agreement should be based on the following elements.

■ *Merchandise Trade.* The agreement should guarantee unrestricted access to the U.S. market for the broadest range of products, including those in which Latin American countries have some competitive strengths and face high tariff and nontariff barriers, i.e., agricultural and tropical products, textiles and apparel, leather, and steel. In exchange, Latin American countries should grant roughly equivalent access to their markets, although the timetable for the phaseout of trade restrictions need not be strictly symmetrical. A strong case could be made for having different phaseout periods in particular products.

■ *Services.* Services are critical to the modernization process and the development of competitive advantages in Latin America. However, it is unlikely that these countries would be ready to expose certain sensitive and strategic sectors to the full rigors of international competition without a prolonged transition period, if at all.

On the other hand, Latin American countries already have or could develop competitive strengths in both knowledge-intensive and labor-intensive service activities. Thus, even though full parallel treatment for capital and labor movements may not be allowed, the agreement should at least include provisions for the temporary movement of labor associated with a service contract, to enable Latin Americans to exploit whatever competitive advantages they might have in labor-intensive services.

■ *Trade Remedies and Dispute Settlement.* The agreement must contain commitments by the United States concerning discipline in the use of trade remedies (countervailing, antidumping, safeguards) to reduce uncertainty about future access to the U.S. market. Limiting the possibility of future restrictions to the U.S. market and putting in place an appropriate mechanism for fair and speedy settlement of trade disputes is essential if Latin America is to capitalize on the potential benefits of increased investment. This would also be an important sign that the United States is prepared to undergo its share of structural adjustment under the FTA.

■ *Investment.* Attracting foreign and domestic investment is a major objective of the FTA. Accordingly, "national treatment" and "right of establishment" must be integral parts of the agreement. Nevertheless, countries may find it necessary to reserve certain areas for national control. Insisting on across-the-board acceptance of these principles may exacerbate domestic opposition to privatization and other badly needed reforms and make it impossible for countries to join the FTA.

■ *Intellectual Property Rights.* This is a complex and sensitive issue where important differences persist between technology producers and technology users, because it is not always clear where normal profits end and rent-seeking starts. The proscription of outright piracy and counterfeiting is bound to be less controversial than the adoption of higher standards in high-technology areas and the whole issue of enforcement. Enforcement will be costly and should be accompanied by technical and financial assistance. The United States should also assist in establishing norms against restrictive or monopolistic business practices to prevent the cost of legitimate technology purchases from skyrocketing.

■ *Relative Reciprocity.* Conceiving the FTA as a reciprocal exchange among equals would be inappropriate. Differential treatment is justified by the vast disparities between the United States and any prospective regional partner in terms of their respective stages of development and the unequal burden of adjustment each is likely to bear as a result of the FTA. Recognition of these disparities is crucial for smaller, less developed economies in the region, but it applies to every country to some degree. Further justification lies in the fact that simply to become eligible to join the FTA, Latin American countries must undergo significant adjustments and might, therefore, be required to meet a less stringent set of additional demands up front. On these bases, a strong case can be built for including transitional measures and financial and technical assistance to support adjustment and the development of competitive advantages in the less developed partners.

■ *Eligibility Criteria.* To join the FTA, prospective members will have to meet a set of eligibility conditions and accept the responsibilities contained in the agreement. Both conditions and obligations should be

Principles	Mexico	Bolivia	Colombia	Ecuador	Chile	Costa Rica	Honduras	Mercosur	Nicaragua	Guatemala	El Salvador	Panama	Caricom (draft)
Desire to develop further both parties' international trade and economic interrelationships	●		●	●	●	●	●	●	●	●	●	●	●
Respect rights and obligations under the GATT	●	●	●	●	●	●	●	●	●	●	●	●	●
Recognize the parties' differences and disparities of economic development	●									●			
Account for parties' commitment to successful completion and implementation of the Uruguay Round			●		●	●							
Recognize the benefits generated by the Caribbean Basin Initiative						●	●	●	●		●	●	●
Recognize the importance of an open, predictable environment for international trade and investment	●	●	●	●	●	●	●	●	●	●	●	●	●
Recognize that foreign direct investment confers positive benefits on each party	●		●	●	●	●	●	●	●		●	●	●
Recognize increased importance of services in parties' economies and bilateral relations	●		●	●	●	●	●	●	●	●	●	●	●
Recognize the need to eliminate NTBs to facilitate mutual access to markets	●		●	●	●	●	●	●	●	●	●	●	●

TABLE 1. COMPARISON OF THE PRINCIPLES IN U.S.-LAC FRAMEWORK AGREEMENTS (continued)

Principles	Mexico	Bolivia	Colombia	Ecuador	Chile	Costa Rica	Honduras	Mercosur	Nicaragua	Guatemala	El Salvador	Panama	Caricom (draft)
Recognize importance of adequate, effective protection of intellectual property rights	•		•	•	•	•	•	•	•	•	•	•	•
Recognize the desirability of resolving trade and investment problems expeditiously	•	•	•	•	•	•	•	•	•	•	•	•	•
Recognize mutual interest in establishing a bilateral mechanism to encourage trade and investment liberalization		•	•	•	•	•	•	•	•	•	•	•	•
Recognize that trade and investment should account for the need to develop natural resources in a manner consistent with environmental concerns					•					•			
Recognize that Latin America's integration would reduce hemispheric trade and investment barriers								•					•
Recognize the importance of liberalization of agricultural trade, including the avoidance of export subsidies								•					
Recognize significance of observance and promotion of internationally recognized worker rights			•	•	•	•	•	•	•	•	•	•	•

Note: The United States has signed framework agreements with the following LAC countries or groups: in 1987, Mexico; in 1990, Bolivia, Colombia, Ecuador, Honduras, Chile, and Costa Rica; in 1991, Venezuela, El Salvador, Peru, Mercosur, Nicaragua, Panama, Caricom, Guatemala, and the Dominican Republic.

fair, transparent, objective, and consistent. Any country that meets all the requirements should be able to join the FTA, without extraneous factors affecting the order of accession.

Finally, one of the more positive aspects of the EAI is that it could encourage the consolidation of subregional integration arrangements as building blocks for the hemispheric free trade area. A subregional approach is preferable to a bilateral one, as it would help to ensure GATT consistency and would also enhance the region's attraction as an investment site. Foreign investment is likely to be attracted not only by advantageous access to the U.S. market but also by the size of the regional market.

The fact that not all countries in the region, or in a particular subregion, may be ready to enter a FTA agreement with the United States at the same time raises the proverbial "convoy problem." It poses a serious policy dilemma for all concerned: avoid individual negotiations to better observe GATT rules and encourage regional integration in Latin America, or allow individual negotiations and risk incurring important costs as a result. The fact remains that atomization of the FTA into bilateral negotiations will work against integration in Latin America and is an approach less likely to be consistent with the GATT.

MACROECONOMIC IMPLICATIONS OF TRADE LIBERALIZATION

Trade and financial liberalization impose certain macroeconomic policy disciplines on liberalizing countries. The use of certain instruments to manage the balance of payments is further restrained by liberalization in the context of a FTA. Finally, the existence of a dominant trading partner within the FTA poses additional policy restrictions.

Unilateral Liberalization

Trade liberalization entails more than tariff reductions. It also implies the elimination of quantitative restrictions (quotas, licenses), surcharges, prior import deposits, and a host of other measures commonly used by developing countries either with protective intent, or in order to suppress balance-of-payments pressures. The elimination of these trade and payments controls has important consequences for macroeconomic management.

The evidence from countries that have simultaneously attempted to liberalize their trade and payments regimes and deregulate their domestic financial markets suggests that the sequence of policy measures is crucial to the success of liberalization efforts.[5] The following are among the main lessons from this body of experience.

- The removal of import restrictions should be accompanied by a compensatory currency devaluation to forestall a sudden surge in imports and improve export profitability. Since trade liberalization calls for expenditure switching from inefficient import-substitution sectors to export-oriented activities, a key ingredient of successful liberalization is the maintenance of a competitive and stable (though not necessarily constant) real exchange rate.

- Fiscal balance and monetary restraint are preconditions for the successful elimination of exchange controls. The elimination of direct trade and balance-of-payments controls increases the burden on internal instruments to achieve external equilibrium. As long as significant fiscal deficits exist, exchange controls will be needed to curb capital flight and capital account imbalances.

- The current account should be liberalized before the capital account. By their nature capital markets adjust much faster than product markets. The slower pace of adjustment in trade in goods and services gives time to react, and implement compensatory measures. Eliminating exchange controls while important distortions remain in product and financial markets could be highly destabilizing.

- Basic internal financial reform should also precede liberalization of the capital account. If substantial financial repression persists in the form of low domestic interest rates, eliminating exchange controls will allow unrestricted capital flight. Conversely, exorbitant domestic real interest rates could invite excessive capital inflows and an undesirable exchange rate appreciation. Either way, a stable and competitive real exchange rate would be hard to maintain.

- Stabilization should precede liberalization. The main aim of liberalization is to adjust relative prices to reflect costs, and inflation reduces the information content of relative prices. Inflation also distorts real interest rates, encourages speculation at the expense of productive investment, and causes real exchange rate instability.

In sum, successful liberalization requires stable and competitive real exchange rates, heavy reliance on fiscal and monetary policy to attain external balance, and fiscal neutrality to avoid distorting domestic interest rates and permitting exchange controls to be eliminated. In terms of sequencing, the proper order appears to be: 1) attaining basic macroeconomic stabilization and inflation control; 2) liberalizing the current account of the balance of payments while maintaining a stable and competitive real exchange rate; 3) achieving fiscal balance and deregulating domestic financial markets; and 4) freeing the capital account.

Macroeconomic Policy Coordination in a FTA

When liberalization occurs in the context of a FTA, some additional restrictions on macroeconomic management are imposed on this basic paradigm.

Over time, a FTA strengthens its members' economic interdependence. In turn, this greater interdependence will increase the speed and intensity with which economic disturbances—such as shifts in the volume and value of trade flows, fiscal and monetary imbalances, and exchange rates and interest rates—are transmitted among FTA members. Membership in a FTA, thus, exacerbates the weight of external constraints, making it more difficult for countries to act "defensively" against shocks originating in other FTA members and to deal with their own macroeconomic disequilibria. Moreover, because in a FTA tariff cuts are deeper and less easily reversed than when trade is liberalized unilaterally, the need for fiscal restructuring to replace foregone trade revenues is also more pressing.

Confronting the disturbances caused by fellow FTA members or by their own liberalization measures, FTA members can choose between fully absorbing the shock, temporarily or permanently separating from the countries causing or experiencing serious instability, or taking defensive action to block the transmission of the disturbance. These measures, however, would either be too costly internally or would undermine the FTA.

A better course of action would be to forestall the buildup of macroeconomic imbalances, through two sets of complementary measures. One involves the coordination of macroeconomic policies, particularly the fiscal and monetary stance, interest rates, and the exchange rate. The other entails the design of compensatory mechanisms or transitional support measures, such as financial support for countries with temporary balance-of-payments problems and net transfers of financial, technological, or investment resources to severely affected or backward areas.

Policy Harmonization in the Context of the EAI

The presence of a dominant trading partner within the hemispheric FTA places further constraints on macroeconomic management. While the United States coordinates some aspects of its macroeconomic policy with other members of the Group of Seven, the United States could not realistically be expected to assume similar commitments with countries in Latin America.

The difference in incentives for macroeconomic policy coordination reflects the fundamental asymmetry between the United States and Latin American countries in terms of economic size, openness, and reciprocal importance as trading partners. In general, larger, less open countries are under less pressure to coordinate macroeconomic policy than their smaller, more open trading partners. Moreover, the incentive to harmonize macroeconomic policies with particular trading partners is a function of the relative importance of such trade flows. On all these grounds, Latin America would have far more interest in policy coordination than the United States.

In any event, countries that enter into FTAs with the United States will need to follow policies broadly consistent with whatever U.S. policy happens to be. In the absence of coordinating or compensatory mechanisms, from time to time these countries are likely to be confronted with unpleasant choices between honoring their external commitments and pursuing other worthy socioeconomic objectives.

Finally, because the EAI is supposed to promote integration not only with the United States but also among the Latin American economies, the issue arises of policy harmonization within and between subregional groups. Because intragroup trade is low, so too are the incentives for macroeconomic policy coordination within the various groups. Yet, the less policy convergence there is, the more difficult it will be for intragroup trade to develop. Ultimately, therefore, to maximize benefits under the EAI this vicious circle will have to be broken and macroeconomic policies will have to be harmonized regionwide.

RELATIVE RECIPROCITY AND TRANSITIONAL MEASURES

For years, trade and development experts have dismissed the possibility of free trade areas between developed and developing countries by pointing out the difficulties that are likely to arise when countries at different levels of development join in a free trade agreement.[6] The norm between developed and developing countries has been one-way preferential arrangements such as the European Community (EC) Lomé Convention or the United States Caribbean Basin Initiative (CBI).

Numerous efforts to establish FTAs among developing countries have foundered over perceived inequities in the distribution of costs and benefits. The least developed members of the group invariably feel shortchanged, a feeling reinforced by the tendency of new investment to concentrate in the more developed regions of the integrated area.

A critical issue posed by the EAI, therefore, is how to design a satisfactory reciprocal arrangement between the United States, Canada, and a large and heterogeneous group of far less developed countries. Indeed, vast disparities exist between the United States and all prospective regional partners in terms of:

■ *Economic market size.* The United States represents nearly 80 percent of the combined regional GDP, and in terms of GDP per capita the ratio between the United States and Latin America is eleven to one.

■ *Reciprocal importance as trading partners.* While exports to the United States make up 52 percent of Latin America's total external sales, they represent only 13 percent of total U.S. imports. Conversely, only 14 percent of U.S. exports go to Latin America, yet they constitute 45 percent of the region's imports. This asymmetry reaches extremes in the case of the small Central American and Caribbean countries, which send over half their exports to the United States but supply no more than 1.5 percent of total U.S. imports.

■ *Initial degree of protection.* Both tariffs and nontariff barriers are much higher in Latin America than in the United States. Consequently, the burden of adjustment posed by the elimination of trade barriers in the context of a FTA falls squarely on Latin America.

■ *Productivity levels.* Significant differences in productivity exist not only across a broad spectrum of industries and products but also in terms of "structural competitiveness," i.e., the amount and quality of support services such as transport, finance, communications, training and education, science and technology.

■ *Health, safety, labor, and environmental standards, as well as the quality of productive factors and processes.*

To the extent that these differences persist, a FTA cannot be conceived as a reciprocal exchange among equals. Reciprocal trade liberalization among unequal partners may be feasible only if supplemented by additional measures to prevent an unacceptably skewed distribution of gains and by mechanisms to support rapid growth of exports, investment, and competitiveness in the less developed partners.

Historically, efforts to deal with these problems have taken many forms, including longer phaseouts of trade restrictions by the less advanced members, financial assistance, and technical support.

Phaseouts and Adjustment Provisions

The United States should contemplate asymmetric liberalization schedules, provided that the final outcome is virtually free trade both ways. Indeed, an orderly and gradual process of adjustment is not exclusively a Latin American concern. In the case of NAFTA, for instance, the U.S. Department of Commerce has recommended that tariffs and NTBs on import-sensitive products be eliminated in small increments over enough time to ensure orderly adjustment, and that the agreement allow temporary reimposition of duties and other restrictions to prevent injury from any import surges.[7]

Although safeguards may be necessary for the sake of prudence, the emphasis should be on provisions to facilitate, not resist, adjustment. To this end, the U.S. administration is considering funding a worker adjustment program to assist dislocated workers who may encounter adjustment difficulties, even though "immediate or substantial job dislocations are not expected."[8] In countries where important structural transformations and import penetration *are* expected following the FTA, compensatory mechanisms are critical, especially after the serious damage inflicted by a decade of brutal shocks and massive resource drain on the region's social fabric, productive capacity, and physical infrastructure.

Because pressing fiscal constraints in Latin America make internal compensatory financing virtually impossible, a facility should be set up in conjunction with the FTA to help retrain and redeploy workers in the region. The new Multilateral Investment Fund at the Inter-American Development Bank (IDB) might serve this purpose, but its funding is totally inadequate to meet the anticipated regional needs.

Transitional Support Measures

Trade deficits and other macroeconomic disequilibria may emerge as a direct result of the new trade and specialization pattern and the process of economic transformation stimulated by the FTA. If exports expand more slowly than imports as trade barriers fall, the external constraint on GDP growth could be exacerbated.

A sufficiently large inflow of capital from abroad—of foreign or domestic origin—could finance the trade deficit for a while (as in Mexico). If this capital inflow does not materialize, however, the trade imbalance will constrain growth. Multilateral and bilateral financing could make a crucial contribution during this transition period. But given that the trade imbalance is directly linked to the FTA, a strong argument could be made for the FTA to include an additional pool of resources to meet these transitory contingencies.

Technical Cooperation

One of the longer-term benefits of a hemispheric free trade area will be to induce an improvement of standards across a broad spectrum: from pollution abatement to intellectual property protection. Because Latin American countries will have to upgrade their standards upon joining the FTA, the agreement should provide for technical and financial assistance to enable the less developed countries to comply with those higher standards.

Support for the Development of Long-Term Competitiveness

International competitiveness hinges on the provision of a critical mass of adequate support services. Once policy reform has been implemented, supply difficulties are usually the most important obstacle to export expansion. Size is an important disadvantage in this regard. For instance, after eight years of relatively unhampered access to the U.S. market for a broad range of products, CBI countries still have serious payments imbalances, including a large trade deficit with the United States.[9] For these countries, the United States should consider providing special support through programs such as those developed in the context of the Lomé Convention between the European Community and African, Caribbean, and Pacific States (ACP). This support includes concessional resources channeled through the European Development Fund and the European Investment Bank; risk capital facilities; stabilization of export earnings from agricultural commodities (STABEX); and microproject financing.[10]

In fact, the competitive disadvantage of the small economies is such that they should insist on a "fourth pillar"[11] to the EAI: a science and technology package to include training and retraining programs; education; marketing and information technology; industrial restructuring; support for small and medium enterprises; and other critical areas of competitive advantage.

Evidently, the inclusion of all these elements in a free trade agreement would turn it into something quite different from a typical FTA. Whether or not technical and financial cooperation of the kind suggested here is included in the agreement is not the point. What matters is recognizing the importance of these complementary policies to ensure the viability of free trade areas between countries at different stages of development. In practice, these aspects could be included in parallel agreements or in economic support programs by multilateral and bilateral agencies.

Bridging these disparities is the most challenging aspect of the Enterprise for the Americas Initiative for all concerned. The incentive to participate, progress in the negotiations, and the success of the hemispheric system of free trade will largely depend on finding satisfactory answers to this challenge.

CONCLUSIONS

Latin America has enthusiastically embraced the vision and the challenge of hemispheric free trade, but it has done so, quite correctly, with a prudent and strategic vision. Even before the EAI was announced, most countries in the region had unilaterally undertaken trade and financial reforms, cutting tariffs to about 20 percent and removing many nontariff barriers. However, moving beyond this point to the virtual elimination of all trade barriers vis-à-vis a country of the size and competitive muscle of the United States is an entirely different proposition.

A free trade agreement with the United States would entail significant benefits as well as costs for Latin America. The main potential benefits include a possibly substantial increase in exports to the United States, larger investment flows, and productivity gains associated with domestic efforts to enhance external competitiveness. For these benefits to materialize, however, access to the U.S. market must be effectively enlarged and assured through the removal of U.S. tariff and nontariff barriers, discipline in the use of U.S. trade remedies, and nonexclusionary rules of origin. The ability to exploit such trade and investment opportunities is not an automatic by-product of liberalization, however. Additional measures will be required to boost supply response, including a stable macroeconomic environment, a clear and consistent framework for long-term investment, and the removal of structural rigidities and bottlenecks that could thwart export growth. The main costs of the FTA will be those linked to import penetration. Those costs are likely to be much higher for Latin America than for the United States. Yet, Latin America would only be able to sustain import liberalization if the United States also allowed greater penetration of imports from the region. Otherwise, Latin America would experience unsustainable disequilibria in its balance of payments.

For Latin America, a free trade agreement with the United States would entail much more than removing cross-border trade barriers. Such an arrangement would have profound effects on the size, role, and prerogatives of the state, macroeconomic management, and the adoption of international standards in a number of areas. In addition, hemisphere-wide market forces would shape Latin America's productive sectors, and global investment trends would further dilute control over national economies. Hence, broad cultural and social issues are also involved.

The extreme heterogeneity of the region poses a critical challenge to hemispheric free trade. Vast differences in size, productivity, level of development, and reciprocal importance as trading partners imply that a regional FTA cannot be conceived as a reciprocal exchange among equals. Reciprocal trade liberalization among unequal partners may only be feasible if supplemented by additional measures to prevent an unacceptably skewed distribution of gains and by mechanisms to support rapid growth of exports, investment, and competitiveness in the less developed partners. Whether or not those technical and financial support measures are included in the agreement is not essential.

Even if the vision of hemispheric free trade takes years to complete, as it probably will, its legacy is already apparent: it has given a new impetus and a new sense of direction to regional integration efforts. Although important differences regarding optimal transition strategies toward freer trade and investment regimes still persist, today few in Latin America question that this is the way to go.

Notes

[1] Based on these criteria, Latin American countries can be divided in two groups. The first includes countries that have nearly half their exports concentrated in the U.S. market and over 40 percent of their imports supplied by the United States—Mexico, most of Central America, and the Caribbean. This group stands to gain the most from enhanced and assured access to the U.S. market but is likely to have the most import penetration as a result of the FTA with the United States. The second group—including most of South America—has far less intense commercial ties to the United States and would therefore be less affected by a FTA. See Winton Fritsch, "The New Minilateralism and Developing Countries," Jeffrey J. Schott, (ed.) *Free Trade Areas and U.S. Trade Policy* (Washington, DC: Institute for International Economics, 1989).

[2] This issue has been a point of controversy in the case of the Mexican auto industry, where the United States insists on rules of origin that protect U.S. investments in Mexico and discriminate against new investment of Japanese and other origin.

[3] For a full discussion of the merits of the hub-and-spoke model relative to those of an expanding FTA, see Ronald J. Wonnacott, *The Economics of Overlapping Free Trade Areas and the Mexican Challenge*, Canadian American Committee (Toronto: C.D. Howe Institute in cooperation with National Planning Association, 1991).

[4] The Caribbean Community (Caricom) includes Antigua and Barbuda, The Bahamas, Barbados, Belize, Dominica, Grenada, Guyana, Jamaica, Montserrat, St. Kitts and Nevis, St. Lucia, St. Vincent and the Grenadines, and Trinidad and Tobago. The Southern Cone Common Market (Mercosur) includes Argentina, Brazil, Paraguay, and Uruguay.

[5] Jagdish Bhagwati and Anne O. Krueger, *Foreign Trade Regimes and Economic Development: Anatomy and Consequences of Exchange Control Regimes* (Cambridge, MA: Ballinger, 1978); Sebastian Edwards, "The Order of Liberalization of the Balance of Payments. Should the Current Account Be Opened Up First?" *World Bank Staff Working Papers*, No. 710 (Washington, DC: 1984); Arnold C. Harberger "Observations of the Chilean Economy 1973-83," *Economic Development and Cultural Change*, pp. 451-462; Vittorio Corbo and Jaime de Melo, "Lessons from the Southern Cone Policy Reforms," *World Bank Research Observer* Vol. 2, No. 2 (1987); Roberto Zahler, "Estrategias Financieras Latinoamericanas: La Experiencia del Cono Sur," *Colección Estudios CIEPLAN*, No. 23 (March 1988); Ronald I. McKinnon and D.J. Mathieson, "How to Manage a Repressed Economy," *Essays in International Finance* (Princeton, NJ: Princeton University Press, 1981).

[6] Ronald J. Wonnacott and Mark Lutz, "Is There a Case for Free Trade Areas?" Schott (ed.), *Free Trade Areas*, op. cit., Chapter 10; Jeffrey J. Schott, "More Free Trade Areas," Schott (ed.), *Free Trade Areas*, op. cit., Chapter 1.

[7] U.S. Department of Commerce, *North American Free Trade Agreement: Generating Jobs for Americans*, Update (May 1991), p. 43.

[8] Ibid.

[9] For evaluations of export performance under CBI see: Edward Ray, "Trade Liberalization, Preferential Agreements, and Their Impact on U.S. Imports from Latin America," in Claudio González-Vega and Michael Connolly (eds.), *Economic Reform and Stabilization in*

Latin America (New York: Praeger, 1987); Stuart K. Tucker, "Trade Unshackled: Assessing the Value of the Caribbean Basin Initiative," William Ascher and Anne Hubbard, (eds.) *Central American Recovery and Development*, Task Force for the International Commission for Central American Recovery and Development [Sanford Commission] (Durham, SC: Duke University Press, 1989); Ennio Rodríguez and Associates, *Análisis de las Oportunidades de Expansión Brindadas por la Iniciativa de la Cuenca del Caribe* (San José: Alternativas de Desarrollo, 1989); Diego Salazar and Allen Vargas, "Evaluación Econométrica de la Iniciativa de la Cuenca del Caribe para Costa Rica, República Dominicana y Guatemala," Juan Vargas and Félix Delgado (eds.), *Progreso Técnico y Estructura Económica: Dimensión Interna y Comercio Internacional* (San José: Centro de Economía Aplicada, 1989).

[10] See Europe Information Development, *Ten Years of Lomé: A Record of ACP-EEC Partnership 1976-1985*, report on the implementation of financial and technical cooperation under the first two Lomé Conventions, report prepared by the Directorate-General for Development of the Commission of the European Communities, Commission of the European Communities, September 1986.

[11] This was suggested by FEDEPRICAP (Federation of Private Enterprise of Central America and Panama) in a document submitted to Ambassador Carla Hills, United States Trade Representative, on behalf of the private sector of Central America. See FEDEPRICAP, *A Central American Private Sector Perspective on Some of the Main Issues as Regards NAFTA and the Formation of a FTA Between our Countries and the U.S.* (San Pedro de Montes de Oca, Costa Rica: FEDEPRICAP, November 21, 1991).

Chapter Three

Getting There: The Path To A Western Hemisphere Free Trade Area And Its Structure

Richard G. Lipsey

Is Western Hemisphere free trade a pipe dream or realistic expectation? . . . Administrative nightmare? . . . Mutual self-interest or U.S. imperialism? . . . Help or hindrance in a nation's climb out of poverty? . . . Irrelevant to those that do not trade heavily with the United States? . . . Thin icing on the cake baked by unilateral, internal and external, economic liberalization?

These are some of the questions that leap to mind when *hemispheric free trade* is mentioned. In this chapter, two main questions are discussed: Why would the various potential members want a Western Hemisphere Free Trade Area (WHFTA)? And, what should its institutional structure be if it did happen?

IS IT A PIPE DREAM?

This question can be persuasively argued both ways.

Yes. WHFTA is close to a pipe dream because some of its preconditions are 1) that the current trilateral negotiations go through to a completed North American Free Trade Agreement (NAFTA); 2) that the U.S. administration and the governments of Latin America be willing to enter a comprehensive arrangement with each other despite the many political and economic worries associated with it; 3) that a solution be found to countless problems on how to craft a deal that can be expanded to cover all the hemisphere's countries; and 4) that the people, and their elected representatives, accept such a deal.

No. WHFTA is not a pipe dream because nothing is impossible. Who in 1938, contemplating 400 years of European history, would have predicted the signing of the Treaty of Rome less than 20 years later, or the evolution of the European Community (EC) to "Europe 1992," and thereafter? Who in 1977, contemplating Canadian fears of U.S. economic and political domination, combined with the conventional Canadian political wisdom that a free trade agreement with the United States was political suicide, would have predicted that, only 15 years later, the countries would be busy adjusting to the most comprehensive free trade area (FTA) the world has ever seen? The message from these examples is that governments should get on with discovering, and advocating, what is desirable, without being deflected by assertions that some desirable things are politically impossible.

DO WE REALLY WANT A WHFTA?

A WHFTA will only come about if each country calculates that its self-interest lies in joining the group. Once self-interest has been determined, local considerations will matter, but every country will have to weigh some general issues as well.

WHFTA and the General Agreement on Tariffs and Trade

The first step in considering any new international arrangement relating to trade and investment is to ask how it relates to the General Agreement on Tariffs and Trade (GATT).

GATT AS A VEHICLE FOR TRADE LIBERALIZATION. The GATT is the world's major tool for preserving and advancing trade liberalization. Under GATT auspices, the bulk of tariffs on trade in manufactured goods among developed countries were removed in successive rounds of multilateral trade negotiations (MTNs) between 1947 and 1985. This enormous achievement was obtained largely through U.S. initiative.

The basic purpose of the GATT is to arrive at a cooperative solution to the trade-policy game and thus avoid the prisoner's dilemma nature of the game's Nash equilibrium.[1] Left to themselves, each country perceives a political and economic gain from raising trade restrictions. But when all do this, growing trade restrictions reduce the gains from trade and lead to loss of income in all countries. Membership in the GATT requires each country to abandon the option of raising its trade restrictions unilaterally.

The Uruguay Round is the most serious test of the GATT since its inception. If the round fails, crisis action will be required to rescue not only the GATT but also the multinational trading system it defends. Either way, the GATT is, and will long remain, the world's most important institution affecting international trade.

IS THE GATT ALL WE NEED? The GATT and a FTA each have their uses, depending on the job to be done. Certain objectives can be achieved either through the GATT or a FTA, the most obvious example being mutual tariff reductions.

Other issues are more easily handled through the GATT than through a FTA, notably politically sensitive issues subject to strong interest-group pressures. Negotiations and agreements for a FTA usually have a high public profile compared with those under the GATT. Even the Uruguay Round, which has had vastly more press than any previous GATT round, has had much less public attention than the NAFTA. Allegations that Mexico has unnecessarily lax environmental controls, labor unions weakened by public policy, and workers exploited through unduly low wages, have persuaded many ordinary citizens to be skeptical of the NAFTA. These same citizens had no opinion, one way or the other, about the corresponding aspects of the countries with which Canada and the United States negotiated major tariff reductions in the Kennedy and Tokyo Rounds.

Some other actions, however, are more easily agreed upon through a FTA, where a small number of like-minded countries bargain over matters of mutual interest and concern. Elsewhere, Murray Smith and I argue that

> [T]here is no way that many of the pathbreaking and powerful trade liberalizing measures included in the Canada-U.S. Free Trade Agreement could have been obtained by Canada through any foreseeable round of multilateral negotiations. In some cases, the two signatories would have been unwilling—for political and/or economic reasons—to extend certain sections of the agreement to all GATT members; in other cases, other GATT countries would have been unwilling to accept some sections; in yet other cases, agreements reached on specific sections would have been unacceptable to one country or the other if judged individually instead of as part of an overall package.[2]

WHFTA: COMPLEMENT OR COMPROMISE TO GATT? The question of whether a WHFTA will complement or compromise the GATT raises one of the most contentious issues surrounding the prospect of a WHFTA.[3] The GATT itself has severely criticized the impending NAFTA agreement and, by implication, a WHFTA.

At one extreme, many observers feel that *any* new regional economic union should be avoided as being too much of a threat to the GATT.

Proponents of this view should ask themselves whether it would be preferable if the EC had never been formed. The EC has been, on balance, a beneficial force in trade liberalization. There is no reason why a WHFTA should be regarded differently as long as it embodies outward-looking principles.

At the other extreme are people who feel that *no* new FTA need be a threat to GATT. My rejection of this view follows from contemplating the possible rise of three great FTAs covering Europe, the Western Hemisphere, and much of East Asia—each of them engaging in much intra-area trade, while erecting increasingly severe nontariff barriers on inter-area trade. This would have serious consequences for countries excluded from the three trading blocs. It could also be a major step toward managed trade and a general decline in multilateralism to everyone's long-term detriment.

Between these two extreme views are those who say that some FTAs can complement GATT multilateralism even though others may threaten it. The main prerequisites for acting as a complement to the GATT would seem to be that the FTA:

- leave its members outward-looking, multilaterally oriented, and active participants in the GATT,
- result in net trade creation rather than net trade diversion, and
- not provoke other countries to form their own regional groupings for purely defensive reasons.

On the first point, there are no compelling reasons for a WHFTA to become inward looking itself or to cause its members to weaken their commitment to multilateralism. One circumstance in which this might happen is if the FTA reallocated resources in a different direction than would follow from multilateral reductions in trade barriers. Such trade diversion would create vested interests that would gain from the FTA but would lose from multilateral trade liberalization. To avoid this outcome, steps would need to be taken to ensure that each addition to the evolving WHFTA be trade creating on balance, and to enshrine a commitment to outward-looking and multilateral policies within the FTA.

On the second point, the concern is with the welfare effects of a FTA. The conditions that give rise to a presumption for welfare gains (a large balance of trade creation over trade diversion) are the same ones that would tend to minimize the creation of vested interests that would profit from the FTA but would lose from further multilateral reductions of trade barriers. On balance, trade creation should predominate over trade diversion in a WHFTA provided that the conditions identified below are fulfilled.

On the third point, Asian countries could have two motives for pushing for their own regional FTA in reaction to the formation of a

WHFTA. First, concerned about trade diversion affecting their exports to the hemisphere, they could decide to gain from trade diversion within their own area. This motive could be diminished by reducing the external tariffs of countries joining the WHFTA, but it can never be eliminated. Of course, if Asian companies were worried about trade diversion, their best defense might be to step up their foreign direct investment (FDI) in the Western Hemisphere (as they no doubt would do in any case). Second, concern about the bargaining power within the GATT of the two major blocs, might prompt Asian governments to create their own power group in self-defense. This incentive would be reduced if the hemispheric arrangement were a FTA rather than a customs union, as discussed below.

The reaction of other countries, particularly those in Asia, remains one of the strongest arguments for caution in the movement toward a WHFTA. There can be little doubt that Asian exporters to the hemisphere would be upset if the movement gained force. They have already expressed strong concern over the move toward a NAFTA, involving Canada, Mexico, and the United States.[4]

Grouping the world's major trading countries into three large FTAs carries serious risks that many people would wish to avoid at almost any cost, but the three blocs may continue to be outward looking. If so, negotiations within the GATT might be eased by having the three power groups bargain to liberalize trade and investment in ways that benefit all countries, whether or not they belong to any of the groups. I would not want to bet large sums on this favorable outcome, but neither would I want to assign it a vanishingly small probability.

What's in a WHFTA for Latin America?

A WHFTA will not get off the ground unless each potential member country feels it has much to gain. For Latin America a WHFTA offers a number of possible benefits.

INCREASED ACCESS TO U.S. MARKET. By far the most important achievement of the FTA would be increased access to the U.S. market. This objective is more or less attractive to countries depending on the amount of their current trade with the United States, and the type of goods they export. Many traditional Latin American exports already enter at low or zero tariffs and are subject to few nontariff barriers.

SECURING ACCESS TO U.S. MARKET. Almost of equal importance is the protection that the FTA would provide against a resurgence of U.S. protectionism, a matter of serious concern to all countries that trade with the United States. Although the balance of U.S. sentiment alternates between trade protectionism and trade liberalism, the long-term result is an increase in protectionist measures.[5] Any country that currently does substantial trade with the United States, or might do so in the future, should welcome increased security of access to the U.S. market.

ATTRACTING FOREIGN DIRECT INVESTMENT. Another important gain from a FTA would be the increased attractiveness as a locale for FDI (and for domestic investment) on account of the preferential access to the markets of member countries.

PROMOTING HEMISPHERIC TRADE. Some commentators have discounted the benefits of hemispheric free trade, noting that some countries in Latin America trade very little with the United States and that most of Latin America's existing exports are subject to low entry barriers in the United States. This is only part of the story, however. A WHFTA of the type I am discussing would provide essentially free trade among *all* of its members. The total amount of trade creation among all the countries of the hemisphere under a comprehensive WHFTA would be substantial for each and every country in the hemisphere. Some of these advantages could, of course, be obtained through comprehensive regional FTAs and common markets that did not include the United States and Canada. In the past, however, such regional groupings have covered only a few countries and a relatively limited list of products.

AVOIDING TRADE DIVERSION. If Latin America had, for instance, four genuine regional FTAs or common markets, there would always exist contiguous countries with the potential to trade substantially with each other across the boundary of two groupings. Thus, even though there might not be major gains for every Latin American country from removing tariffs with the United States, there would always be major gains in removing tariffs with some countries outside the regional group to which any one country belongs. The upshot is that the only way to obtain the full potential for hemispheric trade is to evolve toward a single WHFTA, rather than several regional trade arrangements.

EXPANDING HIGH VALUE-ADDED PRODUCTION. Production of higher value-added goods and services requires trade. Since the domestic market rarely supports the scale required for such production, a FTA creates one of the necessary conditions for growth of such nontraditional types of production. The wider the geographical area and the more comprehensive the sectoral coverage, the broader the potential scope for such production.

CONSOLIDATING MARKET-ORIENTED REFORMS. Liberalizing trade is a key part of the outward-looking, market-oriented policies that most Latin American countries have already turned to, or may be expected to adopt soon.[6] In today's globalizing world, market access on the most liberal terms possible is a key part of the success of any outward-looking growth policy. Thus, the liberalization of international trade is more than just a bit of icing on the cake of domestic reforms. The two go hand-in-hand as equal parts of a market-oriented strategy for enhanced economic growth.

Enshrining trade liberalization in an international treaty does constrain the ability of future governments to shift toward more inward-looking policies, since trade restrictions could not be imposed without abrogating the treaty. Abrogation is less likely the larger the number of countries involved—because the greater the self-inflicted injury in doing so. Once a nation's economy is integrated into the hemispheric trading and investment system, threatening to leave the agreement could cause a massive flight of international capital. Turning back from certain other aspects of domestic reform would also be made much more difficult if trade was regulated by treaty. This "lock-in" effect is independent of the size of a country's volume of trade with any of the other members in a WHFTA, including the United States.

Commitments under the WHFTA are not immutable however. If the majority of signatories to a WHFTA came to feel that more government intervention was desirable, for instance, they would be able to change their agreement correspondingly—although it is not obvious what would happen if the majority included all countries except the United States. If one country came to that conclusion unilaterally, it could abrogate the agreement—provided that it felt that the benefits from the proposed intervention exceeded the benefits to be forgone through abrogation. The restraints would thus be significant but, if genuine advantage were perceived, the policy could be changed. If, as I suspect, the advantages of the WHFTA turn out to be large and cumulate over time, then there would be a lock-in effect in the sense that no government would seriously contemplate leaving the agreement. The lock-in effect would act through self-interest, *not* coercion.

What's in a WHFTA for the United States?

The interest of the U.S. administration in a WHFTA is no doubt a mixture of economic and geopolitical motives (with the degree of the mix much altered by the end of the Cold War).

First, there would be a real economic gain to the United States by promoting growth and trade among countries with a combined population significantly larger than the current population of the United States and Canada. Should sustained growth at catch-up rates result, the expansion of the hemispheric market would allow large mutual gains from a rapidly rising volume of intrahemispheric trade.

Second, sustained growth at catch-up rates may contribute to political stability and reduce the chances of some Latin American countries' turning to the type of left-wing governments that the United States seeks to avoid. This is by no means certain, however, and the effects on political stability, particularly in the initial phases, would depend on the magnitude of the dynamic adjustment costs and the distribution of the static gains.

Third, codifying the rules of trade and investment and securing them by treaty would reduce the chances of a repeat of past direct or indirect confiscations of U.S. investments and sudden upsets to its trade with Latin American countries.[7]

What's in a WHFTA for Canada?

Canadian reasons for entering such an agreement would be the normal ones. First, a desire to share fully in the gains resulting from increased trade and growth within a market of over 700 million people. Second, fear of major trade diversion if Canada stayed out. Third, fear of a major loss of investment (both foreign and domestically owned) as firms found the United States a more attractive location because of its free access to Latin American markets not available to Canadian-based firms.

What are the Disadvantages to Potential Members?

Each country would have to assess its own specific costs, but several general classes of potential costs can be identified.

ADJUSTMENT COSTS. Latin America is no stranger to adjustment to market-oriented, liberalizing policies. Enormous adjustment problems are being faced today in many countries as they liberalize their economies. Nonetheless, the cost of adjusting to a WHFTA could be an additional strain, which is one reason for phasing it in relatively slowly. These costs would be greatly diminished if the entry into a WHFTA is preceded by entry into a regional trade arrangement, which in turn is preceded by substantial unilateral reductions in trade barriers and domestic economic liberalization.

The WHFTA should not stand in the way of any country providing generous assistance to workers who are displaced by the adjustment process. As long as adjustment assistance goes to help people to move and retrain, rather than to subsidize firms to resist adjustment, there should be no problem with existing fair trade laws and GATT commitments. Furthermore, generally available assistance to firms, such as tax credits for research and development and investment, should pose no conflicts with external commitments. Since some poorer countries may face major adjustments, some of the free trade and investment provisions might well be suspended for the transition period. This should be acceptable, as long as these exemptions are only granted for specified periods of time so that all countries eventually move all the way to the WHFTA's liberal trade and investment regimes.

DYNAMIC EFFECTS. In many instances, the dynamic effects of trade liberalization will be beneficial, resulting in higher productive efficiency, investment, and growth. This appears to have been the case with most of the EC, for example.[8]

There is, however, another side to the dynamic issue: can the free market system accentuate the problems of areas on the economic periphery? A long line of economists, including Gunnar Myrdal and Nicholas Kaldor, have argued that market forces accentuate regional inequalities by drawing mobile factors, including entrepreneurial talent, from the peripheries into the economically central areas. If so, do the dynamic gains to overall income growth outweigh the redistributive effects as activity is transferred to the central areas from the peripheries? This is not an easy issue to settle. For one reason, misguided economic policies, rather than the overwhelming attractions of the center, have often contributed to the decline of peripheral areas. For another, peripheral and central areas can change places over time.[9] Less economically powerful countries on various peripheries will have to assess the chances that integration into the world economy would start them on a downward rather than an upward spiral.

CONSTRAINTS ON DEVELOPMENT POLICY. The old interventionist, import-substitution policies are discredited. Today, most governments have accepted the market-driven private sector as the main creator of wealth. (This acceptance does not, however, preclude government intervention to redistribute wealth in the interests of social justice.) Within the broad consensus on the importance of the private sector as the generator of wealth, two main approaches can be distinguished.

Some countries, including the United States and the United Kingdom, espouse a laissez-faire policy. They believe that the state should provide the background in terms of law and order, enforcement of contracts, sound money, good education, and infrastructure where it has a "public good" aspect. Beyond that, the private sector can be left alone to generate the optimum rate and direction of growth.[10] Other countries such as Japan, and the successful newly industrializing countries (NICs), espouse a policy of "nudging" the private sector to influence the amount and direction of its economic growth, creating what can be called "government-assisted, free-market economies."[11] Specific policies designed to create externalities during the early stages of industrialization include education and training to upgrade the quality of the labor force, various transitory tax exemptions, subsidies on the cost of public services, and low-interest loans from state-controlled banks. The list worries many market-oriented economists. However, such measures are justified, at least in principle, by the enormous externalities that accompany early industrialization, by the need to facilitate the diffusion of technologies, and by the pervasive market failures that can be found in most less developed economies.[12]

Both approaches share the goals of privatization, deregulation, avoidance of major distorting interferences in relative prices, and encouragement of competition, both domestically and through relatively liberalized trade. Thus the advocates of both approaches can applaud most of what is going on in the current bout of economic reforms in Latin America. But at some point in the liberalization process, the paths dictated by the two approaches diverge. At that point, the key question for those who would reject laissez-faire policy and embrace the concept of government-assisted, free-market economy is: how much would the constraints imposed by a WHFTA inhibit the adoption of the required economic policies? Many development policies need not run seriously afoul of the basic rules of a WHFTA, but extreme care would be needed here. The successful growth experience of the newly industrializing countries suggests that the ability to duplicate many of their policies should not be lightly abandoned by any developing country.[13]

PRECONDITIONS FOR A WHFTA

The U.S. administration has recently identified a number of preconditions that, in its view, need to be fulfilled before a NAFTA could be extended to other Latin American countries. In this section the main preconditions dictated by sound economic policy are addressed.

■ *Macroeconomic stability.* As a first prerequisite, inflation must be brought under reasonable control. This means that budget deficits must be no more than are sustainable, preferably leading to a constant (or declining) debt-gross domestic product (GDP) ratio.

■ *Market-oriented microeconomic policies.* No country should contemplate accepting the disciplines of a WHFTA unless it is well on its way to installing outward-looking, market-oriented, domestic economic policies and to eliminating the use of such interventionist tools as inefficiency-supporting subsidies and market-distorting administered prices.

■ *Adequate infrastructure.* Good transportation and communications systems are important prerequisites. Without them, much of the potential gains from opening the economy to the forces of global competition will go unexploited. The growth of nontraditional exports through FDI and domestic investment will be seriously hampered by a lack of such infrastructure. As competition becomes increasingly globalized, the harmful effects of such deficiencies are magnified.

■ *Trade and payments regime.* Full GATT membership should, of course, be mandatory for any country that wishes to be considered for WHFTA membership. Furthermore, quotas and other forms of trade restrictions should be converted into tariff equivalents and then reduced unilaterally. The remaining tariffs should be relatively uniform and moderate in height. In addition, exchange rates should either be market determined or be stabilized somewhere near the market equilibrium rate. They should not be sustained by foreign-exchange controls (which are market distorting and subject to administrative abuse), although some control over financial flows may be accepted.

Cutting high tariffs before entering a WHFTA has a number of advantages. First, it will reduce the harm done by trade diversion when imports switch from the tariff-burdened products of third countries to tariff-free, but higher real-cost, imports from WHFTA partners. Second, it will help to allay fears of outside countries that they will lose heavily through trade diversion. Third, the unilateral cuts provide a reversible test case as to how the economy adopts to an infusion of foreign price competition. If the process seems too painful, with too few gains, there is time to reconsider joining the WHFTA.

A country with traditional exports that are not subject to heavy tariffs in other member countries, or do not have the capacity to grow, may find entry into the WHFTA accompanied by a major increase in imports and downward pressure on the exchange rate. If traditional exports do not respond much to exchange depreciations,[14] the capacity to develop new exports is required.

Export promotion may be needed wherever multinationals, with their own export-promotion strategies, are not already in place. However, too many market distortions can prevent firms from responding to export incentives. Moreover, absence of infrastructure can seriously impede a strong response to the export incentives provided by joining the WHFTA. In some cases, though, particularly for small- and medium-sized firms, export-promotion assistance may make a significant contribution to a smooth transition.

Experience with the NAFTA may suggest what other preconditions may need to be met before a country can successfully enter into the WHFTA. In this regard, the WHFTA will be much less of a leap in the dark than the NAFTA.

THE INSTITUTIONAL STRUCTURE

Support in principle for a liberalizing free trade agreement is one thing. Knowing what this entails in practice is quite another matter.

What a WHFTA Should Not Be

Much of the discussion of a WHFTA has assumed that it would take forms that I believe it would not take. This makes it easy to dismiss the whole concept. For example, economist Anne Krueger, when discussing the possibility of bilateral FTAs involving the United States, said:

> I conclude that the American discussion of FTAs—not genuine, no-restrictions and no-trade-barriers FTAs, but the kind that require 16 months to negotiate and consist of 900 or more pages—is doubly tragic: it uses the language of free trade to perpetuate protectionism, and is simultaneously highly unrealistic since it cannot possibly be extended one country at a time over a large number of countries. Possibly even worse, it detracts attention from the current Uruguay Round of multilateral trade negotiations.[15]

Krueger's assessment seems unduly pessimistic. Neither the time taken by the negotiations, nor the number of pages filled by the text is an indication of an agreement's liberalizing force. Yet, Krueger's discussion of what could happen under the wrong institutional arrangement points to several "don'ts" en route to hemispheric free trade.

First, the path should not consist of a series of overlapping, mutually inconsistent agreements between groups of countries. Such a path leads to serious confusion and much inefficiency.

Second, the path should not consist of agreements covering a limited number of specific sectors. The number of such agreements would need to be almost the number of pairs of countries, since one country's weak sector, to be protected vigorously, is another country's strong sector, ripe for tariff elimination. Furthermore, such sectoral agreements usually bring small benefits because the set of sectors that both partners are willing to free up usually excludes the ones most in need of adjustment.

Third, it should not be a series of bilateral agreements, with the United States at the hub, and single Latin American countries at the other end of each spoke. It should be a single comprehensive agreement that can be extended piecemeal to include, in principle, all of the countries in the Western Hemisphere.

Finally, the WHFTA should be a "GATT-plus" not a "GATT-minus" agreement. It should build on GATT principles but push disciplines even further. For the WHFTA movement to be a real historical force, ideas of limited and selective sectoral intervention would need to be replaced by the concept of sweeping, across-the-board liberalization of the sort that is readily acceptable to the GATT under Article XXIV.[16]

What a WHFTA Should Be

The arrangement should be a free trade area, not a customs union or a common market.[17] Many supporters of the WHFTA concept see it as a transition stage toward a full economic union. The desirability of this development is not acceptable for two important reasons.

First, as a superpower, the United States naturally sees trade policy as a tool of foreign policy. It has used trade policy to discipline governments of which at one time or another it disapproved, such as Cuba, China, the Soviet Union, Vietnam, and Nicaragua. The United States is unlikely to relinquish its unilateral power to levy trade restrictions such as quotas, voluntary export restraints, and prohibitions against "unfriendly" countries. In contrast, Canada has traditionally seen foreign policy as a tool of trade policy. As a smaller more open economy, maintaining an open trading system has been its most vital national concern on the international scene. Canada is, therefore, unwilling to accept U.S. choices on matters of commercial policy.

This issue was not much of a concern to many countries in Latin America when they were operating inward-looking, import-substitution policies. Now that they are committed to outward-looking, export-oriented policies, however, they will come to see international relations more as Canada does. For this reason, they will probably also wish to preserve their policy independence with respect to trading relations with third countries.

The solution to this conflict of interests is to form a FTA, which leaves each member free to set its own external barriers, constrained by the knowledge that, if these get too far out of line, trade deflection—goods entering the member country having the lowest tariff and then slipping into the other countries—will become a problem. This freedom is not possible in a customs union. The latter requires members to have a common external commercial policy, including common tariffs, common quotas, and (to a great extent) common nontariff barriers. In such a regime, the United States would inevitably set most of the area's commercial policy, because the U.S. Congress would not give up significant power in setting the foreign-policy aspect of commercial policy to a large group in which the United States was but one of many parties.

A second reason why a free trade area is preferable to a customs union is that it reduces the risk that large regional groups will become inward-looking, trade-restricting monoliths. In a customs union, a central body sets external policy, whereas in a FTA, each country can set its own course. Therefore, a fear that more regional grouping will harm multilateralism is better founded when these groups are large and take the form of customs unions rather than FTAs. To supporters of multilateralism, who see large regional groups as complementary rather than competitive with the GATT, this is an important point.

ALTERNATIVE FTA ARRANGEMENTS. There are two polar models for the evolution of hemispheric free trade, the *hub-and-spoke model* and what I have called elsewhere *plurilateral regionalism.*[18] The choice between the two will have major consequences for the countries in the Western Hemisphere.

In the *hub-and-spoke model*, the United States has a separate, bilateral, free trade agreement with each participating country. Latin American countries, as well as Canada, should resist adoption of the hub-and-spoke model for several reasons.

First, as the hub country, the United States becomes the only country with tariff-free access to the markets of all participating countries. As spoke countries, the other participants have tariff-free access only to the U.S. market. Thus, this model creates trade diversion in each spoke-country market; the beneficiary is the United States; the losers are the other spoke countries.

Second, the United States will benefit from investment diversion at the expense of the spoke countries. Locating a plant in any spoke country provides tariff-free access only to the United States and the local spoke market. Locating a plant in the United States, however, provides tariff-free access to the United Sates and to the markets of all of the spoke countries.

Third, in the hub-and-spoke model the United States is placed in a superior bargaining position. It negotiates separate agreements with each of its smaller partners so that they have no chance to make common cause against it in areas of mutual, small-country interest. This gives the United States a dominance that it may not particularly desire, but which the logic of the model thrusts upon it.

What I call plurilateral regionalism refers to agreements between regional groups in which *each* member has the same privileges and obligations as all the other members. Whereas hub-and-spoke is a model of U.S. hegemony over the Americas, plurilateral regionalism is a model of equals. All members have the same access to each other's market, all bargain together, and all are free to make common cause with others of like-mindedness in common trade negotiations.

Between these two pure cases, lie a number of *hybrid cases.* The simplest is one in which Latin American countries form a small number of nonoverlapping regional trade arrangements, and each signs a free trade agreement with the United States. This is a hub-and-spoke model, except that the spokes are regional trade arrangements rather than individual countries. The same arguments apply, only slightly weaker, to rejecting this as an acceptable model for hemispheric trade liberalization. The United States still has a dominant, and asymmetric, position vis-à-vis all its FTA partners. Also, there would be substantial trade diversion as, inevitably, there will be contiguous countries with a potential for a large volume of trade between themselves but which belong to different regional FTAs.

An even less attractive hybrid case arises when a series of overlapping regional trade arrangements occur in Latin America. This sets up a pecking order of economic advantage, depending on how many other markets any one country has access to. Also, overlapping regional agreements with different rules of origin and differing provisions on other matters are a potential source of administrative complexity that would greatly hamper the free flow of goods and services.

A whole new set of possibilities arises if the United States rejects the NAFTA. Mexico might then become the hub of a Latin American hub-and-spoke model. There would be substantial self-interest pressures on Mexico to play that role. Nevertheless, its commitment to multilateralism should lead it instead to push for a single WHFTA, excluding only the United States. If that worked, and if catch-up growth rates ensued, the Latin American economies would have the satisfaction a decade or two down the line of having the United States apply to join the Latin American FTA!

STRUCTURE OF THE AGREEMENT. Only when the structure of the NAFTA agreement becomes clearer, will it be possible to chart the route forward with any precision. In the meantime, some general rules should guide all future negotiations.

The basic principle for a WHFTA is that there should be *one* free trade agreement that can be acceded to sequentially by any country in the Western Hemisphere. This is the same principle as is used by the EC. Within this framework, there are two main possibilities.

The first and easiest approach would be to have a single agreement that is suitable to all countries. Countries would join the WHFTA merely by signing on to the existing agreement.

The Canada-United States Free Trade Agreement (CAFTA) does not provide a model for this case, because it contains a number of provisions that would be unsuitable for extension to all other hemispheric countries. It would be possible, though perhaps not likely, for the NAFTA to become such a model, provided it did not contain too many conditions specifically tailored to the three countries involved.

The second approach would consist of a core agreement common to all and a penumbra, where special conditions applicable to particular countries would be specified. The core treaty would cover such central items as free trade in goods, free trade in covered services, a liberalized investment regime, and a dispute-settlement mechanism. This core agreement would be nonnegotiable, and any new member country would have to accept it.

Flexibility could be added, as in the EC, by defining two levels of countries. Class A countries could, on signature, receive all the benefits and assume all the obligations that go with membership in the WHFTA, including a phase-in period for the elimination of their tariffs. Class B countries would escape some of the obligations, *for a finite period of time*, by virtue of being significantly less developed than the average class A country. Class B countries might, for example, be allowed a longer phase in for reductions in their tariffs, and even an asymmetric adjustment in which other members' tariffs against their goods fall faster than their tariffs against other members' goods. Exemption from the agreement for certain well-specified development policies might also be allowed—but only for defined time periods.

The penumbra agreement might cover such matters as agriculture, energy, government procurement, some aspects of investment, financial services, and special exemptions. A sentence or two on each is all that this space allows.

Agriculture is too large and sensitive a sector to be routinely accepted for free trade by all members. For the United States and Canada to allow free importation of all agricultural goods from all hemispheric countries would either end their own domestic stabilization programs or eliminate much of their imports from outside the hemisphere. Other countries would justifiably complain if the latter alternative were chosen.

Energy is a difficult problem for many governments. In the Canada-United States agreement, a number of provisions were included to ensure that Canada would not capriciously turn off its energy supply, and the United States would not capriciously turn off its energy demand. Energy will probably be at least partially excluded from the NAFTA, since Mexico's constitution precludes foreign ownership of its oil reserves. Other countries might have similar reservations in this area.

Ideally, *government procurement* should be included. However, many countries see procurement as a developmental tool, which with care it may be. (Strong evidence presented by economist Michael Porter suggests, however, that providing a protected procurement market for local firms can be a route to stagnation rather than innovation.[19])

Investment should be liberalized within the core agreement to some significant degree. But all nations exert some control over foreign direct investment, particularly when in the form of takeovers and mergers. Canada was unwilling to give up *all* such control, and few Latin American countries are likely to be willing to do so either.

Financial services are subject to varying degrees of control across countries. If realistic hopes are to be held for accession of most countries in the hemisphere, financial services may need to be partially, or even totally, exempted.

Special exemptions, ideally, should not apply to any goods and traded services, although existing precedents (i.e., U.S. maritime shipping, Canadian beer, and cultural industries) suggest that is next to impossible. The next best solution would be to allow no further exemptions. That would pose problems for new applicants, who would rightly ask, "If the Canadians and Americans each protected a few sacred cows, why shouldn't we be allowed to do the same?" However, it would be dangerous to allow such negotiations piecemeal each time a new country enters, so I would try to hold out for no further exemptions.

From a NAFTA to a WHFTA: Implications of Enlarged Membership

WHAT IS BARGAINED? Exactly what issues are negotiated between the existing members and a new member will depend on the form that the evolving WHFTA takes. It seems safe to say, however, that a WHFTA will have a core of basic agreements that will have to be accepted by new members, and some form of penumbra that will call for country-specific negotiations. At one extreme, the penumbra would include only phase-in arrangements for a transition period. In this model, the countries would evolve toward a single, common, agreement on all matters, after completion of the phase-in period (which might take a long time). This would require all special exceptions to be terminated at specified future dates rather than grandfathered (e.g., Canada's exemption for its cultural industries and the United States' exemption for shipping). Unfortunately, this seems unlikely. Instead, the penumbra is likely to contain some permanent, country-specific items that will have to be negotiated between each new member and the existing members at the time of entry. Every effort must be made to keep these permanent, country-specific, items to a minimum so that all countries end up being members of as nearly common an agreement as possible.

Transitional arrangements will need to be carefully considered. Because none of the Latin American countries is close to the level of development of the United States, phase-in periods may need to be quite long and might even be asymmetric. Some leeway for innovation and regional policies may also be required. Bargaining will no doubt be hard, particularly with the United States.

A useful principle in designing any FTA is "never say never"—just say "a very long time." Exclude something for 50 years if you must, but never exclude it forever. Time discounts are such that even strong special interest groups will often settle for protection in their own lifetimes. Time, however, ticks on inexorably, and an agreement with no "nevers," but only some "very long exclusion times," would slowly evolve to a complete, unequivocal free trade area. (Think, for example, of the great boon to the world if, in the negotiations leading up to the 1957 Treaty of Rome that launched the EC, instead of adopting the common agriculture policy indefinitely, the countries had insisted that the measures be terminated after 40 years. That would have seemed forever in 1958, but as 1998 approaches, the difference between never including agriculture in free trade and including it after 40 years would seem more and more important.)

Another aspect of this rule concerns grandfathering. In the CAFTA, *all* measures in either country that conflicted with the terms of the agreement, but which were in existence on the day of the agreement, were grandfathered. It will be hard to reverse this unfortunate precedent. I would settle for a blanket, 50-year rule for all existing measures, but purists might want to subject the sunset provision to negotiations. Since such negotiations might be acrimonious, a possible compromise would be to say that all existing measures in conflict with the agreement would be eliminated after 50 years, unless a shorter time period were negotiated.

There is little hope that the never-say-never rule will be adopted. Yet, few more important rules exist. Current measures that conflict with the rules of liberal trade and investment should not be given a blanket exemption for all future time. As the experience of the common agricultural policy shows, such exemptions are often a time bomb ticking away, waiting to explode into major problems at some unknown date.

THE BARGAINING UNIT. If negotiation of any kind is needed over the accession of a new member, there is the vexing problem of who will do the bargaining for the existing members. This would be a serious problem with the core-penumbra model, but it arises if anything other than a mechanical signing of an unalterable agreement is envisaged.

What are the possibilities? First, the United States could do the bargaining for all existing members. Second, all existing members could bargain as a group with the new applicant. Third, a secretariat could be established for the WHFTA, and it could do the bargaining. Fourth, in the case of the penumbra, a series of bilateral bargains between the new entrant and each existing member might be negotiated.

No doubt there are other alternatives. This is enough, however, to show the existence of a serious problem. The basic message is that there is a premium on keeping special-case bargaining to a minimum. A broad core of agreements with no penumbra, no exceptions, and only transitional arrangements to be negotiated, would provide the easiest case. But, a look at the nongeneralizable conditions in the CAFTA suggests that some flexibility will be needed. Perhaps a secretariat (some version of the European solution) would be workable. But would the United States accept it?

The more issues covered by the negotiations, the stronger the case for a secretariat, it might be argued. Conversely, the fewer the issues, the stronger the case for countries representing themselves. I am inclined to think that for the first few accessions, the only acceptable solution will be for each existing member to send bargainers to a common set of negotiations where all members and new applicants will be individually represented, but a mutually acceptable result will still be required.

Similar problems will arise on the applicants' side if they belong to regional FTAs or common markets that wish to join the growing WHFTA group as a bloc. Will they bargain as one unit or as individual countries?

AN ACCESSION CLAUSE. It would seem desirable to include some form of accession clause in the NAFTA agreement currently being negotiated. This would spell out the terms under which a new entrant's application would be acceptable as well as the items that would require negotiation and, by implication, the core of nonnegotiable items.

An accession procedure, whether written into the NAFTA agreement or invented ad hoc the first time a new entrant seemed a serious possibility, will require some way of automatically invoking the U.S. fast-track procedure. No country would rationally enter into a delicate set of negotiations with the United States (which should result in a carefully balanced series of concessions), without the fast track to prevent the U.S. Senate from approving the foreign concessions and rejecting the U.S. concessions. There are some sensitive issues here, because Congress may not be willing to provide an automatic provision for future uses of the fast track in circumstances it cannot currently envisage.

The best solution would be prior agreement to extend fast-track authority to the entry application of any country that met previously stipulated economic policy conditions. Eligibility conditions would presumably include: reasonable fiscal balance; market determination of most prices, including interest rates and exchange rates; absence of indiscriminate domestic subsidies (although new members should not be subjected to greater discipline than is observed by existing members, including the United States); membership in the GATT; and relatively low external tariff and nontariff barriers.

Such conditions cannot be specified precisely nor can they be judged to be fulfilled with any precision. Instead, the intent would be clear, and a committee chosen by WHFTA members should investigate the policies of any new applicant and report in detail on whether, in their opinion, the conditions were met on overall balance. In the event of rejection, an appeal to a high-level council of WHFTA members could be envisaged, with the council being empowered either to sustain the refusal or to send it back to the committee for further investigation.

WHO COULD APPLY? Presumably, all nations in the Western Hemisphere, including those of the Caribbean Basin, could apply for entry—if they met the published, noncountry-specific preconditions. The main issue is whether countries from outside the hemisphere would be eligible. Two countries that might be interested are Australia and New Zealand—provided that membership in a WHFTA did not compromise their close trading relations with East Asian countries.

To preserve the outward-looking image and reality of the WHFTA, countries outside the Western Hemisphere that met the preconditions should be welcomed. The purpose behind the agreement is not to divert trade to the parochial advantage of countries in the Western Hemisphere, but to use regional initiative to move faster toward general trade liberalization. If outsiders were willing to meet the stiff conditions for trade liberalization implied by membership in a broad-based WHFTA, there is no reason not to welcome them. Doing otherwise would confirm the fears of those who suspect an inward-looking agreement.

ACCEPTANCE. Each country will wish to retain its policy independence to reject any agreement with respect to a new entrant once the bargain is struck by the negotiators.[20] Here the best model would seem to be the GATT rather than the European Community. Once the protocol of accession of a new member is negotiated, each country's legislature should be allowed to ratify or reject that accession. This is their only chance to reject the applicant. If a member does reject the applicant, it denies rights proposed to be given by existing members to the new member. In turn, the new member would deny these rights to the objecting existing member.

It is hoped that such eventualities would remain as an unused escape clause, since frequent use would make the WHFTA similar to a series of overlapping FTAs, with all of their accompanying disadvantages. Some discipline might be built in to deter member countries from denying rights to prospective new members for what appear to be less than strongly compelling reasons.

CONCLUSIONS

Enormous structural changes are sweeping the world. Foreign direct investment has become a major instrument of growth and development. To be left outside major flows of international capital is to be marginalized in today's globalizing economy.

Liberalized, outward-looking, market-oriented (but not necessarily market-worshipping), economic policies are key conditions for playing a strong part in the evolving world economy. A Western Hemisphere Free Trade Area could be a key institution in encouraging and enshrining these developments.

If it is to help in this way, a WHFTA must be a union of equals based on plurilateral regionalism, not on a hub-and-spoke model. It must be outward looking, which calls for a FTA not a customs union. It must have low external tariffs. And it must be open to all serious new applicants. The organization should be based on a core of nonnegotiable free trade and investment principles, some important transitional arrangements for new members, and a minimum of country-specific exceptions and special arrangements negotiated with new entrants. Whenever possible, long but specified periods for exceptions are greatly preferable to permanent grandfathering. Clear conditions under which serious negotiations would take place with any new applicant from anywhere in the world should be set down and known in advance of any new application. Under these conditions, a WHFTA could be a complement, rather than a hindrance, to further multilateral trade liberalization.

Notes

[1] A Nash equilibrium occurs when each player, acting on its own, can make no move that will benefit itself, given what all the other players are currently doing.

[2] Richard Lipsey and Murray Smith, "The Canada-U.S. Free Trade Agreement: Special Case or Wave of the Future," in Jeffrey J. Schott (ed.), *Free Trade Areas and U.S. Trade Policy* (Washington, DC: Institute for International Economics, 1989), p. 321.

[3] Schott, *Free Trade Areas*, op. cit.

[4] For example, the November 11, 1991, issue of the *Toronto Globe and Mail* carried a story on page B3 under the headline "North American Free Trade Concerns Japanese" and reported that "spearheaded by the powerful ministry of international trade and industry, Japanese officials are challenging the North American free-trade agreement talks as a threat to the international trade system."

[5] Murray Smith and I have argued this important point at length in Richard G. Lipsey and Murray G. Smith, *Global Imbalances and U.S. Policy Responses* (Toronto: C.D. Howe Institute, and Washington: the National Planning Association, 1987).

[6] For a full discussion, see John Williamson (ed.), *Latin American Adjustment: How Much Has Happened?* (Washington, DC: Institute for International Economics, 1990).

[7] This was a major U.S. motivation in the Canada-United States Free Trade Agreement (CAFTA). Its provisions preclude a reimposition of the confiscatory aspects of investment policies such as the Canadian National Energy Policy of the early 1980s, which confiscated a significant part of the Canadian investments by U.S. oil companies.

[8] I have discussed these dynamic effects at some length in Richard G. Lipsey, "Some Unsettled Issues in the Great Free Trade Debate," *Canadian Journal of Economics*, Vol. 22, No. 1 (November 1988).

[9] For instance, the Canadian Atlantic provinces seem stuck in a (relative) poverty trap largely as a result of national policies that have created a culture of dependency. In contrast, in the United States there appear to have been significant regional differences in per capita incomes since measurements began, but individual states have moved toward either end of the distribution spectrum over time.

[10] To be sure, countries that espouse this view do in practice adopt some substantial micro-interventionist policies, often at subnational levels of government.

[11] See, for example, Marcus Noland, *Pacific Basin Developing Countries* (Washington, DC: Institute for International Economics, 1990).

[12] For a detailed exposition of these policies, see H. Pack and L. E. Westphal, "Industrial Strategy and Technological Change," *Journal of Development Economics*, Vol. 22 (1986), pp. 87-128.

[13] The Canadian political left worried during the debate over the CAFTA that the ability to run an industrial policy would be compromised by the agreement. Their support went, however, to the older industrial policies based on subsidies. Because the agreement did not cover subsidies, it left the status quo unchanged. Subsidies can be used but risk a countervailing challenge when the subsidized firms export to the United States. Because there was no well-worked out policy for creating a modern, state-assisted, free-market economy, the CAFTA does not provide a test case of how a FTA, with the United States as one of its partners, would constrain the type of policy that is part of this package.

[14] "A country does not export more basic products when it depreciates, given current world market conditions." Victor L. Urquidi, "Panel Discussion on Latin American Adjustment: The Record and Next Steps," in Williamson, (ed.) op. cit., p. 334.

[15] Anne O. Krueger, "Comments on a Free Trade Agreement with Australia," in Schott (ed.), *Free Trade Areas*, op. cit., p. 199. By Krueger's criteria, the CAFTA was protectionist, yet it accomplished more liberalization of Canadian-U.S. trade than did any GATT round.

[16] GATT Article XXIV requires that substantially all trade among prospective members of a FTA be liberalized within a reasonable time frame. It also requires that tariff barriers against nonmembers not be raised as a result of a FTA.

[17] This section relies heavily on Richard G. Lipsey, *Canada at the U.S.-Mexican Free Trade Dance: Wallflower or Partner?* (Toronto: C.D. Howe Institute, 1990); and Richard G. Lipsey "The Case for Trilateralism," in S. Globerman (ed.), *Continental Accord: North American Economic Integration* (Vancouver: Fraser Institute, 1991).

[18] I have not traced the origins of this concept. I first came across it at the conference held by the Institute for International Economics in Washington, DC, in late 1988. See Y. C. Park and J. H. Yoo, in Schott (ed.), *Free Trade Areas*, op. cit., who refer to the concept as a "star-shaped" FTA.

[19] See Michael Porter, *The Competitive Advantage of Nations*, (New York: Macmillan, 1990).

[20] I am indebted to Jeffrey Schott for this discussion on acceptance and for the suggestion that the GATT is the appropriate model.

Chapter Four

U.S.-Latin America Free Trade Areas: Some Empirical Evidence

Refik Erzan and Alexander Yeats

INTRODUCTION

Although much of the analyses involving free trade agreements (FTAs) has focused on United States objectives,[1] this chapter examines trade gains that Latin America might experience from such arrangements with the United States. Specifically, a trade-policy simulation model developed by the World Bank is used to project the size and product composition of Latin American and Caribbean countries' export expansion resulting from a preferential removal of U.S. trade barriers. Aside from identifying the major (tariff-line level) products affected by trade restrictions, statistics on the importance of U.S. import duties and nontariff barriers (NTBs) facing Latin America are also analyzed. To set the stage for this discussion, we first examine information on the level and composition of Latin America's imports and exports and also assess the importance of intra-American trade for these countries. Secular changes in Latin American and other regional countries' trade are also compared with world trade to assess the global importance of a FTA for the Americas.[2]

CHARACTERISTICS OF INTRA-AMERICAN TRADE

If a free trade area for the Americas was established, how important would it be from a global perspective? Table 1 provides relevant information by showing the value of world trade (exports) for several years over 1970-1988, as well as the value and share of this exchange accounted for by selected regions. As indicated, the intra-American trade share ranges between 9 and 11 percent, or about one-third the size of developed Europe's intra-trade (in 1988 intra-trade in the Americas was less than half that of the members of the European Community). North American exports between Canada and the United States now total about $150 billion—nearly 60 percent of total intra-American trade—with about $85 billion (3 percent of world trade) occurring between the countries of North and South America. Table 1 also shows that Latin America's intra-trade is only about one-quarter that of the developing countries of South and Southeast Asia.

Turning from the global figures, Table 2 examines the relative importance of intra-American trade for individual Latin American countries as well as for Canada and the United States. Shown here is the value of each country's total exports and the share of this trade destined for the Americas. The latter is disaggregated further to show the relative importance of various countries or country groups—such as the Central American Common Market (CACM) or Caribbean Community (Caricom).[3]

Table 2 shows some marked differences in the regional concentration of both North and South American countries' exports. Argentina, Chile, and Uruguay—as well as the United States—ship between 33 to 39 percent of total exports to hemispheric markets. The corresponding shares for Ecuador, Mexico, and Canada average over 70 percent. Within the region, the United States is generally the most important single destination for exports, although a somewhat higher share of Argentina, Bolivia, Paraguay, and Uruguay's trade is with Latin American Integration Association (LAIA) member countries.[4] Except for the United States, Canada is a relatively unimportant destination for exports, absorbing only 1 to 2 percent of Latin American trade (3.7 percent in the case of Venezuela).[5]

What do North and South American countries trade with each other? Table 3 shows the total value of each individual country's export to: 1) Canada and the United States combined and 2) all other countries in the Americas. Also shown are the shares of total trade accounted for by five broad types of goods: foods and feeds; agricultural materials; energy products (coal, natural gas, and petroleum); ores and metals; and manufactured goods, which are shown along with four of their major components (textiles and clothing, transport and machinery, chemicals, and iron and steel).

Table 3 indicates that there are some marked differences among several of the Latin America countries' exports to North America that could make it easier to accommodate their interests in a free trade agreement.[6] For example, Venezuela's exports are highly concentrated in energy products (90 percent of total), while about one-third of Mexico's and Colombia's trade consists of these goods. A preferential removal of the U.S. excise tax on petroleum, if part of an agreed FTA, could benefit these countries, but the gains from any related tariff preferences appear small (U.S. import duties on crude and refined petroleum average under 1 percent and there are no "hard core" nontariff barriers on energy products). Similarly, Chile and Bolivia have a high concentration (48 to 63 percent, respectively) of ores and metals in total exports, while three-quarters of Ecuador's trade consists of foods (largely coffee). Four Latin American countries—Argentina, Brazil, Paraguay, and Uruguay—have manufactured exports that comprise 50 percent or more of their total exports, but even in these instances there are important differences in the product composition of goods shipped. Table 3 shows that about 50 percent of Uruguay's exports to North America consist of textiles and clothing, while these goods account for only about 5 percent of Argentina's and Brazil's exports.

As far as North-South trade is concerned, Table 3 shows that North American exports to Latin America are concentrated in manufactures, which account for about 75 percent of all shipments. Within this group, capital intensive manufactures predominate with over one-half the value of these exports consisting of machinery (electric and nonelectrical) and transport equipment. With the exception of energy products, intra-Latin American trade is also concentrated in manufactures. Sixty percent or more of Bolivia, Chile, Ecuador, Mexico, Paraguay, Uruguay, and Venezuela's imports from other Latin American countries consist of manufactures. Capital intensive goods such as machinery and transportation equipment comprise a relatively high share of these items (24 percent on average).

Tables 4a and 4b take a more disaggregated look at the composition of trade between Latin America and the United States. Table 4a lists, in descending order of importance, the 25 largest three-digit SITC products exported to the United States and provides the 1988 value of trade along with the item's share in total exports. Table 4b provides similar information for products Latin America imports from the United States. As indicated, more than 21 percent of Latin American trade with the United States consists of crude and refined petroleum. Since the tariffs on these products are low—averaging less than 1 percent—there appears to be little scope for the United States to extend meaningful preferences to these items under a FTA. In addition, a number of other major export products face zero or very low U.S. import duties, and no apparent nontariff barriers (e.g., coffee, copper, aluminum). Several products have relatively high (more than 5 percent) U.S. tariffs under most-favored-nation (MFN) treatment, but Latin America and other developing countries already receive important preferences for these items under the Generalized System of Preferences (GSP) or the U.S. Caribbean Basin Initiative (CBI). Clothing (SITC 84) is an exception; Latin American exports face tariffs that often range between 20 and 35 percent as well as quantitative restrictions under the Multi-Fibre Arrangement (MFA).

From a U.S. perspective, FTAs with Latin America may appear to have considerably more potential. More than 45 percent of major U.S. export products consist of transport and machinery (SITC 7), and most of these items face relatively high tariff and nontariff barriers. In addition, published estimates[7] show that these products generally have the highest import demand elasticities, which suggest that preferential market access could produce a significant expansion of U.S. exports.

LIKELY EFFECTS OF FTAS ON LATIN AMERICAN EXPORTS

As noted, the potential for extending preferences to some Latin American exporters is limited because tariffs are already low due to cuts under the GSP and previous multilateral tariff negotiations. Some countries whose exports are concentrated in raw materials face zero or low import duties. Before proceeding to the trade projections, it would be useful to examine this proposition in more detail.

Table 5 provides some basic statistics relating to U.S. capacity to extend FTA preferences to Latin America. The table shows total exports to the United States from Latin American countries as well as the number of tariff-line products in which trade occurs (U.S. customs schedules distinguish between 5,861 tariff-line items). The next two columns show the import values and shares for all dutiable trade (i.e., items to which nonzero import duties are applied). Because some products in this group encounter very low tariffs (and also may not be major trade items) two additional groups were added. The first consists of products subject to tariffs of 5 percent or more with trade of at least $50,000; the second retains these trade and tariff limits but adds a further requirement that the tariff line be affected by at least one type of nontariff barrier.[8] For comparison, the Republic of Korea, Hong Kong, and Singapore have been added to compare the positions of Latin America and several newly industrializing countries (NICs).

For Latin America as a whole, $6.3 billion or 16 percent of exports (by value) encounter tariffs of 5 percent or more, with about 7 percent of all exports facing these "significant" tariffs and one or more NTB. However, these overall totals are strongly affected by Mexico, which has a far broader base in terms of the number of tariff lines and diversity of products exported. Excluding Mexico, the totals show that only 11 percent of Latin American exports face significant tariffs, and less than half of these shipments ($1.3 billion of trade) are also affected by NTBs.[9]

Table 5 indicates several countries (Bolivia, Chile, Ecuador, Peru, and Venezuela, and members of CACM and Caricom) would experience only a marginal trade expansion in a FTA with the United States. Less than 6 percent of these countries' total exports are subject to "non-nuisance" tariffs and, except for Peru, fewer than 11 tariff-line products are also directly covered by NTBs. In contrast, more than 30 percent of Brazil's major exports to the United States face tariffs of at least 5 percent, while about one-quarter of Argentina, Mexico, and Paraguay's exports face important import duties.[10] As such, the table suggests that a distinction should be made between Latin American countries specializing in raw material exports, subject to low barriers, and countries like Mexico and Brazil whose products encounter more formidable restraints.

A crucial assumption about the trade effects of a FTA is that nontariff barriers applied to products whose tariffs are preferentially reduced would be removed (or relaxed) to allow realization of the full effects of import-duty cuts. If action on NTBs is not taken, the trade response to the FTA tariff cuts could be greatly reduced.

What specific U.S. NTBs need be removed and how important are these measures for Latin American exporters? For an initial evaluation, the share of these Latin American countries' total exports subject to 25 different types of restrictions was tabulated along with the share of total exports covered by all nontariff barriers.[11] In compiling this information, data on 1990 U.S. NTBs were drawn from the United Nations Conference on Trade and Development (UNCTAD) Data Base on Trade Control Measures and applied to 1986 U.S. tariff-line import data compiled by the General Agreement on Tariffs and Trade (GATT). The results, which show the extent to which individual Latin American countries' total exports face NTBs, are reported in Table 6. Table 7 examines the sectoral distribution of these measures and also differentiates between "hard core" and other restrictions.

The coverage figures (Table 7) show that the importance of U.S. nontariff barriers varies considerably for individual Latin American exporters. Only between 4 and 7 percent of Bolivia's and Uruguay's exports face U.S. nontariff measures, but 85 percent of Venezuela's trade is subject to these restrictions.[12] The latter figure is largely explained by the specific excise tax applied to petroleum imports—a measure that also causes the relatively high NTB coverage ratios for Colombia, Ecuador, Mexico, and Peru. Seasonal tariffs on vegetables are important for Chile (Table 6), covering more than one-fifth of all exports (they also are applied to about 3 percent of Mexico's trade). A flexible import fee on sugar—a measure similar to the European Community's variable import levies—covers 14 percent of Paraguay's total exports, over 12 percent of Caricom's exports, and from 1 to 4 percent of Argentina, Brazil, Colombia, CACM, and Peru's trade. Supplementary studies[13] indicate that the tariff equivalents of U.S. NTBs on sugar may range from 60 to 200 percent and are in the 20 to 50 percent range for textiles and clothing.

Tables 6 and 7 suggest that individual Latin American countries will have different priorities for the removal of specific U.S. NTBs. Approximately 7 percent of Brazil's and Colombia's exports have been subject to antidumping and countervailing duty (CVD) undertakings, but these actions have not been applied (or are minor) elsewhere. Similarly, a far higher share of Argentina, Brazil, Colombia, and Peru's exports (5 to 13 percent) are subject to antidumping and countervailing duties than is the case for other Latin American exporters. More than 5 percent of Peru's and Uruguay's exports encounter MFA and other textile restrictions, while Brazil has been singled out for voluntary export restraints (VERs). The latter nontariff measures are applied to a wide variety of fabricated iron and steel products exported by Brazil.

Overall, the important point that follows from Tables 6 and 7 is that the benefits of a U.S. FTA for Latin American countries would be seriously constrained without appropriate action to liberalize nontariff barriers. Table 5 shows that about half the tariff lines where Latin America faces import duties of 5 percent or more are also covered by one or more forms of NTBs. These measures would curtail any export expansion associated with FTA tariff preferences and could limit the results of tariff cuts to increased economic rents collected by U.S. importers. Given the importance of U.S. barriers on textiles and clothing, the annex to this chapter presents a more detailed assessment of their effects.

SIMULATION RESULTS FOR U.S.-LATIN AMERICA FTAS

To assess the likely magnitude of effects of a U.S. FTA for Latin American exports, we use a trade simulation model developed by the World Bank and examine four alternative scenarios. In the first two, we estimate the likely effects if: 1) each Latin American country entered into an exclusive agreement with the United States, and 2) all countries joined FTAs with the United States but not with each other.[14] The two situations chosen represent the upper and lower bounds of potential benefits to Latin America from FTAs. In other words, if some combination of four, five, or six countries signed agreements with the United States, the benefits would lie between those projected for situation one and two. In both the exclusive and the multiple country FTA projections, we make two alternative assumptions concerning nontariff barriers. In the first, we assume that all NTBs are removed or modified so that the full beneficial effects of the tariff preferences can be realized.[15] In the second, we assume that no action is taken on NTBs. In this case, all tariff lines covered by hard core nontariff barriers are excluded from our projections.[16]

Table 8 summarizes the simulation results for exclusive free trade agreements between each Latin American country and the United States. The first section of the table shows each country's total 1986 exports to the United States as well as trade in five major product groups. The second section shows the projected trade expansion when all U.S. tariffs are preferentially reduced, and NTBs are relaxed to allow the full effect of the tariff reduction to play out. The third section of the table shows the corresponding projections when tariffs are preferentially reduced but hard core nontariff barriers are assumed to remain in place.

A key point that emerges from the data is that the expansion of Mexico's exports under an exclusive FTA with the United States ($1.6 billion annually) exceeds that for all other countries combined, and that Mexico and Brazil together account for almost 90 percent of the total gains. However, the percentage expansion in Brazil's exports (14 percent) is almost 4 points higher than that for Mexico—due largely to the high share of petroleum in Mexico's trade (because tariffs on energy products average less than 1 percent, the benefits from a FTA are minimal). Of the five major product categories, the average percentage trade expansion for manufactures (16.9 percent) is more than four times the rate for the food and agricultural materials groups, and approximately 10 times the projected expansion for energy products. [17]

The projections show that accompanying action on nontariff barriers is important if some Latin American countries are to achieve maximum benefits from a U.S. FTA. If tariff-line items subject to hard core nontariff barriers are excluded from the simulations, the projected trade gains for Latin America fall by about $600 million. A failure to liberalize NTBs would reduce both Peru's and Colombia's export gains by at least 60 percent. In terms of absolute values, however, the $350 million reduction in Mexico's projected export gains accounts for over half the total NTB-related decline in Latin American trade expansion. Our lower level product projections show that MFA and other textile and clothing restrictions account for about 80 percent of the projected export expansion that is constrained by nontariff barriers.

In Table 9 we examine how FTA benefits would change (be shared) under multiple arrangements between the United States and the Latin American countries, as opposed to a single exclusive arrangement with the United States. These simulations assume that all Latin American countries enter individual agreements with the United States (but not with each other) and that the value of preferences *each* receives is eroded by other Latin American countries. Aside from Mexico, the trade expansion projections under this alternative scenario decline about 5 percent on average, with the simulation for Ecuador falling almost 12 percent below that for an exclusive FTA between it and the United States. In absolute terms, Table 9 shows that the multiple FTA scenario cuts about $75 million off the exclusive arrangement figures, with Mexico incurring about one-third of the decline. Finally, Box 1 shows the amount of other countries' exports that would be displaced by an exclusive U.S.-Mexico FTA.

POTENTIAL EFFECTS ON RAW MATERIAL PROCESSING

Numerous studies show that trade barriers in industrial countries have a common structure.[18] Typically, no (or low) tariffs and NTBs are applied to raw material imports, and the trade barriers increase or "escalate" as a product undergoes processing.[19] Many developing countries view escalating trade barriers as an important constraint on further processing of domestically produced commodities and have sought to have these barriers removed in multilateral trade negotiations (MTNs).

Given the nature of these concerns, Latin American countries would want trade-barrier escalation to be addressed in any FTA with the United States. The objective would be to negotiate a preferential removal of U.S. tariffs (and NTBs) on fabricated products which would, in turn, stimulate investment and the expansion of commodity processing in Latin America. If enough new investment and production capacity were generated in commodity processing activity, it might cause the actual trade effects of FTAs to exceed our projections.

There are several reasons, however, for believing that the potential trade expansion from natural resource processing has not been seriously underestimated in this study. First, the concluded Canada-United States Free Trade Agreement (CAFTA) already extended preferences in the U.S. market to Canada, which is a major supplier of many of the same raw materials (particularly ores) exported by Latin America. As such, this agreement diluted the potential value of FTAs as a means of stimulating raw material processing in Latin America. Second, previous MTNs and the GSP have reduced barriers facing many processed commodities, and their tariffs now generally average well under 10 percent.[20] Third, it has been increasingly recognized that other constraints such as transportation costs, capital requirements, market power of transnational firms, and the internal policies of developing countries themselves often have a

BOX 1. THE INFLUENCE OF A U.S.-MEXICO FREE TRADE AGREEMENT ON OTHER REGIONAL EXPORTERS

Mexico is the largest Latin American exporter to the United States and the country whose FTA discussions with the United States are the farthest along. How will a FTA between these two countries affect other Latin American exports to the United States? For answers the World Bank projection model was used to simulate the origin and value of trade that would be diverted. These projections are summarized below.

Three points are evident from these simulations. First, Brazil would be by far the largest loser, with some $18 million in exports displaced. This represents about 52 percent of the regional trade diverted. Second, the regional losses are highest in foods and agricultural materials ($15.8 million), with the displaced manufactures trade being about $2.4 million lower. Third, most of the losses occur outside the region. Some $405 million in nonregional exports are displaced, about 92 percent of the total trade diverted.

DISPLACED EXPORTS UNDER A U.S.-MEXICO FTA ($ thousands)

Exporter	Food and Agricultural Materials	Energy Products	Ores and Metals	All Manufactures	All Items
Argentina	-743	-188	—	-270	-1,201
Bolivia	—	-1	—	-18	-19
Brazil	-9,834	-209	-1	-8,263	-18,308
CACM	-3,856	-25	-1	-3,406	-7,288
Chile	-509	—	-240	-46	-795
Colombia	-419	-464	—	-484	-1,368
Ecuador	-190	-458	—	-22	-669
Paraguay	-9	—	—	-2	-11
Peru	-22	-293	-55	-78	-448
Uruguay	-1	—	—	-164	-165
Venezuela	-192	-4,278	—	-608	-5,078
Subtotal	-15,775	-5,916	-296	-13,361	-35,350
Total Displaced Exports	-35,027	-22,391	-1,843	-381,374	-440,636

Note: Numbers may not add due to rounding.

Source: Data and projections from the World Bank and UNCTAD Software for Market Analysis and Restrictions on Trade (SMART) model maintained in Washington, DC, and Geneva.

major influence on the location of processing industries in developing countries. Taken together, it is argued convincingly that the locational influence of tariff and nontariff trade barriers may be smaller than often supposed.[21]

TRADE BARRIERS FACING THE UNITED STATES IN LATIN AMERICA

The previous analyses (Table 5) demonstrated that the capacity of the United States to extend FTA tariff preferences to most Latin American countries was limited by three factors: 1) the U.S. CBI and the GSP under which important tariff preferences have been extended to these countries; 2) the tariff cuts previously achieved in MTNs; and 3) the concentration of some Latin American country exports in raw materials that have traditionally faced zero or low import duties in the U.S. market. As a result, our simulations suggested that full tariff preferences might expand Latin American exports by an average of 8 to 9 percent, but the increase for countries like Bolivia or Peru would be much lower. This leads to the question of whether or not there would be major imbalances in FTA trade gains in North and South America. In other words, would the expansion of U.S. exports be of roughly the same magnitude as Latin America's or would there be a major disparity in the gains?

Table 10 provides information relevant to this question by showing average weighted and unweighted Latin American tariffs on total imports.[22] Two points should be noted concerning these statistics. First, in almost all the countries (excluding Chile) important surcharges or "paratariffs" are added on top of these rates. While we have been unable to secure comprehensive data on these taxes, they likely add a further 5 to 10 points to rates shown in Table 10.[23] Second, these statistics do not reflect the influence of LAIA preferences because we could not get comprehensive information on these duties. These preferences seemingly cover some 30 to 40 percent of all tariff-line items in LAIA member countries with a margin of preference about one-third lower than MFN duties.

The key points that follow from Table 10 are that the average level of tariff protection in most Latin American countries is much higher than that in the United States, and that the potential for a FTA-induced expansion of U.S. exports appears significantly greater than that for Latin American exports to the North American market.[24] For the 11 countries combined, tariffs facing U.S. exports average about 20 percent—exclusive of the paratariff charges that are not included—compared to the approximately 3 to 4 percent average duties facing Latin American exporters. Some of the highest import tariffs in Latin America are applied to machinery and transport products, which, as noted, have relatively high import demand elasticities, so that a large percentage expansion of imports should result from a FTA.

Evidence on the use of nontariff barriers suggests that these restrictions would pose at least as much of a problem in Latin American markets as in the United States, but for some countries they are clearly of greater importance. Table 11 shows the value of total Latin American imports covered by nontariff barriers as well as similar data for major product groups. The U.S. NTB coverage ratio of 39 percent on all Latin American exports (Table 7) is somewhat higher than that for Latin American imports (Bolivia, Ecuador, and Peru are exceptions), but some evidence suggests that Latin America may use more hard core restrictions. Chile is one country where NTBs would not constitute a problem since almost all NTBs have been removed.

Finally, the data suggests that Latin American countries should be concerned lest a series of bilaterally negotiated agreements with the United States grant the United States preferences in regional markets that put other Latin American countries at a competitive disadvantage in their own region. The major danger from independently negotiated FTAs with the United States stems from the fact that a high share of some Latin American countries' exports are destined for the region (Table 2) and, with the exception of LAIA preferences, this trade occurs under MFN rates. However, if a country, say Brazil, negotiates a FTA with the United States, most, or all, exports from the latter will be admitted to Brazil duty free, while exports from other Latin American countries continue to face the prevailing tariffs. As a result, existing exports from other Latin American countries to Brazil would be displaced by the competitive advantage tariff preferences given the United States.

Table 12 provides summary statistics on competition between the United States and Latin American countries in five of the largest markets: Argentina, Brazil, Chile, Mexico, and Venezuela. The table shows the total number of four-digit SITC products each country exports to these markets and also indicates the number of items that compete with U.S. shipments.[25] Also shown is the value of trade in which these product conflicts occur, and the share of each country's total exports that are subject to such competition.

The key point from Table 12 is that most Latin American countries compete with the United States in regional markets across a broad range of products, and often a high share of the total value of their exports is involved. For example, Mexico exports 73 different four-digit SITC products to Brazil, and 69 of these items compete with similar shipments from the United States. This direct product competition covers some $125 million in trade, 92 percent of Mexico's exports to Brazil. However, various country combinations in the table indicate an even higher level of product competition is occurring. More than 98 percent of Colombia's exports to Brazil and Venezuela face competition from the United States, while 100 percent of Chile's exports to Venezuela are similarly affected. As such, Table 12 indicates that an important segment of Latin American intra-trade would be adversely affected by regional FTAs with the United States unless some compensating action—such as the extension of full regional preferences—is adopted.

SUMMARY AND CONCLUSIONS

The purpose of this simulation exercise was to examine the short-term impact of removing trade barriers in the context of free trade agreements between the United States and Latin American countries. The analysis focused on the first-round trade effects of eliminating trade barriers rather than on the broader welfare implications or the longer-term dynamic effects of trade liberalization.

The major conclusion to be drawn from our analysis is that the potential for many Latin American Caribbean countries to expand exports through FTAs with the United States may be far smaller than is often thought. As a result of general U.S. tariff cutting in previous MTNs, the extension of GSP and CBI preferences to some Latin American countries, and the concentration of Latin America's exports in primary products facing zero or low barriers, only a small share of Latin America's total exports currently face important tariff and nontariff barriers in the U.S. market. Mexico and Brazil are somewhat exceptional, but even there, the average tariffs they face, and the share of their total exports subject to NTBs in the United States, are well below those encountered by countries such as Hong Kong, Korea, or Taiwan. By contrast, the potential for a FTA-induced expansion of U.S. exports to Latin America appears considerably greater, because protection levels in most Latin American countries are significantly higher than those in the United States.

Our estimates indicate that the potential trade gains for most Latin American countries from FTA negotiations with the United States are relatively modest: a step increase in aggregate Latin American exports on the order of 8.8 percent, if tariffs are removed and "hard core" NTBs in the U.S. market are liberalized, 6.6 percent if only tariffs are eliminated. A successful completion of the Uruguay Round would further reduce the worth of FTAs to Latin America, as any reduction in MFN tariffs would lower the margin of preference that could be extended to Latin American exporters. Our simulations suggest that Uruguay Round tariff cuts in the 30 to 40 percent range would reduce Latin America's FTA-induced U.S.-bound export growth by about one-third from our baseline projections.

In view of the limited potential of the FTA approach, Latin American countries might do better by assigning relatively greater importance to multilateral liberalization efforts within the GATT. If FTA negotiations do move forward, however, they should do so in as plurilateral a fashion as possible. Bilateral agreements between individual Latin American countries and the United States—the "hub-and-spoke model"—would appear to be the least desirable way to proceed, because such arrangements would maximize the risk of intra-Latin American trade displacement by increasing exports from the United States. The danger of such adverse consequences seems so important that we strongly recommend that negotiations on hemispheric FTAs proceed on a multilateral basis to ensure that the interests of individual countries are protected.

Our analysis also indicates that the way nontariff barriers are handled in free trade negotiations with the United States is an issue of utmost importance to Latin America, particularly in sectors such as sugar, textiles, and clothing. Considering the United States' past reluctance to make concessions in such sensitive sectors, either multilaterally or bilaterally, the question arises as to whether the United States has the political will to liberalize such barriers in the context of hemispheric FTAs. Before proceeding too far, Latin American countries should get a clear statement of U.S. intentions.

Origin of Exports	Value ($ millions)				Share of World Trade (percent)			
	1970	1980	1985	1988	1970	1980	1985	1988
World	311,905	2,000,858	1,928,404	2,824,010	100	100	100	100
Intra-trade of:								
The Americas	35,837	177,224	202,531	249,550	11	9	11	9
North America	19,379	75,281	113,073	148,207	6	4	6	5
Developing America	3,029	23,080	16,463	15,274	1	1	1	1
Developed Europe	89,332	550,337	490,936	875,662	29	28	25	31
European Community	57,526	355,837	321,674	634,379	18	18	17	22
Eastern Europe	18,388	78,657	91,625	126,459	6	4	5	4
Developing Countries	11,241	138,742	134,035	152,996	4	7	7	5
Africa	672	2,970	2,892	3,412	—	—	—	—
West Asia	781	11,120	14,328	12,296	—	1	1	1
South and Southeast Asia	2,904	29,877	36,398	60,849	1	1	2	2

Note: Throughout the tables in this chapter the symbol — indicates that the amount is nil or negligible.

Source: Compiled from United Nations Conference on Trade and Development, *Handbook of International Trade and Development Statistics* (New York: United Nations, 1990), Table A1 (Total Exports), pp. A2-A7.

TABLE 2. INTRA-REGIONAL TRADE IN THE AMERICAS (percent)

Exporter	Year	Total Exports ($ millions)	Share of Total Exports to Region	Of Which						
				United States	Canada	LAIA	Andean Pact[a]	CACM	Caricom	Other America
Argentina	1988	9,134	34.7	13.3	0.9	19.3	5.4	0.5	0.2	0.4
Bolivia	1988	570	74.6	16.9	—	57.4	5.4	—	—	0.3
Brazil	1987	26,229	42.8	27.3	2.2	11.6	4.4	0.5	0.4	0.8
CACM	1987	3,387	66.3	45.5	1.4	1.1	0.6	14.4	0.7	3.1
Canada	1987	92,886	78.0	75.8	—	1.7	0.6	0.1	0.2	0.1
Caricom	1987	2,200	70.5	50.6	5.5	2.3	1.0	0.5	9.1	2.5
Chile	1988	6,794	32.6	18.3	0.6	13.0	4.5	0.2	—	0.5
Colombia	1988	5,026	56.6	39.3	1.2	11.1	7.1	1.0	0.1	2.9
Ecuador	1988	2,192	67.3	45.9	0.1	12.5	8.1	0.6	—	1.6
Mexico	1987	22,532	73.6	64.6	1.5	3.9	1.7	1.5	0.9	1.4
Paraguay	1988	510	45.9	3.8	—	38.5	2.8	—	—	3.6
Peru	1987	2,152	49.5	29.9	1.6	16.3	6.4	0.8	—	0.8
Uruguay	1988	1,443	39.4	11.2	0.8	27.1	0.8	—	0.1	0.2
United States	1988	303,380	35.1	—	21.5	11.2	2.5	0.7	0.7	0.8
Venezuela[b]	1986	8,613	65.6	52.9	3.7	4.4	1.9	2.0	1.2	1.3

Note: Numbers may not add due to rounding.

[a]All Andean Pact countries are included in the LAIA countries. Therefore, the share of total exports to region is calculated by excluding the amount for the Andean Pact.

[b]Reliable 1987 and 1988 data were not available from the U.N. data base as Venezuela's oil exports were not recorded at the time this report was prepared.

Source: United Nations Statistical Office, *U.N. COMTRADE Data Base,* New York. Statistics reported by the exporting countries.

TABLE 3. PRODUCT COMPOSITION OF INTRA-REGIONAL TRADE IN THE AMERICAS
(percent share of all products exported to the Americas[a])

Exporter and Destination	Exports to the Americas ($ millions)[b]	Foods & Feeds	Agricultural Materials	Coal & Petroleum	Ores & Metals	All Manufactured Goods	Selected Manufactures (percent)			
							Textiles & Clothing	Transport & Machinery	Chemicals	Iron & Steel
Argentina										
Canada and United States	1,298	33.2	0.8	4.5	5.7	55.6	6.6	5.0	8.5	15.7
Other Americas	1,857	37.8	3.3	3.1	2.4	53.4	2.2	18.8	16.0	4.1
Bolivia										
Canada and United States	96	8.8	15.2	5.5	62.5	7.2	6.3	0.0	0.2	n.a.
Other Americas	329	10.0	5.8	76.2	6.5	1.4	0.1	—	0.5	n.a.
Brazil										
Canada and United States	7,763	23.2	2.7	7.8	3.9	62.3	4.5	27.6	2.9	6.2
Other Americas	3,488	10.5	2.3	3.6	6.6	76.9	2.5	37.3	13.9	9.8
CACM										
Canada and United States	1,587	83.5	3.0	1.1	0.9	11.2	5.2	0.8	0.3	0.1
Other Americas	662	19.5	6.3	1.2	2.2	69.4	8.5	6.0	27.5	2.7
Canada										
United States	70,401	5.1	8.3	11.4	5.2	69.6	0.9	46.2	4.4	2.5
Other Americas	2,048	24.3	7.1	3.1	10.1	55.1	1.5	28.7	7.8	2.8
Caricom										
Canada and United States	1,234	5.3	0.4	49.3	6.1	38.8	8.5	1.2	25.7	2.0
Other Americas	344	15.2	0.1	36.6	1.1	46.7	1.5	4.1	17.2	10.8
Chile										
Canada and United States	1,282	34.5	2.9	0.3	48.0	14.3	2.3	0.8	3.7	1.2
Other Americas	932	13.1	13.4	0.8	47.5	25.1	0.7	3.1	6.4	2.4
Colombia										
Canada and United States	2,037	29.5	8.1	42.8	0.6	18.1	5.8	0.5	1.2	1.0
Other Americas	761	7.3	5.3	5.6	0.2	67.0	17.9	5.7	23.0	0.2
Ecuador										
Canada and United States	1,009	74.0	1.7	22.6	0.3	1.4	0.3	0.0	0.1	—
Other Americas	323	23.1	—	67.0	0.4	9.2	0.9	2.2	2.8	0.2

TABLE 3. PRODUCT COMPOSITION OF INTRA-REGIONAL TRADE IN THE AMERICAS (continued)

Exporter and Destination	Exports to the Americas ($ millions)[b]	Foods & Feeds	Agricultural Materials	Coal & Petroleum	Ores & Metals	All Manufactured Goods	Selected Manufactures (percent)			
							Textiles & Clothing	Transport & Machinery	Chemicals	Iron & Steel
Mexico										
Canada and United States	13,577	17.2	1.0	32.0	5.5	44.2	1.9	27.8	3.6	2.2
Other Americas	1,580	2.4	3.2	42.7	4.1	47.5	2.1	11.1	19.1	5.6
Paraguay										
Canada and United States	19	20.8	3.4	n.a.	0.0	75.8	33.5	0.0	6.0	0.0
Other Americas	215	35.4	59.2	n.a.	0.4	4.9	—	—	1.6	1.6
Peru										
Canada and United States	679	21.3	0.8	29.8	27.2	20.8	10.0	1.7	1.3	0.1
Other Americas	387	9.6	8.7	13.2	50.9	17.6	3.9	3.1	7.3	0.6
Uruguay										
Canada and United States	173	17.3	6.1	—	—	75.5	52.7	1.0	0.2	0.3
Other Americas	395	33.1	8.0	—	0.4	58.2	9.9	8.8	24.2	1.1
United States										
Canada	65,287	2.9	1.5	2.1	2.6	68.9	1.1	50.9	5.6	1.0
Other Americas	40,793	10.9	3.2	3.5	2.2	76.1	4.4	44.8	13.0	1.3
Venezuela										
Canada and United States	4,882	2.3	—	89.2	3.3	5.2	—	0.5	0.8	1.8
Other Americas	764	2.6	0.2	62.3	6.4	28.5	—	0.7	1.8	1.1

[a]The following product groups and SITC numbers were used in computing the export statistics shown in this table: Foods and fees (0 + 1 + 22 + 4); Agricultural raw materials (2 less 22, 27, 28); Coal, natural gas, and petroleum (3); Ores and metals (27 + 28 + 68); Manufactured goods (5 through 8 less 68); Textiles and clothing (26 + 65 + 84); Nonelectrical machinery (71); Electrical machinery (72); Transport equipment (73). The product shares may sum less than 100 since they do not account for SITC 9 (goods not classified), which are in the value totals.

[b]Export statistics are for the latest year. See Table 2 in this chapter.

Source: United Nations Statistical Office, *U.N. COMTRADE Data Base,* New York. Statistics reported by the exporting countries.

**TABLE 4A. MAJOR LATIN AMERICAN EXPORTS TO
THE UNITED STATES, 1988** (percent and $ millions)

SITC	Product	Share (percent)	Value ($ millions)
331	Crude petroleum	12.6	6,656
332	Petroleum	8.7	4,570
732	Road motor vehicles	5.8	3,042
724	Telecommunication equipment	5.1	2,669
841	Clothing not of fur	4.7	2,466
071	Coffee	3.9	2,035
051	Fresh fruits	3.5	1,822
711	Nonelectric power machinery	3.2	1,706
722	Electric power machinery	3.1	1,634
031	Fresh fish	2.8	1,466
723	Electrical distribution machinery	2.4	1,283
931	Special transactions[a]	2.4	1,279
851	Footwear	2.2	1,181
729	Electric machinery	2.1	1,129
053	Preserved fruit	1.8	971
719	Machines nonelectric	1.6	851
682	Copper	1.4	746
714	Office machines	1.3	698
054	Fresh vegetables	1.1	588
821	Furniture	1.0	535
674	Iron and steel plate	0.9	463
684	Aluminum	0.8	439
512	Organic chemicals	0.8	438
861	Scientific instruments	0.8	406
611	Leather	0.7	372
Total		**74.8**	**39,445**

Notes: These data include shipments from Mexico's free processing zones. Numbers may not add due to rounding.

[a]Excludes animals, military sales, firearms, and nonmonetary gold; includes unclassified items and returned goods.

Source: Data compiled from United Nations Statistical Office, *U.N. COMTRADE Data Base*, New York.

TABLE 4B. MAJOR LATIN AMERICAN IMPORTS FROM THE UNITED STATES, 1988 (percent and $ millions)

SITC	Product	Share (percent)	Value ($ millions)
732	Road motor vehicles	6.6	2,695
719	Machines, nonelectric	6.2	2,518
729	Electrical machinery	5.4	2,196
714	Office machines	4.1	1,670
913	Special transactions[a]	4.0	1,624
724	Telecommunication equipment	3.8	1,562
512	Organic chemicals	3.7	1,499
711	Nonelectric power machinery	3.5	1,423
722	Electric power machinery	3.5	1,415
734	Aircraft	3.0	1,235
718	Machines for special industry	2.9	1,164
581	Plastic materials	2.8	1,159
841	Clothing not of fur	2.4	949
332	Petroleum products	2.4	964
723	Electrical distribution machinery	2.0	828
599	Chemicals	2.0	819
861	Scientific instruments	1.7	700
044	Unmilled maize	1.5	572
221	Oilseeds and nuts	1.4	567
041	Unmilled wheat	1.3	526
081	Animal feeds	1.3	512
251	Paper pulp	1.2	478
642	Articles of paper	1.0	428
561	Manufactured fertilizer	1.0	411
045	Cereals, unmilled	0.8	331
Total		**69.2**	**28,245**

Notes: These data include shipments from Mexico's free processing zones. Numbers may not add due to rounding.

[a]Excludes animals, military sales, firearms, and nonmonetary gold; includes unclassified items and returned goods.

Source: Data compiled from United Nations Statistical Office, *U.N. COMTRADE Data Base*, New York.

TABLE 5. INCIDENCE OF U.S. TARIFFS AND NTBs ON LATIN AMERICAN EXPORTS

Exporter	All Exports 1986		All Dutiable Trade[a]		Major Exports Affected by Tariffs[b]		Major Exports Affected By Tariffs and NTBs[c]		
	Number of Lines	Value ($ millions)	Value ($ millions)	Percent of Exports	Value ($ millions)	Percent of Exports	Number of Lines[d]	Value ($ millions)	Percent of Exports
Argentina	771	840.8	479.9	57.0	211.3	25.1	55(35)	89.6	10.7
Bolivia	140	123.2	6.3	5.1	2.9	2.4	10(0)	2.7	2.2
Brazil	1,927	6,681.2	3,701.5	55.4	2,021.7	30.2	168(148)	835.1	12.5
CACM	81	2,255.8	223.5	9.9	196.9	8.7	7	57.7	2.6
Caricom	79	2,887.3	933.8	32.3	3.7	0.1	1	0.2	0.0
Chile	586	818.6	456.0	55.6	41.6	5.1	36(6)	11.2	1.4
Colombia	682	1,865.1	705.2	37.8	209.9	11.2	76(70)	195.3	10.4
Ecuador	300	1,466.8	581.9	39.6	7.5	0.5	13(3)	4.8	0.3
Mexico	2,350	17,071.6	11,767.0	68.9	3,629.8	21.3	214(191)	1,447.0	8.5
Paraguay	61	30.4	9.2	30.3	8.5	28.1	3(1)	4.7	15.5
Peru	590	757.8	328.6	43.4	41.9	5.5	53(52)	41.1	5.4
Uruguay	249	472.5	76.0	16.1	68.0	14.3	44(20)	56.9	12.0
Venezuela	654	4,978.0	4,232.1	85.0	44.0	0.9	22(11)	34.1	0.7
Total	**8,310**	**40,249.1**	**22,343.6**	**55.5**	**6,287.2**	**15.6**	**694(537)**	**2,722.5**	**6.8**
Excluding Mexico	5,960	23,177.5	10,576.7	45.6	2,657.4	11.4	480(346)	1,275.5	5.5
Memo items									
Korea, Republic of	2,331	12,681.9	11,685.0	92.1	7,225.1	57.0	512(279)	6,985.2	55.1
Hong Kong	2,439	8,848.0	8,273.6	93.5	5,877.4	66.4	608(264)	4,990.2	56.4
Singapore	1,041	4,712.0	3,664.2	77.7	1,177.2	25.0	491(154)	1,008.1	21.4

Notes: NTB data for 1990; covered trade from 1989 imports.

[a]Exports > $0; tariffs >0 percent.

[b]Exports ≥ $50,000; tariffs ≥5 percent.

[c]Exports ≥$50,000; tariffs ≥5 percent; and NTBs applied.

[d]Parentheses denotes number of tariff lines where NTBs directly cover a country's exports. Other figures show number of tariff lines where the country has exports and a NTB occurs. For example, if a country exported a product where there was a VER against Japan, the tariff line would be included. These items are "affected" by NTBs in that other exporters often restrict their trade to prevent the measure from spreading.

Source: World Bank records on tariffs and trade barriers.

TABLE 6. LAC EXPORTS SUBJECT TO VARIOUS U.S. NTBs, BY EXPORTER AND TYPE OF NTB (percent)

Nontariff Barrier	Argentina	Bolivia	Brazil	CACM	Caricom	Chile	Colombia	Ecuador	Mexico	Paraguay	Peru	Uruguay	Venezuela
Tariff Quotas	0.0	—	—	1.1	—	0.0	—	0.2	0.0	—	—	—	0.1
Seasonal Tariffs	0.1	—	0.0	—	6.0	20.8	0.0	0.1	3.0	—	0.0	—	0.1
Increased Duties	0.5	—	0.1	—	—	—	—	—	0.8	—	—	—	0.0
Safeguard Duties	0.2	—	1.0	—	0.8	—	0.0	0.0	0.4	—	—	0.0	0.0
Retaliatory Duties	—	—	0.7	—	—	—	—	—	—	—	—	—	—
Other Increased Duties	0.3	—	0.3	1.9	17.3	—	—	—	0.2	—	—	—	0.0
Specific Excise Tax[a]	19.6	2.3	11.1	—	—	1.6	26.3	39.1	21.8	—	25.5	0.0	82.5
Antidumping Duties	1.3	—	9.5	—	—	1.5	5.1	0.0	0.6	—	—	0.2	1.2
Countervailing Duties	4.1	—	3.1	3.6	—	0.0	—	0.0	2.0	—	5.6	0.9	1.2
Flexible Import Fees[b]	1.9	1.8	1.4	3.6	12.4	—	1.2	0.5	0.1	14.0	2.9	—	0.0
Quotas (unallocated)	1.9	1.8	1.4	—	2.1	—	1.2	0.5	0.1	14.0	2.9	0.9	0.0
Global Quotas	0.6	0.1	0.0	—	—	0.0	0.0	—	0.1	—	0.0	0.0	0.0
Quota by Country	1.4	—	0.1	—	—	0.0	0.0	0.1	0.0	—	0.0	0.0	0.0
"Voluntary" Export Restraint	—	—	4.4	3.7	1.2	—	3.8	—	0.9	—	5.6	—	0.9
MFA Restraint	—	—	2.9	1.1	1.4	—	—	—	2.7	—	—	5.7	—
MFA Quota	1.0	—	—	—	—	—	—	—	—	—	—	—	1.2
Antidumping Investigation	1.4	—	2.9	—	—	—	—	—	0.1	—	—	—	—
Countervailing Duty Investigations	—	—	2.9	—	—	—	—	—	—	—	0.1	—	—
Antidumping and Countervailing Undertakings	—	—	6.9	—	—	—	7.1	—	0.4	—	—	—	—
Health and Safety Regulations	—	—	0.1	5.0	0.1	—	—	—	1.7	—	—	—	—
Technical Standards	0.5	—	—	—	—	—	—	—	—	—	—	—	—
All Measures	**28.6**	**4.2**	**26.1**	**15.8**	**22.1**	**24.0**	**38.6**	**39.9**	**34.2**	**14.0**	**34.4**	**6.8**	**84.7**

Note: The entry 0.0 indicates that exports subject to the NTB accounted for less than one-tenth of total trade. The NTB data pertain to 1990, while the "covered" trade is computed from 1986 imports. For details on coverage and methodology, see Refik Erzan and Alexander Yeats, "Prospects for United States, Latin American Free Trade Areas: Empirical Evidence Concerning the View from the South" (Washington, DC: World Bank, 1991).

a. Excise taxes are applied to 86 TSUS lines which mainly consist of fuel, tobacco and alcoholic beverage products. The high coverage figures for some Latin American countries are largely explained by petroleum products.

b. These measures are applied to two TSUS lines covering sugar imports. These charges are similar to the European Community's variable import levies.

Source: UNCTAD Data Base on Trade Control Measures, Geneva.

TABLE 7. LATIN AMERICAN EXPORTS SUBJECT TO "HARD CORE" AND OTHER U.S. NTBs, BY MAJOR PRODUCT GROUPS (percent; hard core coverage in parentheses)

Exporter	Food and Feeds	Agricultural Materials	Coal and Petroleum	Ores and Metals	All Manufactured Goods	Selected Manufactures		All Items
						Textiles and Clothing	Nonelectric Machinery	
Argentina	24(11)	12	99	—	12	55[a]	39	29(4)
Bolivia	32(32)	—	100	—	—	—	—	4(2)
Brazil	25(5)	—	99	2	24(13)	81(81)	38	26(9)
CACM	2	3	—	—	8(6)	38(38)	—	16(7)
Caricom	38(22)	2	100	—	9(6)	40(39)	—	22(8)
Chile	64	—	1	3	—	—	—	24
Colombia	3(3)	100	95	—	26(26)	82	6	39(5)
Ecuador	1(1)	4	100	—	—	—	2	40(1)
Mexico	43(1)	8(2)	98	11	13(7)	91(88)	7	34(4)
Paraguay	18(18)	—	—	—	—	—	—	14(4)
Peru	10(10)	28(5)	100	—	36(36)	95(84)	—	34(9)
Uruguay	13(13)	—	—	—	27(26)	39(37)	9	7(7)
Venezuela	7	—	96	24	17(16)	—	49	85(1)
Total	**26(3)**	**32**	**97**	**7**	**16(9)**	**81(77)**	**14**	**39(5)**

Note: Hard core nontariff barriers consist of quantitative restrictions and flexible import fees (i.e., the counterpart of the European Community's variable levies). Quantitative restrictions that were in effect include the following: quotas, global quotas, quotas by country, voluntary export restraints, Multi-Fibre Arrangement quotas, Textile Restraint Agreement and Prohibitions.

[a]Fifty-five percent of Argentina's textile and clothing exports to the United States are subject to antidumping duties.

Source: *UNCTAD Data Base on Trade Control Measures*, Geneva.

Exporter	Food and Feeds	Agricultural Materials	Energy Products	Ores and Metals	Manufactured Goods	All Exports 1986
I. Baseline: Actual Trade Values						
All Countries	9,229.5	482.2	10,604.9	2,509.9	15,989.8	40,057.9
Argentina	286.2	10.0	130.0	45.7	358.9	840.8
Bolivia	7.2	0.3	2.9	72.2	6.9	123.2
Brazil	1,870.4	144.5	378.9	408.1	3,766.7	6,681.2
CACM	1,608.2	27.6	26.6	6.4	371.0	2,064.8
Caricom	622.5	8.9	989.1	202.5	1,141.3	2,887.2
Chile	285.3	40.6	0.5	354.0	55.8	818.6
Colombia	874.9	133.6	513.9	8.4	272.9	1,865.1
Ecuador	857.5	16.1	573.8	0.3	10.8	1,466.7
Mexico	2,394.1	84.8	3,539.2	833.5	9,498.8	17,071.6
Paraguay	23.2	0.7	0.0	0.0	5.5	30.4
Peru	223.7	7.0	192.6	168.2	117.0	757.8
Uruguay	34.2	7.1	0.0	164.3	101.9	472.5
Venezuela	142.1	0.9	4,257.4	246.4	282.2	4,978.0
II. Trade Expansion with All U.S. Tariffs Removed and Nontariff Barriers Relaxed						
All Countries	292.9	15.9	162.5	18.5	2,717.9	3,207.8
Argentina	17.9	0.3	11.7	—	45.0	64.9
Bolivia	—	0.0	0.1	0.0	3.2	3.3
Brazil	163.8	0.1	7.0	2.2	774.2	947.3
CACM	0.1	—	0.5	—	156.9	157.5

Table 8 continued on next page

TABLE 8. CONTINUED

Exporter	Food and Feeds	Agricultural Materials	Energy Products	Ores and Metals	Manufactured Goods	All Exports 1986
Caricom	0.2	—	16.8	—	108.3	125.3
Chile	6.4	0.5	0.0	6.0	9.8	22.8
Colombia	1.4	12.4	9.2	—	56.9	79.9
Ecuador	1.0	0.1	11.8	0.0	1.6	14.4
Mexico	96.4	1.9	51.7	5.3	1,484.5	1,639.8
Paraguay	1.7	0.0	0.0	0.0	1.2	2.9
Peru	0.2	0.1	2.4	2.6	20.0	25.3
Uruguay	0.6	0.5	0.0	—	45.4	46.6
Venezuela	3.2	—	61.3	2.4	10.9	77.9

III. Trade Expansion with All U.S. Tariffs Removed But "Hard Core" Nontariff Barriers Retained

Exporter	Food and Feeds	Agricultural Materials	Energy Products	Ores and Metals	Manufactured Goods	All Exports 1986
All Countries[a]	263.2	15.8	145.1	18.5	1,870.5	2,313.1
Argentina	15.2	0.3	1.7	—	44.8	62.1
Bolivia	—	0.0	0.1	0.0	3.2	3.3
Brazil	138.4	0.1	7.0	2.2	638.4	786.1
Chile	6.4	0.5	0.0	6.0	9.8	22.8
Colombia	1.4	12.4	9.2	—	7.8	30.8
Ecuador	1.0	0.1	11.7	0.0	1.6	14.4
Mexico	96.4	1.9	51.7	5.3	1,135.1	1,290.3
Paraguay	0.4	0.0	0.0	0.0	1.2	1.6
Peru	0.2	—	2.4	2.6	0.8	6.1
Uruguay	0.6	0.5	0.0	—	23.4	24.5
Venezuela	3.2	—	61.3	2.4	4.4	71.3

[a]Difficulties in allocating the influence of U.S. NTBs among member countries of Caricom and CACM prevented us from making these simulations.

Source: Data and projections from the World Bank and UNCTAD Software for Market Analysis and Restrictions on Trade (SMART) model maintained in Washington, DC, and Geneva.

TABLE 9. COMPARISON OF EXPORT EXPANSION UNDER SINGLE AND MULTICOUNTRY FTAs ($ millions)

Exporter	Value of Exports 1986	Expansion with All U.S. Tariffs Removed and NTBs Relaxed		Expansion with All U.S. Tariffs Removed But Hard Core NTBs Retained	
		Single Exclusive FTA	Multicountry FTA	Single Exclusive FTA	Multicountry FTA
Argentina	840.8	64.9	59.9	62.1	57.8
Bolivia	123.2	3.3	3.2	3.3	3.2
Brazil	6,681.2	947.3	923.4	788.0	763.7
Chile	818.6	22.8	21.5	22.8	21.4
Colombia	1,865.1	79.9	76.4	30.8	28.6
Ecuador	1,466.7	14.4	12.8	14.4	13.0
Mexico	17,071.6	1,639.8	1,614.2	1,290.3	1,266.5
Paraguay	30.4	2.9	2.6	1.6	1.5
Peru	757.8	25.3	23.1	6.1	4.8
Uruguay	472.5	46.6	45.3	24.5	23.6
Venezuela	4,978.0	77.9	70.1	71.3	63.7
Total	**35,105.9**	**2,925.0**	**2,852.5**	**2,315.2**	**2,247.8**

Note: Numbers may not add due to rounding.

Source: Data and projections from the World Bank and UNCTAD Software for Market Analysis and Restrictions on Trade (SMART) model maintained in Washington, DC, and Geneva.

Importer/ Source	Foods and Feeds	Agricultural Materials	Coal and Petroleum	Ores and Metals	All Manu- factures	All Imports
Argentina						
World	24	23	1	13	29	24(27)
United States	19	20	1	18	29	26(29)
Bolivia						
World	9	19	20	20	14	13(20)
United States	6	18	20	20	17	13(20)
Brazil						
World	21	31	1	14	41	24(42)
United States	15	32	3	14	38	31(42)
Chile						
World	11	11	11	11	11	11
Colombia						
World	29	9	15	9	16	16(22)
Ecuador						
World	13	19	17	13	16	16(23)
United States	11	19	19	14	15	14(23)
Mexico						
World	5	7	2	7	16	13(23)
United States	5	7	2	8	17	13(23)
Paraguay						
World	8	10	2	5	8	7(10)
United States	1	13	1	7	12	10
Peru						
World	25	22	14	21	40	36(48)
United States	16	22	16	16	41	33(47)
Uruguay						
World	23	22	34	21	26	27(28)
United States	22	21	30	24	24	24(27)
Venezuela						
World	16	6	15	9	16	15(31)
United States	13	4	16	13	16	15(31)
Total						
World	17	17	12	13	22	19(26)
United States	11	16	11	13	20	18(24)

Note: Data are average tariff rates, trade-weighted. Numbers in parentheses are unweighted averages if different from weighted averages. Tariff rates do not incorporate any preferences or paratariff changes.

Sources: Latin American Integration Association, United Nations Statistical Office, World Bank, *UNCTAD Data Base on Trade Control Measures*, Geneva, 1986.

TABLE 11. SHARE OF IMPORTS SUBJECT TO NTBs IN SELECTED LATIN AMERICAN MARKETS
(percent of total)

Importer and Source[a]	Foods & Feeds	Agricultural Materials	Coal & Petroleum	Ores & Metals	All Manufactures	Selected Manufactures				All Imports
						Textiles & Clothing	Nonelectric Machinery	Electrical Machinery	Transport Equipment	
Argentina										
World	4	8	—	2	42	32	28	6	83	31
United States	18	5	—	3	29	19	10	12	1	25
Bolivia										
World	70	19	1	16	17	58	2	29	2	27
United States	79	52	1	5	17	69	1	24	3	39
Brazil										
World	13	0	88	26	15	27	2	37	37	39
United States	18	0	4	19	14	31	2	47	12	14
Colombia										
World[b]	95	8	68	45	82	76	70	98	81	78
Ecuador										
World	82	32	99	21	27	1	0	0	0	32
United States	89	43	97	44	34	1	0	0	0	44
Mexico										
World	99	46	79	0	6	9	7	0	12	23
United States	99	47	82	0	6	5	10	0	17	28
Paraguay										
World	70	13	47	9	10	7	4	7	8	24
United States	5	8	6	21	5	2	7	1	13	5
Peru										
World	100	29	91	70	39	69	14	22	77	53
United States	100	38	93	68	38	86	16	18	79	55
Uruguay										
World	6	26	99	2	20	53	10	6	86	31
United States	0	7	84	0	7	41	3	11	25	8
Venezuela										
World	55	20	6	4	4	21	0	0	0	11
United States	66	10	8	5	4	6	0	0	0	8
Total										
World	51	18	53	18	24	32	12	19	35	32
United States	43	19	34	15	14	24	4	10	14	21

Note: For a list of nontariff barriers, see Table 6 in this chapter.

[a] Chile is not listed below since almost all nontariff barriers have been removed.

[b] Due to a lack of required import data separate trade coverage ratios for U.S. exports to Colombia could not be compared.

Sources: Latin American Integration Association, United Nations Statistical Office, World Bank, and UNCTAD Data Base on Trade Control Measures, New York, 1986.

TABLE 12. U.S.-LATIN AMERICAN COMPETITION IN REGIONAL MARKETS

Exporter/Product Conflicts	Importer				
	Argentina	Brazil	Chile	Mexico	Venezuela
Argentina					
Number of major export products	—	191	258	48	93
(with major U.S. competition)	—	(144)	(215)	(48)	(89)
Value of exports ($ thousands)	—	434,846	225,269	39,443	109,023
Share of exports (%)	—	59	81	99	97
Bolivia					
Number of major export products	21	14	12	6	2
(with major U.S. competition)	(10)	(9)	(6)	(5)	(2)
Value of exports ($ thousands)	8,253	3,496	4,838	3,472	1,715
Share of exports (%)	4	30	41	74	99
Brazil					
Number of major export products	254	—	288	219	167
(with major U.S. competition)	(196)		(247)	(219)	(156)
Value of exports ($ thousands)	713,423	—	502,772	29,758	538,182
Share of exports (%)	74	—	91	100	97
Chile					
Number of major export products	70	55	—	51	35
(with major U.S. competition)	(47)	(40)		(51)	(35)
Value of exports ($ thousands)	127,570	168,020	—	45,995	94,087
Share of exports (%)	89	46	—	99	100
Colombia					
Number of major export products	21	19	64	49	119
(with major U.S. competition)	(15)	(18)	(57)	(49)	(110)
Value of exports ($ thousands)	22,835	13,798	43,980	24,065	155,210
Share of exports (%)	50	98	35	99	99
Ecuador					
Number of major export products	12	6	25	17	12
(with major U.S. competition)	(5)	(4)	(15)	(17)	(12)
Value of exports ($ thousands)	739	1,726	10,176	18,215	4,718
Share of exports (%)	6	14	18	99	98
Mexico					
Number of major export products	84	73	82	—	118
(with major U.S. competition)	(80)	(69)	(77)		(114)
Value of exports ($ thousands)	99,247	124,592	66,154	—	128,191
Share of exports (%)	82	92	96	—	92
Paraguay					
Number of major export products	28	20	14	3	3
(with major U.S. competition)	(12)	(9)	(9)	(3)	(3)
Value of exports ($ thousands)	12,223	98,115	28,947	373	740
Share of exports (%)	18	83	57	90	92

| Exporter/Product Conflicts | Importer | | | | |
	Argentina	Brazil	Chile	Mexico	Venezuela
Peru					
Number of major export products	27	23	74	6	31
(with major U.S. competition)	(20)	(16)	(59)	(6)	(30)
Value of exports ($ thousands)	8,341	33,180	20,145	22,276	80,883
Share of exports (%)	45	37	61	99	98
Uruguay					
Number of major export products	141	134	37	14	6
(with major U.S. competition)	(90)	(94)	(32)	(14)	(6)
Value of exports ($ thousands)	65,096	218,817	8,772	8,096	3,385
Share of exports (%)	61	70	77	98	96
Venezuela					
Number of major export products	17	13	29	11	—
(with major U.S. competition)	(16)	(11)	(26)	(11)	
Value of exports ($ thousands)	29,948	54,103	36,188	3,242	—
Share of exports (%)	93	35	22	94	—

Note: Major exports are defined as products of the 4-digit SITC level where exports exceed $25,000 for each country.

Source: United Nations Statistical Office, *U.N. COMTRADE Data Base*, New York. Statistics reported by the exporting countries.

DISMANTLING PROTECTION IN SENSITIVE SECTORS

Textiles and Clothing

Would a preferential elimination of U.S. quotas on textiles and clothing from Latin America generate—and divert—substantial amounts of trade?

To infer the short-term impact of such an occurrence, the restrictiveness of the quotas faced during 1985-89 by five Latin American countries under the Multi-Fibre Arrangement (MFA) in the U.S. market was examined (see Table A1). The five countries in question—Brazil, Colombia, Mexico, Peru, and Uruguay—account for only about 5 percent of total U.S. textile and clothing imports, in comparison to 50 percent for the East Asian Four (China, Hong Kong, Korea, and Taiwan). The share of these products subject to quotas (59 percent on average), is somewhat lower for the Latin Five than the overall average for developing-country exporters to the United States (70 percent), and much lower than the corresponding figure for the East Asian Four (76 percent). Of the Latin Five, Mexico, Brazil, and Peru had significantly higher quota coverage than Colombia and Uruguay.

The existence of quotas may have a harassment effect on exports long before they are filled, but quotas become binding constraints only after the limits are approached. Accordingly, we defined quotas with utilization rates above 90 percent as binding and tabulated the percentage of trade subject to such quotas. These "restriction indices" reveal that Latin American countries face fewer restrictions in the U.S. market than do East Asian exporters and developing-country exporters as a group. Furthermore, quota utilization rates for the Latin Five averaged only 54 percent compared to 87 percent for the East Asian Four, and 75 percent for developing countries as a whole.[26]

On the basis of these indicators, we conclude that in the *short run*, the abolition of U.S. textiles quotas on Latin America would almost certainly *not* lead to an overall export explosion. However, certain product categories subject to binding quotas may experience substantial growth. Such categories account for 21 percent of Brazil's textile and clothing exports to the United States and 18 percent of Mexico's but are much less for the other Latin American countries. In product lines not currently facing binding quota limits, significant trade expansion could, nevertheless, result from the abolition of duties that often exceed 20 percent. Unfortunately, we do not have reliable ad valorem equivalents for quotas on Latin American exports. Estimates ranging from 10 to 50 percent would double

TABLE A1. U.S. TEXTILE AND CLOTHING IMPORTS: INDICATORS OF COVERAGE AND RESTRICTIVENESS, 1985–89 (percent)

| Supplier | U.S. Market | | | | | Memorandum Items: |
	(1) Share of Total U.S. Imports[a]	(2) Share of Imports Restricted[b]	(3) Imports Subject to Binding Restrictions[c]	(4) Average Quota Utilization Rates	(5) Average Unit Value[d]	(6) Average Quota Utilization Rate in the European Community Market[e]
Latin American Five	4.3	59.4	15.5	53.5	1.48	63.4
Brazil	1.2	59.3	20.9	67.7	1.21	70.3
Colombia	0.4	17.7	1.5	35.3	1.11	34.8
Mexico	2.2	73.5	17.9	51.5	1.70	6.8
Peru	0.2	50.8	7.8	37.9	0.84	90.9
Uruguay	0.3	27.0	3.0	56.9	5.20	40.3
East Asian Four[f]	50.2	76.1	54.9	86.9	2.44	87.2
All MFA Suppliers	78.6	70.3	46.4	75.1	2.18	77.3

Note: Shares (columns 1-3) are calculated using value in current dollars. Quotas refer to Multi-Fibre Arrangement (MFA). Utilization (columns 4-6) is based on volume of shipments. Textile products are defined broadly as SITC (Rev. 2) codes 65 plus 84.

[a] As a percentage of total U.S. imports of textile and clothing products from all sources.

[b] Imports subject to bilateral quotas as a percentage of total imports from the given supplier.

[c] Imports with quota utilization rates of 90 percent or greater as a percentage of total imports from the given supplier.

[d] Expressed in current dollars per square yard equivalent.

[e] EC-10 in 1985; EC-12 thereafter. Of the 11 Latin American countries in the study, only the five listed in this table were subject to MFA quotas in the U.S. market. In the EC market, only these five plus Argentina were restricted. Argentina first came under quota in the EC market in 1987, and utilized roughly 30 percent of its quota limits.

[f] East Asian Four includes China, Hong Kong, Korea, and Taiwan.

Sources: World Bank computer files on the Multi-Fibre Arrangement, Washington, DC; and United Nations Statistical Office, *U.N. COMTRADE Data Base,* New York.

or triple the estimated trade expansion in quota-bound items compared to the removal of tariffs only.

In the *longer run*, allowing for domestic and foreign investment, trade diversion could be practically limitless provided that MFA quotas remain in place on other developing exporters. This has two obvious caveats, however. First, relaxation of the MFA regime in any phaseout scenario currently under negotiation in the General Agreement on Tariffs and Trade (GATT) would counter the investment incentives. Second, and more important, any conceivable free trade agreement (FTA) between the United States and the Latin American countries would almost certainly have some transitional safeguard provisions to close the "back door" in textiles and clothing.

The Sugar Regime

Sugar imports into the United States are governed by a tariff-rate quota system. Under the system, a given quantity of sugar, allocated on a country-by-country basis according to historical trends, is allowed in each year subject to the prevailing most-favored-nation tariff rate—currently 12.6 percent. The Generalized System of Preferences and the Caribbean Basin Initiative beneficiaries receive duty-free treatment on the quantity of sugar allocated to them under the quota. Any additional quantities of sugar imports from any source are subject to a flexible import fee—currently set at 16 cents per pound—that equates import prices with internal U.S. support prices.

The restrictiveness of the U.S. sugar regime is reflected in the fact that in 1986-88, such restrictions were estimated to be the equivalent of an ad-valorem tariff on sugar in the range of 102 to 223 percent.[27] In addition, the United States levies antidumping duties on Canada and has initiated antidumping and countervailing duty actions against every member of the European Community (EC).

Most sugar trade analyses suggest that any meaningful reduction of barriers would essentially wipe out U.S. producers—a minor economic loss, perhaps, but one with major political ramifications. Another factor inhibiting the liberalization of the U.S. sugar regime is the fact of even higher sugar protection in Japan and the EC: in 1986-88, ad valorem tariff equivalents in Japan were on the order of 360 to 542 percent, while in the EC the corresponding range was 170 to 222 percent during the same period.[28]

As the principal sugar suppliers to the United States (66 percent of all U.S. sugar imports) and major potential beneficiaries, Latin American countries have a strong interest in the liberalization of the U.S. sugar regime. This is particularly so for countries in Central America and the

Caribbean, where the losses currently inflicted by the restrictive sugar regime far outweigh the benefits these countries receive under the CBI.

How this issue gets resolved will be an important indicator of the seriousness of the commitment to freer trade in the hemisphere.

Notes

[1] See, for example, Jeffrey J. Schott, *More Free Trade Areas?* (Washington, DC: Institute for International Economics, May 1989).

[2] Some economists and government officials believe FTAs offer a wide range of other benefits in addition to those directly connected with trade. These may include the promotion of new investment opportunities and development of new transport and communication links. Similarly, FTAs may be useful as a device for halting the spread of trade barriers, and these associated gains may exceed those from the measures actually liberalized. The present investigation focuses solely on the likely effects of a preferential liberalization of existing trade barriers and not on these other benefits that may be highly tentative and difficult to project in advance.

[3] The Central American Common Market (CACM) is made up of the following countries: Costa Rica, El Salvador, Guatemala, Honduras, and Nicaragua. The Caribbean Community (Caricom) includes Antigua and Barbuda, Bahamas, Barbados, Belize, Dominica, Grenada, Guyana, Jamaica, Montserrat, St. Kitts and Nevis, St. Lucia, St. Vincent and the Grenadines, and Trinidad and Tobago.

[4] The Latin American Integration Association (ALADI in Spanish) is made up of Argentina, Bolivia, Brazil, Chile, Colombia, Ecuador, Mexico, Paraguay, Peru, Uruguay, and Venezuela.

[5] As far as import dependence is concerned, our tabulations (not shown) reveal a pattern similar to that for exports. On average, the Latin American countries rely on regional trade for 57 percent of total imports (53 percent was the corresponding export share). The United States is generally the major supplier—except for Argentina, Bolivia, Paraguay, and Uruguay where LAIA countries are the principal suppliers. Argentina, Chile, and Uruguay are much more regionally dependent. North and South American countries' shares of their imports average about 15 points higher than their corresponding export shares (Table 2).

[6] If a country signs an exclusive FTA with the United States, its exports will increase through *trade creation*, newly created trade opportunities that materialize when the landed price of foreign goods falls below the price of a domestically produced substitute. *Trade diversion* results when domestic products displace similar items shipped by other (nonpreference receiving) exporters. However, if a second country then signs a FTA with the United States, the first country's exports may be displaced by the new preference receiver. The potential for FTA erosion of preferences is greater the more similar are the (dutiable) exports of the countries signing agreements. Stated differently, if the two countries export different baskets of dutiable goods to the United States they do not compete with each other, and the potential for erosion of individual preferences is small. Table 3 shows some important differences in the composition of Latin American exports.

[7] Robert Stern and Associates, *Price Elasticities in International Trade* (London: Macmillan, 1976).

[8] It has been suggested that the many tariffs below 5 percent that resulted from across-the-board, tariff-cutting formulas applied in previous MTNs have insignificant trade effects. One proposal in the multilateral negotiations termed them "nuisance tariffs" and suggested they be dropped. Most products that encounter important NTBs have tariffs of 5 percent or more in the United States.

[9] There is a major decline in trade values—a fall of over 75 percent—moving from the dutiable export group to products subject to tariffs of 5 percent or higher. Petroleum is a pri-

mary reason for these results. Crude and refined petroleum imports face tariffs of about three-quarters of a percent, which causes the shipments to be classified in the "dutiable goods" group. However, duties at this level are considered to be "nuisance tariffs," so petroleum is not included in the "important tariff-affected" category.

[10] The results for Paraguay are due almost entirely to three tariff line items that account for 78 percent of dutiable trade with the United States. Derived sugar and molasses (TSUSA-15520) exports face import duties of 12.6 percent with Paraguay's trade in this item totaling $4.3 million. Bovine leather exports came to $1.8 million with an applied tariff of 5 percent, while reptilian leather (exports of $1.1 million) faced a similar 5 percent import duty.

[11] For the formula used in computing trade-coverage ratios and a discussion of this measure's properties, see S. Laird and A. Yeats, *Quantitative Methods for Trade Analysis* (London: Macmillan, 1991), p. 21. The index suffers from the familiar problem of any "own" trade-weighted index in that products facing very restrictive NTBs enter the calculation with zero or low weights. The index is, therefore, downward biased in that it fails to account for the most restrictive trade measures. In addition, economists often focus on "hard core" NTBs whose normal *intent* is the restriction of trade instead of on other measures that can have relatively unimportant effects. Statistics tabulated by Laird and Yeats provide estimated ad valorem equivalents for many hard core barriers. For a list of measures in the hard core group, see the note to Table 7.

[12] The total NTB trade-coverage figure reported in Tables 6 and 7 is generally lower than the sum of the trade-coverage shares for the individual nontariff measures. This is the result of *stacking*, the multiple application of different NTBs on a given tariff-line product. The total trade-coverage measure is not affected by the "double counting" that would result from any attempt to sum individual NTB coverage ratios.

[13] See United States International Trade Commission, *Estimated Tariff Equivalents of U.S. Quotas on Agricultural Imports and Analysis of Competitive Conditions in U.S. and Foreign Markets for Sugar, Meat, Peanuts, Cotton, and Dairy Products*, USITC Publication 2276 (Washington, DC: USITC, April 1990); or Laird and Yeats, *Quantitative Methods*, op. cit.

[14] There would no doubt be an interest in projecting the likely effects of FTAs among the Latin American countries themselves, but several problems preclude such an effort. Lack of data is one difficulty. No systematic records exist on Latin American barriers against other Latin American exports comparable to those of the United States. Second, many parameters required for such projections—like demand elasticities—are not available for Latin America. Third, partial equilibrium models of the sort used for the U.S. projections are not intended for use on such high trade barriers that now exist in some Latin American countries. For a description of the equilibrium models, see Laird and Yeats, *Quantitative Methods*, op. cit., Chapter 3.

[15] These projections do not attempt to estimate the trade effects of the NTBs themselves but assume that the nontariff measure is adjusted to accommodate the FTA tariff preferences. For example, assume a product has a 10 percent tariff with a binding quota on Latin American exporters. If the duty is reduced preferentially to zero by the FTA, our projections assume that the quota will be expanded to allow the full trade effects of the tariff preferences to be achieved. The quota may again become binding (at the higher level) after this modification is made.

[16] We have limited the excluded items to hard core measures due to certain limitations of the NTB data in the UNCTAD Data Base on Trade Measures. Some measures, like health and sanitary restrictions or some import licensing schemes, may have no, or minor, trade effects. Excluding these products from our projections would likely cause the influence of NTBs to be overstated. See the note to Table 7 for a list of restrictions included in the hard core group.

[17] Textiles and clothing play a key role in the simulations for Mexico and a somewhat lesser role for Brazil. Mexico's textile and clothing exports face an average U.S. tariff of 17.3 percent and a $304-million projected increase for these products is about one-fifth the total expansion in manufactures exports. In contrast, the projected $94 million increase for Brazil is only about 10 percent of the total increase in its manufactures exports. The Annex to this

chapter provides details on the influence of textile and clothing NTBs on Latin American exports.

[18] B. A. Balassa, "Tariff Protection in Industrial Countries: An Evaluation," *Journal of Political Economy* (December 1965), pp. 573-594; Giorgio Baseri, "The United States Tariff Structure: Estimates of Effective Rates of Protection for United States Industries and Industrial Labor," *Review of Economics and Statistics* (May 1966), pp. 147-160; and UNCTAD, *The Kennedy Round: Estimated Effects on Tariff Barriers* (New York: United Nations, 1968).

[19] As an illustration, all copper-bearing ores (U.S. tariff classification no. 60230) are imported into the United States free of any import charges. Unwrought black and blister copper—a slightly processed product—faces a 1 percent duty. More highly processed products like master alloys of copper (tariff no. 61220) or copper plates and strips (tariff no. 61245) face duties of 5 percent. In other words, the rate of protection increases as processing adds value to a commodity or product. For a discussion of tariff escalation issues involved in the Uruguay Round negotiations and empirical information on tariffs and NTBs over major commodity-processing chains, see A. Yeats, "The Escalation of Trade Barriers" in J. Michael Finger and Andrzej Olechowski, (eds.), *The Uruguay Round: A Handbook for the Multilateral Trade Negotiations* (Washington: World Bank, 1987); and Alexander Yeats, "On the Analysis of Tariff Escalation: Is There a Methodological Bias Against the Interest of Developing Countries," *Journal of Development Economics*, Vol. 15 (Spring 1984).

[20] Yeats, "The Escalation of Trade Barriers," op. cit., Table 15.2.

[21] David Wall, *Industrial Processing of Natural Resources*, Commodity Working Paper No. 4, Commodities and Export Projections Division (Washington, DC: World Bank, 1979).

[22] Because available data on imports and tariffs came from different sources, with different commodity code classifications, we had to make some simplifying assumptions to prepare Table 10. First, we calculated the mean tariff rate for each customs commodity council nomenclature (CCCN) four-digit heading belonging to a product category in these tables. The resulting data were translated into a four-digit SITC code. Next, we calculated the averages of the tariffs, again by product category, to eliminate overlapping of more than one SITC four-digit code with more than one CCCN four-digit code. We merged these files with the import statistics, translated them into a two-digit SITC code, and aggregated according to the U.N. SITC-based classification for broad product groups (agricultural materials, food, and so on). For lack of data, we could not include many CACM and Caricom countries in Table 10.

[23] See Refik Erzan, et al., "The Profile of Protection in Developing Countries," *UNCTAD Review*, Vol. 1, No. 1, 1989, pp. 29-49; and UNCTAD, *Handbook of Trade Control Measures of Developing Countries* (Geneva: UNCTAD, 1987).

[24] Accurate estimates of developing countries' import demand elasticities are sparse; some rough data are provided by R. Langhammer, "Problems and Effects of a Developing Country's Tariff Concession Round on South-South Trade," *Kiel Working Paper No. 167*, University of Kiel (Kiel, Germany: Institute of World Economics, 1983); and Stern and Associates, *Price Elasticities in International Trade*, op. cit. These estimates suggest that Latin American import demand elasticities are between 1.5 and 3 for most manufactures, between 0.25 and 0.50 for raw materials, and about even for foods. Applying these broad estimates to current trade flows and at present tariff rates suggests that U.S. exports will expand by 30 to 50 percent. A crucial parameter is the coefficient of substitution between U.S. exports (preference receiving under the FTA) and other nation's goods. Our low estimate for this term (1.5) suggests a U.S. export expansion of about 30 percent. If it is in fact twice as high, the trade gains might be in the 45 to 50 percent range.

[25] To remove "insignificant" items from the tabulations, we stipulated that the value of trade in a product had to equal or exceed $25,000 for the item to be counted as a four-digit export. As such, the first figures show the number of distinct four-digit products where exports from the Latin American country were at least this great. The smaller figures in parentheses show the number of competing products where exports from both the United States and the competing country exceed $25,000.

Annex Notes

[26] We also examined the Latin American countries' average quota fulfillment in the EC market. If these rates were on the higher side, hitting quota ceilings, a relaxation of restrictions in the U.S. market could divert these exports. With the exception of Peru, where quota fulfillment rate in the EC was over 90 percent (versus 38 percent in the United States), there does not appear to be an incentive for these countries to divert trade to the U.S. market. In fact, in most cases, utilization rates in the EC market were even lower than in the United States.

[27] See USITC Publication 2276, op. cit., p. xvi.

[28] See United States International Trade Commission, *Estimated Tariff Equivalents of Nontariff Barriers on Certain Agricultural Imports in the European Community, Japan, and Canada*, USITC Publication 2280 (Washington, DC: USITC, April 1990), p. vi.

Part IV
Subregional
Free Trade Agreements

Chapter Five

The North American Free Trade Agreement: A Regional Model?

Craig VanGrasstek and Gustavo Vega

The North American Free Trade Agreement (NAFTA) is an ambitious initiative that will establish a combined market of 363 million people with an aggregate GDP of over $6.2 trillion. It may also be the first step in an even grander project: the establishment of a free trade area spanning the entire Western Hemisphere. To what extent will the NAFTA serve as a model for future trade agreements in the region? Will other Latin American countries enter into free trade agreements (FTAs) with the United States on essentially the same terms as Mexico and Canada, or will they be obliged to undertake further disciplines and obligations?

This chapter summarizes the key provisions of the NAFTA and their relevance for U.S. trade relations with other Latin American and Caribbean countries. Although the negotiations are not yet completed, a draft text of the agreement, leaked in early 1992, offers insight into the agreed and disputed provisions of the accord to date.[1] The areas of disagreement are identified by nearly 2,000 instances of bracketed text in the draft. The end-game of the NAFTA negotiations will largely be a matter of accepting, rejecting, or compromising on the items in these brackets.

This chapter does not present an exhaustive review of the NAFTA's negotiating groups, or the precise architecture of its chapters and annexes. (For a full listing of the negotiating groups, see Table 1.) Instead, it highlights those issues that are of greatest interest to the United States, Mexico, and their trading partners in Latin America. Where appropriate, reference is made to those aspects of the Canada-U.S. Free Trade Agreement (CAFTA) that serve as the basic model, or baseline, for the NAFTA negotiations.

TABLE 1. NAFTA NEGOTIATING GROUPS

1) Market Access

   - Tariffs and nontariff barriers
   - Rules of origin
   - Government procurement
   - Automobiles
   - Other industrial sectors

2) Trade Rules

   - Safeguards, subsidies and trade remedies
   - Standards

3) Services

   - Principles for services
   - Financial
   - Insurance
   - Land transportation
   - Telecommunications
   - Other services

4) Investment (Principles and Restrictions)

5) Intellectual Property

6) Dispute Settlement

Source: Office of U.S. Trade Representative, Washington, DC, June 14, 1991.

U.S. AND MEXICAN PERSPECTIVES ON THE NAFTA

The United States and Mexico approach the NAFTA negotiations from fundamentally different perspectives. These talks can best be viewed as a bargain between a regional regime-builder and a reformed free-rider. Although the two countries' policies have tended to converge in the past decade, they remain wide apart on issues that reflect differences in these countries' places in the global trading system, their level of economic development, and the importance of their bilateral relationships.

The United States is the world's largest economy and the single most influential participant in the global trading system. It would make no sense for the United States to jettison a global trading order in which it is so heavily invested, and that governs economic relations with its principal competitors and markets, in favor of a regional arrangement that accounts for less than one-sixteenth of its trade. The NAFTA, and more broadly the Enterprise for the Americas Initiative (EAI), are emphatically not an alternative to the General Agreement on Tariffs and Trade (GATT). They are, instead, the regional component of a negotiating strategy that employs unilateral, bilateral, and multilateral means to advance a broad range of U.S. goals. These include freer trade in goods and services, more open access for investors, and stricter protection for intellectual property rights as well as a host of other foreign policy objectives.

To buttress market-oriented reforms, the United States has entered into bilateral and plurilateral "framework" agreements with nearly every country in Latin America and the Caribbean and has negotiated bilateral investment treaties[2] and tax information exchange agreements[3] with a number of countries in the region.[4] Each of these talks allows U.S. negotiators to promote policies that—coupled with autonomous reforms and subregional negotiations among the Latin American countries—will prepare countries for FTA negotiations. Although the first priority of U.S. negotiators is to advance the economic interests of the United States, Latin American countries would also benefit from agreements that guarantee secure and open access to the U.S. market on a contractual basis. National economic reforms are made more credible when they are bound by international agreements and thus attract the confidence—and the capital—of investors.

For Mexico, the NAFTA negotiations symbolize a radical break with the past. Economic disaster in the wake of low oil prices and the debt crisis in the early 1980s forced Mexico to rethink its development strategy. In less than a decade, Mexico was transformed from one of the most closed and state-centric economies in Latin America to one of the most open. For Mexico's outward-oriented strategy to succeed, however, secure access to the U.S. market is essential. Concerns about a drift toward protectionism in the United States led Mexican authorities to seek guaranteed access to the U.S. market. The two countries negotiated a series of bilateral accords, including a 1985 agreement on subsidies and countervailing measures,[5] and a 1987 "framework" for bilateral consultations on a range of issues. These agreements, together with Mexico's accession to the GATT in 1986 and autonomous reforms, established a firmer foundation for U.S.-Mexican economic relations.

The NAFTA carries different weight for the two countries. Mexico accounts for only about 7 percent of U.S. exports. By contrast, three-fourths of Mexican trade is with the United States. The NAFTA will thus be Mexico's most consequential economic initiative in a generation. Mexican negotiators might ideally want preferential access to the U.S. market to be shared only by Canada, but they have found that this is an unrealistic expectation. They also seek "asymmetrical" treatment, on account of Mexico's status as a developing country. The United States is unsympathetic to proposals that either set bad precedents for future FTAs or that hark back to the principle of "special and differential" treatment for developing countries.

The NAFTA and the EAI are predicated upon the belief that developing countries stand to gain more from comprehensive economic liberalization at both the domestic and international levels than from isolated and exceptional trade preferences. Yet the NAFTA negotiations highlight one of the central problems of preferential trade agreements: the danger that such arrangements, through discriminatory practices and trade diversion, degenerate into exclusionary, market-sharing arrangements. There are a few areas where the negotiators could legitimately strike special deals in recognition of their shared borders (e.g., on gas pipelines and land transportation). However, with these limited exceptions, the negotiators should avoid making only bargains that cannot be extended to other trading partners.

TRADITIONAL ISSUES: TRADE IN GOODS

Border measures and other barriers to the free exchange of goods were, until recently, the conventional fare of trade negotiations. Today, they are often eclipsed by more controversial topics under negotiation.

Tariff Liberalization

GATT Article XXIV requires that customs unions or FTAs eliminate "duties and other restrictive regulations of commerce . . . on substantially all the trade" between the parties. There is some room to maneuver, however, regarding the base and pace of liberalization. The NAFTA may set a precedent for phasing out tariff rates not from their GATT-bound levels,[6] but from their applied levels—a limited U.S. concession to Mexico's demand for "asymmetrical" treatment that would effectively maintain Mexico's privileges under the Generalized System of Preferences (GSP). The draft NAFTA suggests that there will be three or four distinct schedules for tariff liberalization. Some items will receive immediate duty-free treatment, whereas others will be phased out over periods as long as five, ten, or even fifteen years.[7]

The significance of tariff liberalization is easy to exaggerate. Import duties comprise a relatively minor barrier for most Latin American and Caribbean exports to the U.S. market, since every country in the region (except Cuba) already benefits from at least one preferential tariff program, be it GSP, the Caribbean Basin Initiative, or the Andean Trade Preference Act. U.S. import duties on Latin American exports are about 3 percent on average and around 4.5 percent on foodstuffs and manufactures. However, sensitive products—such as textiles, apparel, footwear, sugar, and fruits and vegetables—enjoy higher tariff protection and are also subject to different types of nontariff barriers (NTBs), which are often an even more binding constraint.

For Latin America and the Caribbean, tariff liberalization would be more meaningful. Import duties on U.S. exports are 18 to 24 percent on average, with much higher rates on certain items (see Erzan and Yeats, Chapter 4, Table 10). Because trade taxes are an important source of fiscal revenues in many of those countries, tariff liberalization would require that governments develop alternative sources of revenue to replace forgone import duties.

Rules of Origin

Rules of origin are intended to limit the benefits of a trade agreement to the goods produced in the exporting country, and to prohibit third countries from using one of the parties as a launching platform for the transshipment of goods. Overly strict rules could unfairly discriminate against trade and investment from countries that are not party to the agreement.

The draft agreement provides that a product will be eligible for treatment under the agreement if it meets one of four criteria: 1) it is wholly obtained or produced in one of the three countries; 2) all of the nonoriginating materials undergo a change in tariff classification; 3) it does not meet the preceding rule, but contains a yet-to-be-determined minimum level of North American content; or 4) it is processed or assembled in one North American country from another North American country's materials. The United States also proposed that parties be allowed to exclude goods that are not substantially transformed. There is no agreement yet on what can be counted toward the "direct cost of processing" in determining North American content or on the cumulation of origin for products that are processed in two or more countries.

Special rules of origin and content will apply to specific sectors or products, notably computers, automobiles, and apparel. Negotiators must be careful to craft rules that are neither so loose as to invite abuse by third-country producers nor so strict as to discourage North American producers from trading with firms outside the region.

The United States and Canada have periodically fought over these issues for nearly a generation. The bilateral Auto Pact (first negotiated in 1965) eliminated all tariffs for qualifying products in bilateral automotive trade. Many U.S. policymakers believe that Japanese and Korean automakers took advantage of the agreement by establishing assembly plants in Canada to serve the U.S. market. These concerns give rise to demands for high regional content in automobiles. Mexican negotiators oppose these proposals, insofar as they might dissuade new foreign investment in Mexican automotive plants.

Still undecided is whether the automotive rules of origin in the NAFTA will adopt the norm set by the CAFTA (50-percent minimum North American content), or set higher content requirements. Negotiators may compromise on a 60-percent North American content rule and a grandfather clause granting special protection for established manufacturers over a ten-year period.

Textiles and Apparel

The textile negotiations illustrate the problem of liberalizing regionally when global trade is protected by a complex web of tariffs and quotas under the Multi-Fibre Arrangement (MFA). The MFA itself is under negotiation in the Uruguay Round, with a view to phasing out the restrictions over a ten-year period. If those talks succeed, Mexico (and presumably other Latin American countries under the EAI) could enjoy *temporary* preferences, to the extent that liberalization within the FTA proceeded faster than in the GATT. If the Uruguay Round fails and textile quotas remain in place, any FTA preferences would be at the expense of non-member suppliers. Discrimination against non-FTA members would be even worse if the rules of origin on textiles and apparel were tightened to exclude sourcing of imports from outside the FTA.

The negotiations may lead to a deal that would phase out all tariffs (and about half the quotas) over five years, and the rest by the end of 10 years. The United States would cut its tariffs 50 percent up front and 10 percent a year thereafter, while Mexico would cut its tariffs 20 percent each year. To qualify for duty-free treatment, however, apparel would have to be made almost entirely of North American yarn. To agree to tighter rules of origin, Canada reportedly seeks a large increase in the amount of apparel it can ship to the United States duty-free and without origin requirements as well as the right to continue special duty-remission for goods eventually exported.

Agriculture

Agriculture is among the most politically difficult areas of trade liberalization, for all countries at every level of economic development. Agricultural issues are often treated as a hybrid of social and economic policy, where the welfare of producers takes precedence over the needs of consumers. Mexican agriculture is plagued by low productivity and a growing inability to meet domestic demand for staples. Glut is the chief problem in the United States. Both countries would benefit from market-oriented reforms in agriculture but could incur heavy costs in the transition period.

The prospects for agricultural reform in North America depend heavily upon the outcome of the Uruguay Round. The United States seeks to eliminate import quotas, liberalize tariffs, set strict disciplines on production and export subsidies, and require that sanitary and phytosanitary rules not be manipulated as indirect trade barriers. None of these objectives can be easily achieved through bilateral or regional bargaining in the absence of real progress at the global level. For this reason, the United States and Canada made little effort in the CAFTA to reform agricultural policy beyond a commitment to cooperate in the multilateral negotiations. By the same token, progress in the agricultural chapter of the NAFTA is being held back by the impasse in the multilateral trade negotiations in Geneva.

There are some agricultural issues that the trilateral partners can pursue among themselves. All three insist upon the temporary retention of tariff protection for import-sensitive crops. U.S. negotiators want a slow phaseout of protection for fruits and vegetables, where Mexican producers are quite competitive. Mexican negotiators are similarly protective of corn, beans, and other staples, where Mexican producers are inefficient. Canada, in turn, seeks to protect poultry and dairy products. In addition, Mexico proposes the imposition of quotas on some products that it wishes to protect, whereas the United States seeks the right to employ "snapback" tariffs or tariff-rate quotas for sensitive products in the event of import surges from NAFTA countries.[8] There is a possibility that the differences among the three parties may be impossible to reconcile, and that instead of a trilateral accord, there may be two separate deals on agriculture.

Government Procurement and State Trading

Governments themselves are among the largest procurers of goods and services, especially in significant sectors such as infrastructural investments and defense industries. The public sector can also be a discriminatory purchaser when its decisions are dictated more by "buy-local" laws than by strict economic criteria. The NAFTA government procurement chapter will require that purchasing procedures be transparent, nondiscriminatory, and conducted on the basis of national treatment (i.e., Mexican firms would be treated the same as American firms). Areas of disagreement in this chapter include differences over the threshold value for procurements that will be subject to these rules, and Mexico's objection to including services in the agreement. The countries must also decide whether and to what extent these rules will apply to subnational bodies (e.g., state and provincial governments) and to parastatal enterprises.

Government procurement falls within the broader category of "state trading," which encompasses virtually any government activity that affects trade. In future negotiations under the EAI, the United States may raise concerns over other policies that entail the monopolistic provision of a good or service or the monopsonistic purchase of goods and services. Both Canada and Mexico have defended their state-run monopolies in the NAFTA negotiations.

Exclusions and Exemptions

Although FTA negotiations aim at liberalizing "substantially all trade," they can provide for some exemptions and exclusions. This is an area in which negotiators must exercise caution lest they create wide loopholes or unwelcome precedents. There are several proposed exemptions in the NAFTA negotiations. Canada seeks special consideration for laws affecting "public order and safety," just as Mexico wants an exemption for measures relating to "public morals." Neither proposal seems likely to affect large areas of trade, but the same cannot be said for exemptions concerning "environmental standards" (Canada) or "conservation of natural resources" (Mexico). These provisions could be used to justify laws restricting imports or exports of petroleum products, chemicals, and other items. All three countries favor exemptions on national security grounds, but disagree on the wording of this provision.

The petroleum sector is the most controversial of the proposed exemptions. The Mexican Constitution declares this industry off-limits to foreign investors, and Mexican negotiators proposed that the NAFTA's investment chapter stipulate that its provisions "shall not apply to any measure taken pursuant to a restriction expressly mandated by the Constitution of a Party." The U.S. negotiators have sought some way around this obstacle to allow investment in at least some segments of the Mexican petroleum sector. The dispute has not yet been resolved, but it is generally expected that U.S. firms will win greater access to investment in refining and petrochemicals. Negotiators must also decide whether the United States will have the authority to restrict oil imports for reasons of national security.

NEW ISSUES

It may no longer be accurate to describe investment, intellectual property rights, and services as "new issues," given the prominent place they now hold in the Uruguay Round and other international trade negotiations. The Round is expected to set useful precedents in these areas, on which further progress at a regional level can be built.

Investment

Investment disputes have been a perennial source of friction in U.S. relations with Latin American and Caribbean countries. Quarrels over the nationalization of industries and expropriation of U.S. investments left a legacy of mistrust. With the onset of the debt crisis and the need for new funds, however, investment restrictions came to be viewed as ill-considered disincentives to foreign capital. They are now more receptive to U.S. demands for the right of establishment, national and most-favored-nation (MFN) treatment for its investors, access to arbitration, and the elimination of "performance requirements" (e.g., mandated levels of exports by foreign investors). Mexico has moved in this direction, but still restricts the extent of foreign participation in sectors such as petroleum, transportation, mining, automotive products, and financial services.

Although the trilateral negotiators agree on the essential principle of liberalized investment, many sections in the draft of NAFTA's investment chapter are disputed. In addition to Mexico's insistence that the petroleum sector be protected, the parties disagreed on such matters as the right to screen investments, the obligations of state enterprises, and the retroactive application of the rules to existing investments.

Intellectual Property Rights

Trade-related intellectual property rights (TRIPs) include patents, trademarks, and copyrights. A broad spectrum of U.S. industries depend on the protection of these rights, including producers of pharmaceuticals, computers, books, and motion pictures. The U.S. negotiators argue that protecting these rights is in the interest of developing countries because they help to establish a secure climate for foreign investors. Many developing countries claim that these laws inhibit technology transfer and allow foreign firms to abuse monopoly rents. Mexico, which had earlier subscribed to these views, enacted a new patent law in 1991 that eliminated many of the previous U.S. complaints.

The NAFTA draft indicated substantial concord on copyright and trademark provisions, although it also showed disagreements over such issues as patent protection for biotechnology, layout designs for semiconductors, satellite signals, trade secrets, and the enforcement of rights.

The U.S. negotiators view intellectual property protection as a top priority in Latin America and will not wait for new FTA negotiations to press their demands on this issue. They are particularly insistent that pharmaceutical patents be granted and protected. If not, the United States is prepared to take retaliatory measures. The "Section 301" provision of the 1988 Trade and Competitiveness Act requires the U.S. Trade Representative to review annually infringement of these rights and take retaliatory action against countries that do not protect U.S. intellectual property rights. Half of the countries in the region are potentially subject to action under this statute.[9]

Services

Negotiations on services are complicated by the vast disparities in each country's comparative advantages. The United States is better positioned to compete in capital- and knowledge-intensive services such as computer programming, telecommunications, engineering, and medical services, while Mexico has a natural advantage in such labor-intensive sectors as construction and agricultural services. The U.S. negotiators would prefer a services regime that opens foreign markets to the exports and investments of U.S. service providers but that requires few or no changes in U.S. immigration and shipping laws. Mexican negotiators would prefer to retain restrictions in fields that are considered critical to national security or economic sovereignty.

The draft NAFTA services chapter is full of bracketed text. The parties agreed to the principle of national treatment for services firms but disagreed to one extent or another on almost every other provision and proposed exemptions. The United States successfully kept maritime services out of the CAFTA and the Uruguay Round and seeks the same exemption in the NAFTA. Canada wants to continue protecting cultural industries, and Mexico seeks exemptions in such fields as social security, health care, and public education.

The NAFTA will include separate sections on telecommunications (where both Canada and Mexico permit monopolies), financial services (where Mexico reportedly seeks a seven-year period for opening the sector and quantitative caps on foreign participation), and land transportation.

Temporary entry for business persons is also a difficult topic. The U.S. negotiators are willing to provide special access for executives and specialists in various careers (e.g., architects or medical technicians) who meet certification and immigration requirements. They are much less willing to make concessions of interest to Mexico in sectors employing many unskilled or semi-skilled workers, such as construction or agriculture.

CONSULTATIONS AND DISPUTE SETTLEMENT

Free trade does not mean hassle-free trade. A successful trade agreement should provoke disputes between the partners, by accelerating the movement of goods, services, and capital. An agreement must therefore provide institutional arrangements that set the terms under which conflicts can be resolved. The NAFTA will include provisions allowing for consultations, dispute-settlement, and temporary departure from the terms of the agreement.

Mexican and Canadian negotiators would prefer a regime that subjects all parties to the rule of law and prevents their giant neighbor from treating economic disputes as an exercise in power politics. Not surprisingly, Washington's perspective is different. Historically, Congress has been unwilling to cede broad authority to supranational bodies, and the U.S. negotiators are sensitive to these concerns. The United States is willing to include in the agreement provisions for consultations in the case of disputes and allow a limited degree of adjudication but resists some of the more expansive Mexican and Canadian demands.

Dispute Settlement

Dispute-settlement provisions are intended to resolve disagreements over the interpretation and application of a trade agreement or other causes of friction in a trade relationship. The CAFTA approach, likely to be repeated in the NAFTA, provides for consultations between high-level members of the respective governments, whenever disputes arise. The consulting parties will attempt to reach a solution by diplomatic means but can alternatively pass an issue along to a panel of nongovernmental experts.

The draft NAFTA agreement indicates that the parties will similarly establish a North American Trade Commission, composed of representatives from the three governments and empowered to refer disputes to expert panels. The countries have disagreed on the commission's exact powers and jurisdiction; the relationship between NAFTA, CAFTA, and GATT dispute-settlement mechanisms; the means for selecting panel members; and the issues that panels may examine in their reports. In addition to the state-to-state system that already exists in the CAFTA, the United States has reportedly also asked to include in the NAFTA a dispute-resolution mechanism for private claims against a state.

Dispute-settlement provisions, though an indispensable part of any trade agreement, have limitations. Sovereign states are not cavalier about ceding their authority to supranational bodies, and none of the parties would empower a panel to nullify or alter their respective laws. Dispute-settlement provisions in both the GATT and the CAFTA rely first on the goodwill of the contracting parties and ultimately on the threat of retaliation. The same will probably be true for the North American Trade Commission and any expert panels it may create.

The inclusion of other Latin American and Caribbean countries in the FTA would make the process even more complex. In the NAFTA, Mexico seeks participation on all panels, even when the country is not a party to the dispute (e.g., in disputes between the United States and Canada). In an enlarged FTA, should a dispute—for instance between the United States and Argentina—be resolved through bilateral consultations or by a court representing each country in the region? Latin American countries would find comfort in numbers, but U.S. negotiators and legislators would almost certainly resist proposals to establish a regional trade court.

Trade-Remedy Laws

The NAFTA may also include provisions concerning the application of antidumping (AD) and countervailing duties (CVD) on products traded within North America. This issue is even more controversial than the dispute-settlement provisions. Whereas U.S. industries and legislators often view these trade-remedy laws as necessary defenses against the unfair trading practices of foreign companies and governments, U.S. trading partners frequently argue that the zealous prosecution of these laws can itself be a trade barrier.

Disputes can be sharp in the case of the countervailing duty statute, which allows tariffs to be imposed to offset injury from foreign subsidies. Practically any form of state aid to an industry can be subject to countervailing duties if it is not generally available throughout an economy, and if imports cause or threaten to cause material injury to U.S. producers. The U.S. antidumping law, which allows domestic firms to seek the imposition of duties on foreign competitors that sell products at less than fair value, also offers a formidable barrier to some products (most notably in the steel sector).

Both Mexico and Canada have been subject to harassment under these statutes. Mexican exporters were vulnerable before the 1985 subsidies agreement with the United States, when they did not receive the procedural protection of an injury test. Between 1980 and 1988, U.S. petitioners filed 35 CVD and AD cases against Mexican exporters.

The CAFTA granted special treatment to Canada in the execution of the U.S. trade-remedy laws, but the value of these provisions is debatable. Strictly speaking, the trade-remedy provisions of the CAFTA amount to little more than a "freeze." Canada received a qualified pledge that the terms and interpretations of U.S. law would not further evolve as an instrument to restrict Canadian exports. The CAFTA does not actually prevent Congress from amending the laws as they apply to Canada but does state that proposed amendments can be reviewed for their conformity with the agreement. If Congress does amend the statutes, it must specify whether the changes apply to Canada.

The CAFTA also establishes a system of binational panels to review determinations in AD and CVD cases. These panels do not have the authority to declare a U.S. law invalid or to reverse a determination by fiat, but they can remand a decision back to the U.S. International Trade Commission (USITC) or the Department of Commerce, if they determine that it was not reached in accordance with U.S. law. Moreover, decisions by binational panels may differ from those the Court of International Trade (the first court of appeals in the United States) would otherwise have reached.[10] The panels offer a relatively cheap and efficient alternative to the appeals process in the U.S. judicial system. However, the CAFTA does not prevent U.S. petitioners from resorting to these laws. During the first three years of the CAFTA (1989-1991), five AD and five CVD petitions were filed against Canadian products.

Whatever the real worth of the CAFTA provisions, the Mexican negotiators perceive them to be valuable. Mexico insists that similar provisions be written into the NAFTA. The U.S. negotiators view the CAFTA panel provisions as a lamentable compromise and resist efforts to include identical provisions in the NAFTA. They also express concerns over the inherent difficulties in reconciling the differences between the Anglo-Saxon and Franco-Iberian legal traditions. Those opinions sometimes also convey an unspoken disquiet over the fairness and impartiality of the Mexican judiciary.

Safeguards

Safeguard provisions allow countries to depart temporarily from their obligations under a trade agreement. Escape clauses permit adjustments whenever unanticipated increases in import competition threaten to injure an industry in the importing country. These provisions allow a country to impose tariffs or other restrictions for a limited period, without forcing it to abrogate the agreement altogether.[11]

The NAFTA safeguard provisions will be based upon the two-track CAFTA approach. The "global track" in the U.S.-Canada agreement provides that parties must exclude one another from safeguard actions, unless the imports from the other party are substantial and contribute importantly to serious injury. The agreement's "bilateral track" states that either party can employ a special bilateral safeguard provision against imports that increase at an injurious rate as a consequence of the agreement itself. Action is limited to either a suspension of duty reductions or an increase in duty to the MFN rate and cannot last more than three years.

Snapback provisions are a special form of safeguard. CAFTA Article 702, for example, provides that either party can temporarily restore pre-CAFTA duties on perishable agricultural products when those imports surge and depress prices. The draft NAFTA indicated that a similar provision was still under negotiation. Whereas the CAFTA provision was inserted at Canada's insistence,[12] the United States is the demandeur for the NAFTA snapback. The provision might set less exacting criteria for use of the mechanism than does the CAFTA, and restrictions could take a somewhat different form (e.g., tariff-rate quotas). Mexico opposes the snapback provision for agricultural products but did propose the insertion of similar provisions in the chapters on textiles, services, and investment.

ENVIRONMENTAL AND LABOR ISSUES

The environmental and labor issues create linkages that trade negotiators did not seek but must address. NAFTA critics in the United States, charging that the agreement will damage the environment and harm the welfare of workers, demand that at least it be accompanied by palliative measures. Others are thoroughly opposed to the agreement and cite environmental and labor arguments in their efforts to defeat congressional ratification of the accord.

Trade and the Environment

The link between trade policy and the environment is a recent development but could prove one of the most critical issues of the 1990s. Activists charge that trade negotiations promote economic growth without regard to its environmental consequences and fear that governments might invoke liberal trade rules to invalidate environmental statutes. These concerns were aired during the debate in early 1991, over the extension of fast-track negotiating authority for the NAFTA and the Uruguay Round. Environmental groups objected to the fast-track rules for expedited congressional ratification of trade accords and charged that these rules could prevent Congress from considering the environmental consequences of trade liberalization. This campaign was unsuccessful. The final vote appears to have been influenced more by economic than environmental considerations,[13] but the Bush and Salinas administrations had to make concessions. By pledging in an action plan to address bilateral environmental issues,[14] the White House temporarily defused this source of opposition.

The trilateral negotiators have resisted demands for a comprehensive environmental chapter in the NAFTA. It is hard to imagine a provision that could be so delicately crafted as to reconcile the positions of trade negotiators and the more radical environmental groups. No matter how "green" the final agreement, some activists are bound to claim that it is not green enough. Negotiators have instead decided that, apart from a few references in the NAFTA, most environmental issues will be dealt with on a separate track. The Mexican Department of Environment and Urban Development and the U.S. Environmental Protection Agency jointly released a border plan in early 1992. The plan calls for expenditures of over $1 billion by the governments of Mexico and the United States, by the border states, and by private industry to clean up pollution along the border. It includes commitments for hiring additional Mexican inspectors, tightening U.S. law enforcement, and funding specific projects (e.g., wastewater treatment facilities in border towns).

The environmental issue will undoubtedly be raised when Congress considers ratification of the NAFTA. The administration may be pressed to strike a deal that will satisfy legislators who are predisposed to support the NAFTA but want assurances that the environment will be safeguarded. There are any number of concessions that the administration might decide to make to win their support. It could pledge to propose a "green round" of GATT negotiations, increase funding for border projects, or make a concession on some domestic environmental initiative. Some members of Congress may further demand that environmental transgressions be made a cause of action under retaliatory trade laws, or that environmental standards be written into the renewal legislation for the Generalized System of Preferences.

It is not clear whether environmental issues will be equally prominent in trade negotiations with other Latin American countries. There certainly are environmental challenges elsewhere in the region, ranging from the migration of "dirty" industries to deforestation, but one major problem—pollution at the U.S. border—is unique to Mexico. It is also possible that some tensions may be relieved through environmental assistance to these countries, provided under EAI debt-reduction provisions.[16]

Labor Issues

The labor issue is similar to the environmental problem in several respects. In both cases, the trilateral agreement is opposed by interest groups concerned about potential consequences of the agreement and demanding special protection. The American Federation of Labor-Congress of Industrial Organizations (AFL-CIO) was the sharpest critic of the NAFTA when it was first proposed, out of concern that free trade with Mexico would depress U.S. wages and encourage companies to relocate in Mexico. The AFL-CIO and like-minded members of Congress demanded that the NAFTA include a "social charter." This charter would presumably set minimum standards for the treatment of workers and unions in Mexico and perhaps set a minimum wage closer to the U.S. level.

Negotiators may deal with the labor issue in much the same manner as environmental concerns. In place of a distinct social clause in the NAFTA itself, the administration might propose or accept separate legislation to assist workers. The objective would not be to win the support of the AFL-CIO, which has opposed trade liberalization since the late 1960s, but instead to assuage the concerns of congressional Democrats. Trade adjustment assistance (TAA) programs are intended to provide special unemployment and training benefits to workers injured by trade liberalization. President Kennedy first proposed TAA programs during the early 1960s to prevent labor unions from leaving the free-trade coalition. The programs achieved their immediate objective by securing passage of the Trade Expansion Act of 1962 but have never received full funding. The Reagan and Bush administrations both proposed that TAA be eliminated altogether. President Bush may find it useful to make a tactical retreat from this position and agree to an increase in TAA funding to win additional votes for the NAFTA from Democratic legislators.

ACCESSION TO THE NAFTA

The NAFTA may not be merely the *model* for future FTAs, but in fact the *vehicle* for subsequent negotiations, if the agreement includes an accession clause. The purpose of such a mechanism, also known as a docking provision, would be to define the terms and procedures by which additional countries might become parties to the FTA. It would permit other Latin American countries to enter the existing free-trade club instead of negotiating separate agreements with the United States. This approach would avoid the chief disadvantage of overlapping free trade areas, where the benefits of trade liberalization are confined to discrete sets of partners.

Mexican policymakers are not keen on a docking clause, as they would prefer exclusive preferences in the U.S. market. The United States appears intent upon proceeding with further negotiations in the region, with or without Mexican participation, and Mexico will be better placed to safeguard its interests if it has a seat at the table. Canada went through precisely these calculations in deciding to participate in the trilateral negotiations.[17]

Despite the advantages of an accession clause, the benefits can be easily exaggerated. It should not be assumed that any administrative mechanism can depoliticize negotiations or minimize the demands on new entrants. Moreover, the operation of an accession clause raises vexing issues concerning both the scope of negotiations that it would permit and the ratification procedures for approving new members.

A strict accession clause could delimit the scope of future negotiations. The clause might require countries to adopt the general principles established in the NAFTA and make specific commitments to bring their laws into conformity with the agreement. This approach could run afoul of an established U.S. negotiating practice of making each successive trade negotiation more comprehensive than the one before.

If rigidly drafted, the clause would make it difficult for the United States and its trading partners to raise new issues or reopen matters that were settled in the NAFTA. For example, if Mexico succeeded in preserving constitutional protections for its petroleum industry in the NAFTA, what effect might this have in negotiations with Venezuela? Would the accession clause permit the United States to bring up petroleum issues when negotiating with Venezuela, allow the issue to be raised only if Mexico and Canada concurred, or keep the issue out of bounds altogether? If the issue were raised, would new disciplines affect Venezuela exclusively or apply retroactively to all members of the club? The same questions apply regarding issues that other countries might raise with the United States. For example, if U.S. negotiators successfully resisted Mexican demands for changes in the marketing orders that restrict certain fruit and vegetable imports, would this prevent Chile from revisiting this issue in its accession negotiations? A properly drafted docking clause would allow the NAFTA to expand both geographically and thematically. If the accession clause is too restrictive, U.S. negotiators might feel compelled to fall back on the bilateral option.

An accession clause also raises concern over ratification procedures for new trade agreements and the role of Congress. Latin American countries, like other U.S. trading partners, would prefer that Congress be kept "out of the loop" in trade negotiations. Congress is widely assumed to be a protectionist institution that if given the chance, would attempt to rewrite the terms of an agreement. There are precedents for ratification procedures that effectively exclude Congress, but these experiences offer questionable guidance. For example, the United States pursued a series of interlocked bilateral trade agreements in 1934-1947. The tariff concessions in these agreements were automatically extended to all other countries receiving MFN treatment,[18] and the agreements were ratified with a stroke of the president's pen. The only role that Congress played was periodic renewal of the negotiating authority.

GATT accession procedures are only slightly more complex. They allow GATT members to negotiate with applicants to set the price for entry into the club. The negotiations are one-way affairs, in which only applicants make concessions (i.e., accept GATT disciplines, bind and reduce tariffs, etc.). All of the countries that have acceded to the GATT in recent years already received MFN treatment from the United States and thus gained no significant new benefits in bilateral trade relations as a result of their accession.[19] Again, Congress plays no role in the process.

The legislature is unlikely to be a wallflower in the EAI negotiations. Congress will not permit the executive to grant concessions above and beyond MFN treatment without obtaining their explicit approval. Ratification procedures will probably be based on the fast-track rules that have evolved since the Trade Act of 1974. The conventional interpretation underestimates the authority that Congress retains under the fast track. The process is commonly but inaccurately characterized as one in which the legislative branch is restricted to a simple yes-or-no vote on the agreement.

In fact, Congress votes on the implementing legislation for a trade agreement (i.e., a bill specifying the changes that must be made to bring U.S. law into conformity with the agreement) rather than on the agreement itself, and the congressional trade committees participate in the drafting of this legislation. These committees can bargain with the executive over the interpretation of the agreement and may demand that the implementing legislation include matters that were not in the trade agreement itself. The fast-track rules also stipulate that the president must obtain the approval of the congressional trade committees before initiating any FTA negotiations, consult with those committees during the negotiations, and inform them before signing the agreements. These requirements give the trade committees ample opportunity to influence the negotiating agenda and also permit them to demand some quid pro quo in other areas of trade policy. In brief, the fast-track rules leave considerable authority with the Congress, and legislators would oppose any proposals to deny them this leverage.

Congress will want assurances that additional countries cannot join the NAFTA without congressional approval and that the existing NAFTA provisions cannot be altered without review. The legislative branch will be particularly insistent upon its right to reject any agreements that grant new and additional U.S. concessions to Latin American countries and to participate in drafting any implementing legislation that these agreements require. Procedures could be simplified, if future agreements do not mandate additional changes in U.S. law. It may be possible for these accords to be ratified by means of a lay-over process, in which they are automatically approved unless Congress enacts a resolution of disapproval.

These issues may soon be addressed in both the NAFTA and in U.S. law. The current fast-track authority will expire in mid-1993, and the next administration must convince Congress to grant such authority once again before it can pursue further negotiations under the EAI. The terms of the NAFTA accession clause and the renewed fast-track authority will help determine the pace and shape of future negotiations.

CONCLUSIONS AND RECOMMENDATIONS

Assuming the NAFTA negotiations are successfully concluded, the next task will be ratification of the agreement. This is not expected to be a major hurdle in Mexico, but the process may be more turbulent in Canada and the United States. The Canadian ratification debate could revisit the concerns raised in 1988, when a federal election became a national plebiscite on the CAFTA; the parties opposing the agreement narrowly lost the race. In the United States, the key question is whether or not the executive and legislative branches can arrive at a mutually acceptable price for fast-track approval of the agreement. The White House would be well advised to consider increased funding for trade adjustment assistance programs, as well as border environmental projects, when it submits the agreement to Congress. Besides cushioning some of the negative side effects of increased trade with Mexico, these measures could convince fence-sitting Democrats to vote in favor of the accord. Legislators and trade officials should resist bargaining over matters that might alter the negotiated terms of the NAFTA itself.

Congress and the White House should also agree on the institutional arrangements for new negotiations under the EAI. The legislative branch has a legitimate and necessary role to play in developing U.S. negotiating objectives, overseeing the conduct of commercial diplomacy, and making the final decision to accept or reject agreements. The fast track offers an appropriate balance between these requirements and the need to ensure that trade agreements will not be subject to crippling amendments or dilatory maneuvers. The implementing legislation for the NAFTA should provide a new grant of authority under the fast track for at least three years. The proposed accession clause should be viewed as a useful complement to the fast-track rules. If properly drafted, the docking provision and the fast track will jointly facilitate the entry of other Latin American and Caribbean countries into the free-trade club.

The accession talks need not be limited to the terms agreed in the trilateral accord. The trading partners may want to have the option to negotiate further with one another, as some NAFTA provisions will inevitably fall short of expectations. The agreement might not offer as much access to the Mexican energy sector as the United States seeks, for example, or might not adequately protect Mexican exporters from harassment under the U.S. trade-remedy laws. Whatever these shortcomings might be, the parties might wish to address them in the context of negotiations with other countries. The NAFTA accession clause should be drafted in a way that lets the original contracting parties make additional concessions, in response to requests from one another or from applicant countries.

Finally, the preoccupation with regional trade arrangements should not make countries in the hemisphere lose sight of their stake in the outcome of the Uruguay Round of multilateral trade negotiations. A successful round would not only facilitate reaching regional accords, but would help ensure that those accords truly lead to greater trade rather than protected trade in an enlarged area.

Notes

[1] The draft consists primarily of the so-called "Dallas Composite," which negotiators developed for their talks during February 1992. The draft appears to have been leaked in Canada and was later distributed widely by environmental groups in all three countries.

[2] Bilateral Investment Treaties (BITs) typically provide for national and most-favored-nation (MFN) treatment and the binding arbitration of disputes. The United States concluded a BIT with Argentina in 1991 and is pursuing similar accords with Bolivia, Costa Rica, Haiti, Jamaica, Peru, and Venezuela. U.S. negotiators would prefer to conclude BITs prior to entering into FTA talks. Chile, the next country in line for FTA negotiations, has not accepted this approach, however.

[3] Tax Information Exchange Agreements (TIEAs) permit countries to share tax information on corporations and persons operating in either of the countries to discover tax evasion. The United States has been particularly eager to reach such agreements with countries in the Caribbean Basin, for which it has offered tax inducements. The United States has TIEAs in effect with Barbados, Costa Rica, the Dominican Republic, Grenada, Jamaica, Mexico, and Trinidad and Tobago. TIEAs with Honduras and Peru have been signed and are pending ratification, and negotiations are under way with El Salvador, Guyana, and Nicaragua. In addition to the TIEAs, the United States is negotiating with Mexico and Venezuela for more comprehensive income and estate tax treaties.

[4] The United States has also recently enacted the Andean Trade Preferences Act, which will grant trade preferences in the U.S. market to Bolivia, Colombia, Ecuador, and Peru in exchange for their continued participation in the fight against drug traffic.

[5] The main benefit of the subsidies agreement was the extension of an injury test in countervailing duty cases against Mexican products. Prior to this agreement, petitioners could win the imposition of countervailing duties on imports from Mexico, merely by proving that these products benefited from subsidies that are countervailable under U.S. law. Since the agreement, petitioners are also required to convince the U.S. International Trade Commission that these imports cause or threaten material injury.

[6] In GATT parlance, a "bound rate" is the maximum rate that a country is permitted to impose on imports from countries that received MFN treatment. Countries often apply tariffs at levels below the bound rates.

[7] An issue of some contention is the fate of the maquiladora and in-bond programs. Tariff preferences under these programs will naturally be eroded by general tariff cutting within

the NAFTA. Moreover, production under these programs may not meet the local content and rules-of-origin criteria to qualify for duty-free treatment under the NAFTA. After a transition period, these special regimes will likely be phased out.

[8] Mexico also raised concerns over U.S. "marketing orders," which are allegedly used with protective intent to exclude products that do not meet certain size and shape standards. U.S. officials defend these orders as legitimate quality-control standards.

[9] Brazil is on the special "priority watch list," and Argentina, Chile, Colombia, Ecuador, El Salvador, Guatemala, Paraguay, Peru, and Venezuela are currently on the (nonpriority) "watch list."

[10] This appears to have been true in a critical case involving Canadian pork products, when a panel directed the USITC to reverse its injury determination (and thus invalidate the countervailing duty order).

[11] The United States first included an escape clause in a 1942 trade agreement with Mexico. The mechanism later became standard in bilateral accords and formed the basis for GATT Article XIX. A more generalized escape clause in U.S. trade law (Section 201 of the Trade Act of 1974) allows import restraints to be imposed even when the injurious imports cannot be attributed to a specific trade agreement. Only one-fifth of the petitions filed between 1974 and 1991 resulted in some form of import protection.

[12] The United States has not yet exercised this provision of the CAFTA, but Canada has employed it to restrict U.S. asparagus, peaches, and tomatoes.

[13] See Craig VanGrasstek, "The Political Economy of Trade and the Environment in the United States Senate," in Patrick Low (ed.), *International Trade and the Environment*, Discussion Paper No.159 (Washington, DC: World Bank, 1992). The analysis indicates the Senate vote in favor of fast-track extension can be readily explained in a pluralist framework (i.e., senators vote in accordance with the positions taken by specific industries in their constituencies) and that environmental considerations played only a marginal role in the final decision.

[14] Executive Office of the President, "Response of the Administration to Issues Raised in Connection with the Negotiation of a North American Free Trade Agreement" (Washington, DC: processed, 1991).

[15] Specific environmental disputes are also likely to become entangled in the debate. One candidate is an import ban on Mexican tuna, arising from a determination that Mexican fisheries do not meet U.S. "dolphin-safe" standards. A GATT panel determined in 1991 that the import ban violates Mexico's trade rights, but Congress has not yet approved legislation to bring this law into conformity with the decision.

[16] The program's debt-relief provisions are a means of generating funds for environmental programs by allowing interest payments on the remaining debt to be made in local currency into an environmental trust fund in the beneficiary countries. Those monies are then used for environmental purposes (e.g., to purchase ecologically threatened land). This approach creates a source of funding for these projects at a time when both the United States and its Latin American partners face severe budgetary constraints. The United States entered in environmental framework agreements with Bolivia, Chile, and Jamaica in 1991. Additional agreements are on hold pending authorization and appropriation of new debt-reduction funds.

[17] Mexico does not oppose the docking concept in principle. In fact, the 1991 Mexico-Chile FTA includes such a clause. Such accords are unlikely to form the basis for expansion of the EAI, however, as Mexico simply does not have the market power to play the pivotal role that the United States does.

[18] For example, when Argentina and the United States concluded such an agreement in 1941, Argentina automatically received all of the tariff concessions that the United States had made in the preceding two dozen agreements. Moreover, Argentina and the United States automatically extended to one another all of the concessions that they subsequently made to other parties.

[19] There are two marginal advantages that countries gain in their bilateral relations with the United States when they acceded to the GATT. First, the United States is legally obliged to extend an injury test in countervailing duty cases when the product in question is duty-free, and, second, the GATT signatory has the right to bring any trade disputes with the United States to a GATT dispute-settlement panel.

Chapter Six

U.S.-Chile Free Trade

Andrea Butelmann and Alicia Frohmann

An outward-oriented trade policy has been a top priority in Chile, both under the Pinochet regime and now under the Aylwin administration. Chilean authorities thus reacted quickly and enthusiastically to the Enterprise for the Americas Initiative (EAI). As a result of Chile's efforts and the U.S. administration's interest in making Chile a model for EAI-advocated economic reforms, Chile was the first country to benefit from the EAI's three components:

■ *Investment.* Chile was granted the first sectoral investment loan ($150 million) by the Inter-American Development Bank, under the program set up to support the EAI. Chile also submitted the first loan application to the Multilateral Investment Fund, even though the fund is not yet operational, pending U.S. congressional approval.

■ *Debt Reduction.* Chile was also the first country to benefit from the official bilateral debt-reduction program; the announcement of a $16-million reduction of Chile's concessional debt marked the first anniversary of EAI.

■ *Trade.* In September 1990, Chile signed a framework trade and investment agreement with the United States, and a bilateral working group was set up in June 1991 to deal with bilateral trade issues and clear the way for the eventual negotiation of a free trade agreement (FTA).

Of these three components, trade has received the greatest attention in Chile. The United States has been Chile's most important trading partner for several years (accounting for less than one-fifth of Chile's foreign trade),[1] which enhances the relevance of a FTA. On the other hand,

Chile is relatively insignificant as a trading partner to the United States, which brings to the forefront the political aspect of the negotiations. It is uncertain whether Chile will negotiate a bilateral FTA with the United States or whether it will join the North American Free Trade Agreement (NAFTA).[2] Either way, it will probably be the first EAI-eligible country to sign a FTA. So far, Chile is also the only instance where bilateral negotiations with a single country within the EAI have been contemplated and concrete steps toward it actually have been taken. During President Aylwin's official visit to Washington in May 1992, it was announced that Chile would be the first in line for a FTA after the NAFTA has been completed.

TRENDS IN CHILEAN TRADE POLICY

Chile adopted an import substitution strategy after the 1930s world depression. Despite some failed attempts at trade liberalization in the interim, Chile's trade policy became increasingly protectionist and cumbersome until 1973.

In 1973 the tariff mode was 90 percent, with a maximum tariff of 750 percent. Protection was buttressed by other barriers such as a 90-day noninterest bearing deposit worth 10 times of the value of the merchandise to be imported, licensing, prohibitions, and multiple exchange rates. This bundle of protectionist measures greatly distorted relative prices. However, because of the extensive use of nontariff barriers (NTBs), high tariff dispersion, numerous exemptions, and special regimes, tariffs as such were not important restraints on trade. Estimated tariff revenue with respect to import value did not exceed 26 percent for the late 1960s or early 1970s.[3]

From 1974 onward, a radical process of structural change took place. Trade policy was streamlined, and protection levels drastically reduced. Most nontariff barriers were eliminated at the outset, and tariffs were lowered in steps to a flat rate of 10 percent for practically every item by mid-1979. With the onset of the debt crisis, tariffs were again raised to reach a level of 35 percent in 1984, but the uniform tariff structure was not abandoned, and NTBs were not resurrected. Subsequently, tariffs have been gradually lowered to their present level of 11 percent.

Free trade has been widely accepted as an integral part of Chile's development model, and there is consensus that a return to protectionism is not a reasonable option. The latest proof of this consensus was the lack of opposition to the unilateral reduction of import duties from 15 to 11 percent, approved by the Chilean congress in mid-1991.

The goal of becoming an integral and active part of the international economy is helped by two factors: 1) the peaceful transition to democracy has improved Chile's international image, and 2) most other Latin American countries are also abandoning their inward-oriented policies and seeking to strengthen commercial relations with their hemispheric partners. Sensing a major opportunity to expand and diversify Chile's exports, Chilean authorities have sought to strengthen economic ties with their Latin American neighbors, with whom trade has not been particularly dynamic (Table 1).

In the past, Chile had entered into partial preferential agreements with every member of the Latin American Integration Association (LAIA),[4] each covering different products and margins of preferences. Recently, Chile has favored more effective agreements. LAIA contem-

TABLE 1. CHILEAN EXPORTS, IMPORTS, AND TRADE BALANCE ($ millions and percent)

	1974	1983	1987	1990
World				
Exports	2480.5	3835.5	5101.9	8580.3
Imports	1911.1	2968.8	3793.3	7023.4
Balance	569.4	866.7	1308.7	1556.9
Trade as percent GDP	30.8	46.1	52.0	71.7
United States				
Exports	286.1	1083.3	1140.5	1469.2
Imports	415.7	703.5	773.1	1373.4
Balance	-129.6	379.8	367.4	95.8
Share of total trade (percent)	16.0	26.3	21.5	18.2
Mexico				
Exports	22.7	1.3	2.8	57.7
Imports	29.9	16.9	44.0	100.8
Balance	-7.2	-15.6	-41.2	-43.1
Share of total trade (percent)	1.2	0.3	0.5	1.0
Canada				
Exports	64.7	60.4	71.1	56.2
Imports	39.9	60.9	66.4	224.3
Balance	24.8	-0.5	4.7	-168.1
Share of total trade (percent)	2.4	1.8	1.5	1.8
LAIA				
Exports	410.3	449.5	835.4	1014.3
Imports	627.8	762.0	950.2	1731.1
Balance	-217.5	-312.5	-114.8	-716.8
Share of total trade (percent)	23.6	17.8	20.1	17.6

Note: Numbers may not add due to rounding.

Source: Central Bank of Chile, *Indicadores de Comercio Exterior*, Santiago, several issues.

plates other modes of bilateral integration beyond simple tariff reduction including free trade areas and common markets under the Economic Cooperation Agreements (ACEs).

Framework Agreements

Since 1990, Chile has signed framework agreements prior to negotiating ACEs with Mexico, Venezuela, and Argentina. The agreements with Mexico and Argentina have been signed, and the negotiations with Venezuela are well under way.

MEXICO. The agreement with Mexico envisions the formation of a free trade area, with the elimination of most tariff and quantitative barriers to trade by the end of 1995. The first step will be to lower the maximum tariff to 10 percent in 1992; subsequently, all tariffs will be reduced in equal steps to zero. Some products (i.e, poultry, eggs, tobacco, wood and wood products, certain glass and ceramics products, and motor vehicles) will be put on a slower track of liberalization, while others (i.e., wheat, sugar, oil and oilseeds, certain dairy products, petroleum, apples, and cigarettes) will be permanently excluded from the process of tariff reduction unless a new round of negotiations takes place. With respect to rules of origin, the maximum input share acceptable from third countries is 50 percent for products that have no substantial transformation. The rule is less strict (i.e., allows lower domestic content) for the automobile industry.

The agreement includes safeguard provisions in case of injury to a particular industry or of balance-of-payments crisis. Injury caused by dumping or export subsidies will continue to be dealt with by means of domestic legislation in compliance with codes under the General Agreement on Tariffs and Trade (GATT). The administrative body created by the agreement will review pricing by public enterprises to avoid trade distortions.

With respect to services, some liberalization was achieved in maritime and air transport. Government purchases, technical standards,[5] and other barriers to trade in other service sectors will be the subject of continuing negotiations in the administrative body created by the agreement.

VENEZUELA. The agreement with Venezuela is expected to be similar to the one with Mexico, entailing an initial reduction in tariffs, but no ceilings in the tariff schedule. Before the agreement can be formalized, the problem of its compatibility with Venezuela's membership in the Andean Pact needs to be resolved. (See Alberto Pascó-Font and Sylvia Saborio in Chapter 9 of this volume.)

ARGENTINA. The agreement with Argentina is far less ambitious in terms of trade liberalization. It does not reduce any duties but merely ratifies existing tariff preferences and contains a standstill provision on existing NTBs. The possible extension of further preferences and the elimination of NTBs will be discussed in 1992. The agreement does, however, address a whole set of transborder issues not covered in the Mexican accord, including the movement of productive factors; tourism and transportation services; joint ventures in mining, agriculture, infrastructure, and energy; and mutual use of seaports for exports to third countries. Agreement was also reached on issues related to investment protection, national treatment for investment, expropriation, and repatriation of capital and profits. Mechanisms for dispute settlement were established as well.

OTHER COUNTRIES. Chile has also initiated consultations toward free trade arrangements with Bolivia, Colombia, Costa Rica, Ecuador, and Uruguay. For the time being, the intention is to broaden the scope of tariff preferences already in place.

Trade Patterns and Export Structure

The effect of the deep trade reforms of the 1970s on export performance was slow to emerge, partly because of the time required to adjust the productive structure, and partly because of the simultaneous appreciation of the real exchange rate in response to pre-debt crisis macroeconomic policies.[6] Nevertheless, as shown in Table 1, Chilean exports increased at high rates in the late 1980s. Their share in total gross domestic product (GDP) rose from 31 percent in 1974 to 71 percent in 1990.

One of the expected results of the liberalization process was increased export diversification and lessened dependence on mineral resources. Table 2 shows that export diversification has, indeed, advanced in the desired direction, but that dependence on mineral resources is still high and the percentage of value added to natural resources remains low. For example, in 1989, 32 percent of industrial exports still consisted of wood pulp and fishmeal.

PATTERNS OF TRADE WITH PROSPECTIVE NAFTA MEMBERS

Mexico and Canada

Chile's high specialization on natural resources is reflected in its exports to North America. Neither Canada nor Mexico has been an important trading partner for Chile, but Chile has been running a trade deficit with both countries over the last few years. Chile's trade with Mexico has

TABLE 2. CHILEAN EXPORT STRUCTURE (percent)

Period	Mining	Agriculture and Fishing	Industry
1960-1970	85.6	3.9	10.5
1971-1980	70.6	5.1	24.3
1981-1984	57.2	10.0	32.8
1985-1989	53.1	14.1	32.8

Source: Joaquín Vial, Andrea Butelmann, and Carmen Celedón, "Fundamentos de las políticas macroeconómicas del gobierno democrático chileno (1990-93)," *Colección Estudios CIEPLAN,* Vol. 30, Santiago, December 1990.

increased considerably: in 1990 bilateral trade was more than $150 million, and the FTA is expected to boost the trade flows between the two countries to $500 million in five years.

Canada has not been a significant trading partner in the past either. However, as a result of the increase in Canadian investment in the mining sector in recent years, Chilean imports from Canada have also grown, reaching $224.3 million in 1990. The potential for an increase in the Canadian supply of mining equipment, services, and technology is considerable, and both countries have drawn closer, signing a framework trade and investment agreement in June 1991. It is by no means obvious, though, that Canada or Mexico would be eager for Chile to join NAFTA.

United States

The United States is by far Chile's most important North American market. The significance of the U.S. market, however, has been shrinking lately with sluggish growth in the U.S. economy and Chile's decision to reduce its reliance on the United States as a market for copper exports after several (unsuccessful) claims of dumping against Chilean copper. Since the debt crisis, Chile has had a trade surplus with the United States as well as with the world as a whole. Exports to the U.S. market are a good example of Chilean efforts at export diversification: foods and feeds (mainly fruit, vegetables, and fish) far exceed the share of mining products in total U.S. purchases (Table 3).

The trading relationship of Chile and the United States is, of course, very asymmetrical: the United States is Chile's main trading partner, taking 17 percent of all Chilean exports, whereas Chile is the

TABLE 3. STRUCTURE OF MAIN U.S. IMPORTS FROM CHILE AND ACCESS CONDITIONS TO U.S. MARKET, 1990 (percent)

Product Group (share of total imports)	
Foods and feeds	49.9
Agricultural materials	4.5
Coal and petroleum	0.7
Ores and metals	21.2
Manufactures	14.2
Nonclassified	9.6
Access Conditions to U.S. Market[a] (share of total imports)	
MFN duty-free imports	40.2
GSP duty-free imports	11.2
Tariff-paying imports	48.8
Weighted Tariff Rates	
Foods and feeds	2.14
Agricultural materials	0.75
Coal and petroleum	0.47
Ores and metals	0.86
Manufactures	8.63
All goods	2.50
Imports Paying Tariffs of 5 Percent or Higher	14.9
Nontariff Barrier Coverage Ratio	24.0

Note: Numbers may not add because of rounding.

[a]These are the conditions of access had Chile been in the GSP in 1990, given the structure of exports of that year. Had Chile been included in GSP in 1990, it would have encountered an average tariff of only 2 percent, with over half of Chilean exports entering the United States duty-free.

Sources: U.S. Bureau of Census, *U.S. Imports of Merchandise* (Washington, DC: U.S. Department of Commerce, 1990); and Refik Erzan and Alexander Yeats, Chapter 4 of this volume.

34th-ranked trading partner for the United States, absorbing only 0.4 percent of U.S. exports. This asymmetry is important when considering each country's interest in pursuing a FTA.

TRADE ISSUES. After Chile's transition to democracy in 1990, most lingering difficulties in U.S.-Chilean relations pertained to commercial issues: protection of intellectual property rights by Chile, the U.S. exclusion of Chilean products from Generalized System of Preferences (GSP) treatment for alleged violations of worker rights, marketing orders for Chilean fruit, and the U.S. embargo on Chilean fresh produce after the poisoned-grape case.

Some of these issues were settled—i.e., Chile regained GSP benefits—and others became less dramatic as both sides tried hard to reach a compromise. This was especially true after the U.S.-Chilean Framework Agreement on Trade and Investment was signed, and a bilateral council was set up to address these issues.

The council in turn created a bilateral working group to study the feasibility of a FTA was set up in June 1991 and has met several times since then. The U.S. government has officially announced its intentions of negotiating an agreement with Chile, but not until the North American Free Trade Agreement is completed. Informal negotiations have in fact already started in as much as the working group's task is precisely to identify and study problem areas that might arise in FTA discussions. By the time formal negotiations begin, many technical issues will have been, if not settled, at least clearly identified.

TARIFFS. In 1990 the average U.S. tariff was 3.3 percent with some escalation toward more processed goods. In the case of Chilean exports, the average tariff was even lower.[7] The main reasons for this lower average tariff are Chile's strong comparative advantage in natural resources and its long distance from the main markets, which often makes the transportation of unprocessed goods cheaper. Accepting the importance of these variables, an analysis of the degree of tariff escalation is useful for identifying sectors that might benefit from its elimination.

We examined the incidence of tariff escalation on Chile's main natural resource exports: copper, fruits and vegetables, and fish and forest products (Table 4). On the whole, U.S. tariff escalation does not seem to be a major deterrent to the export of processed goods. The escalation for fruits and vegetables is important, but its elimination would not drastically change the structure of Chilean exports because comparative advantage resides in the ability to ship fresh produce to the U.S. market during the winter.

The figures in Table 4 are strongly influenced by export structure. Had tariffs not been weighted by actual trade—which is heavily concentrated in the lower tariff items—tariff escalation would be much more pronounced. For example, fruit jams and preserves face tariffs in the range of 20 to 35 percent but are not taken into account because Chile does not export them.

In preliminary interviews with producers, tariff escalation does not appear to be a major problem; technical barriers are a more frequent complaint. Transportation costs and distance from the client are additional sources of concern, particularly for custom-made articles.

NONTARIFF BARRIERS. Although tariff barriers are not a major problem, nontariff barriers such as quotas and variable duties do affect trade between developed and developing countries. Nevertheless, accord-

**TABLE 4. TARIFF ESCALATION ON CHILEAN EXPORTS
TO THE UNITED STATES** (percent)

Commodity	Tariff Rate		Percent of Total Exports To U.S.
	Most Favored Nation	Generalized System of Preferences	
Copper			
Unrefined, refined	1.00	1.00	15.63
Alloys, bars, rods, plates	1.20	0.00	1.57
Articles of copper	3.60	0.00	0.02
Fruits and Vegetables			
Fresh fruit and vegetables	1.20	1.00	31.30
Prepared fresh fruit and vegetables	10.80	10.62	4.06
Fish			
Raw fish	0.20	0.03	9.47
Prepared	5.10	0.08	0.72
Fish meal	0.00	0.00	0.44
Wood			
Wood	1.10	0.00	2.31
Raw wood	0.00	0.00	1.56
Plywood	1.48	0.00	0.48
Articles of wood	6.80	0.00	0.27
Wood pulp	0.00	0.00	0.58
Paper	4.80	0.00	0.04
Wood furniture	3.20	0.00	0.68

Source: U.S. Bureau of Census, *U.S. Imports of Merchandise* (Washington, DC: U.S. Department of Commerce, 1990).

ing to UNCTAD data, Chile does not face very significant NTBs.[8] Some 24 percent of all Chilean exports are affected by NTBs; 87 percent of these are seasonal tariffs. Most seasonal rates are imposed on products that enjoy duty-free entry in the U.S. low growing season and very low rates in the high season.[9] The rest of the exports affected by NTBs are subject to specific excise taxes or antidumping duties.

UNCTAD does not consider the marketing order restrictions as a NTB because the quality standards they impose apply to domestic as well as to foreign produce. From the Chilean perspective, marketing orders are intended to protect U.S. growers because the same standards do not apply off-season. That they may be used as a protectionist measure was confirmed by a recent directive to the U.S. Department of Agriculture to obtain "advice and concurrence" from the U.S. Trade Representative (USTR) before subjecting certain imported fruit to quality inspection.[10]

At the moment, marketing orders affect few Chilean fruit exports because they are only applied during the U.S. harvest season. However, as technological advances make more Chilean lands suitable for fruit growing, the productive seasons in both countries will increasingly overlap.

The elimination of all technical NTBs is not a realistic goal for a U.S.-Chilean FTA, though Chile would like to obtain a strict distinction between health and environmental regulations and quality regulations. Marketing orders are not justified by health standards, so consumers should be free to choose the price-quality combination of the goods they buy. But, if marketing orders cannot be eliminated altogether, then the United States should agree to quality checks at Chilean ports and a freeze on the period when marketing orders apply.

Finally, some barriers affecting Chilean exports are not even included in the UNCTAD inventory. The main example is cheese, for which U.S. import quotas are allocated among suppliers according to historic trends; because Chile is not a traditional supplier, it gets no quota share and its potential exports are not taken into account in UNCTAD's list of exports affected by NTBs.

ISSUES FOR U.S-CHILEAN NEGOTIATION

Tariffs

Except for agriculture, no real opposition has emerged in Chile to a zero duty rate for U.S. products. The private sector's main concern is that it have adequate input to the negotiating process. On some agricultural commodities, Chile applies a variable tariff to reduce price variability, which largely results from the distorting agricultural policies of developed countries. Some observers expect these products—wheat, oilseeds, cooking oil, and sugar—to be excluded from the negotiation of a FTA and folded into an eventual Uruguay Round agreement.

Drawbacks

If the Canada-United States Free Trade Agreement (CAFTA) is any guide, both export subsidies and drawbacks would be banned under a U.S.-Chile FTA. Although Chile does not have direct export subsidies, it does have duty drawbacks, some of them similar to export subsidies. A standard drawback system operates in Chile for medium and large exporters who must certify the percentage of imported inputs used in their exports. Small producers of nontraditional exports have a simplified program, however, by which they receive a rebate on a percentage of their exports, irrespective of their imported content. This simplified program is considered by trading partners to be an export subsidy and is likely to be a contentious issue in the FTA negotiation.

Nontariff Issues

A FTA with the United States would involve negotiations in many areas affecting trade flows directly or indirectly, besides tariffs. First are the "traditional issues," including government procurement, subsidies, and other practices codified in the Tokyo Round of multilateral trade negotiations (MTNs). Then there are the "new issues," including investment, intellectual property rights, and trade in services. Finally, there are the "emerging issues" that have arisen in the context of FTAs among countries at different stages of development, notably environmental standards and labor rights.

TRADITIONAL ISSUES. Chile is basically an open economy and quite disciplined in its trade policy, but in a few areas Chile has not made a full commitment to international competition (Table 5). Chile has not yet signed the codes on government procurement, antidumping measures, and customs valuation, for instance, although its domestic legislation in those areas does not differ substantially from the GATT obligations, and Chile has tabled an offer in the Uruguay Round to sign the three codes. That would greatly reduce the scope for disagreement on those issues.

NEW ISSUES. The salient topics for negotiation are:

■ *Investment.* In 1974 Chile opened its economy to foreign investment. Legislation in this area is based on general principles of national treatment and right of establishment. There are no performance requirements and no restrictions on profit remittances, although capital cannot be

---

TABLE 5. FOREIGN TRADE AND EXCHANGE RATE REGIMES IN CHILE, 1991

Foreign Trade Regime	
Tariff rate	11%
Variable duties	Limited
Quantitative restrictions	None
GATT Codes	
Antidumping	Nonsignatory
Customs valuation	Nonsignatory
Government procurement	Nonsignatory
Exchange Rate Regime	Managed float/ Foreign exchange controls

Source: CIEPLAN, Santiago, Chile, 1991.

repatriated before three years. This restriction might have to be negotiated in the context of a FTA.

■ *Services.* The Chilean and U.S. governments are exchanging information on barriers to trade in services and restrictions on right of establishment. Few restrictions on the provision of services have been detected so far, although there is a prohibition on foreign ownership of broadcasting radio and television stations.

With respect to transportation, there is a set-aside for Chilean vessels of under 900 tons in the case of intercoastal transport and freedom of entry for international maritime and air transport, based on reciprocity. No other direct restrictions seem to exist on the freedom of foreign companies to supply services except those related to the validation of foreign professional degrees, the terms and conditions of work visas, and, in some sectors, the proportion of foreign workers that can be employed.

■ *Intellectual Property Rights.* Protection of intellectual property has been a source of conflict in U.S.-Chile trade relations for some time. The United States has been particularly concerned about the lack of protection for pharmaceuticals. Chile's recent law on intellectual property rights does not fully satisfy the United States because it provides patent coverage for only 15 years and is not retroactive. Therefore, medicines coming onto the Chilean market in the near future will not be covered because the original patent will have been obtained abroad before the law was enacted in Chile. This issue might be left out of a U.S.-Chile FTA, considering that it was not included in the CAFTA, that Chile has already made significant progress in this area, and that intellectual property rights are being discussed in the Uruguay Round.

EMERGING ISSUES. The main focus will be:

■ *Environment.* Environmental issues are likely to come up in bilateral negotiations. Environmental conditions are poor in various areas (industry, mining, sewerage, and air pollution), and an environmental consciousness is just beginning to emerge in Chile. The Aylwin administration is beginning to address these problems but faces the usual dilemma regarding developmental priorities and lack of resources. If environmental issues are included in the negotiations, Chile would probably have to try much harder for progress in this area. People, both in and out of government, view this constraint with mixed feelings. Some Chilean environmental groups argue that the overall environmental impact of the FTA is dubious because the benefit from debt-for-nature swaps, the environmental tool of the EAI, is likely to be small compared to the environmental damage of the FTA caused by increased trade and investment. Some industries are reluctant to accept U.S. environmental standards that might compromise their operations. On the other hand, others argue that U.S. pressure and, eventually, support might help clean up the environment and improve Chilean standards in the future.

■ *Workers' Rights.* There has been a dramatic improvement of labor conditions in Chile under the Aylwin administration, and today workers' rights meet international standards. The United States has acknowledged as much in restoring Chile's GSP benefits. Therefore, this should not be a contentious issue in the FTA negotiations.

CONCLUSIONS

Entering into a trade agreement with the United States would have direct and indirect economic implications for Chile. The direct effects include the increase in trade flows, and possibly investment, induced by the agreement. The indirect benefits refer to the role that such an agreement can play in signaling Chile's commitment to free trade and a market economy.

The direct economic impact on Chile has not yet been assessed. An increase in exports is to be expected from the tariff reductions and from the resolution of disputes on nontariff barriers under the FTA. Studies thus far detect only modest direct trade effects. For instance, Refik Erzan and Alexander Yeats estimate that the removal of U.S. tariffs would expand Chilean exports by only about 2.8 percent. (See Erzan and Yeats, Chapter 4 of this volume.) These results are not surprising considering that Chilean exports to the United States currently face low levels of protection, and that most such studies fail to capture the potential increase in sales of products not currently exported because of high trade barriers.

The main goal of Chile's present commercial policy is to raise the value-added of its natural resource exports. Although tariff escalation in the United States is not so steep that it impedes exports of more processed goods, the elimination of tariff escalation in some subsectors would further that goal. Moreover, the purpose would be not only to reduce present tariff escalation but also to prevent future increases in the level of U.S. protection. This point should not be underrated, as prospects dim that the Uruguay Round will reverse protectionist trends.

Free trade areas convey welfare costs as well as benefits, depending on the amount of trade diversion they might cause. Although the United States is Chile's single most important trading partner, it currently absorbs less than one-fifth of all Chilean exports. An 11 percent margin of preference for a country like the United States, could cause significant trade diversion.

The potential for trade diversion also depends on the stringency of the rules of origin, which impose an additional element of discrimination against third parties. They might also harm Chile's international competitiveness by making it very costly for Chilean companies to produce goods using imported inputs from certain countries depending on the export market.

The indirect economic effects of the FTA are expected to be as important as its direct benefits. The government believes such an agreement would send a positive signal of Chile's commitment to free trade and a market economy to the domestic business community and international investors. It would show that democracy is good for business because it offers continuity and stability and legitimizes market liberalization policies.

Discussions about the eventual benefits and costs posed by the FTA have been low profile and mostly among government officials, apprehensive that a more public and vocal debate might inflate expectations and jeopardize the negotiations.

According to opinion polls, the Chilean public favors a FTA. Labor has not yet developed with an official position but does not seem to be strongly opposed. Chilean workers have already paid the cost of liberalizing the economy, and increased trade and investment would probably bring about more and better jobs.

Some political sectors, both on the right and the left, have argued that Chile should seek economic integration with other Latin American countries, and not just with the United States. Although the Aylwin administration has made important strides toward establishing close trade links with other countries in the region, it has not joined any of the subregional groupings, such as the Southern Cone Common Market (Mercosur) or the Andean Pact.[11] The policy has been, instead, to seek special trade relationships with as many countries as possible to enhance Chilean trade prospects, without viewing them as mutually exclusive alternatives. From this perspective, a FTA with the United States seems compatible with trade arrangements with other Latin American countries.

An issue hardly discussed in Chile is how a FTA with the United States (or Venezuela for that matter) would affect Chile's prospects of joining Mercosur. Because Mercosur is a prospective common market constituted under the LAIA legal framework, it must admit any other LAIA member that wishes to join. The Mercosur countries have agreed that applications by third countries will not be considered until five years after the agreement goes into force. Until then, applications will be considered only from countries that are not parties to any other regional or extraregional integration arrangement. Chile is the only LAIA country that presumably meets this condition, though that depends on how "integration" is defined. At present, only about 10 percent of Chilean exports go to Mercosur, but it is clearly a market of great potential as trade barriers are lowered and these economies become more stable. At the moment, Chilean authorities feel comfortable with a wait-and-see attitude, pending definition of the level and structure of Mercosur's common external tariff and the region's success in attaining macroeconomic stability. Although Chile is not considering joining a market that is highly unstable and might raise tariffs on its extraregional imports, clearly Mercosur is an alternative the Chilean authorities cannot ignore.

An important indirect benefit for Chile from the EAI would hinge on the extent to which it produces trade liberalization regionwide. The inclusion of other Latin American countries in a U.S.-centric FTA would increase competition for Chilean exports to the United States but would also open up markets where Chile faces higher barriers than in the United States. And Chile would not have to make a commitment to a common external tariff, as it would upon joining Mercosur or the Andean Pact.

Most discussions about a FTA with the United States focus only on the increased possibilities for Chilean exports. The most important Chilean business associations favor the FTA and have begun lobbying for the FTA in the United States. Exactly what the benefits would be and which sectors would gain the most are not yet clear. The main Chilean exporters to the United States (public mining sector, fruit exporters) think it would be difficult to increase their U.S. market share, with or without a FTA, and that, paradoxically, the negotiation of a bilateral agreement may bring to the fore conflicts that might not otherwise have surfaced. For example, the issue of poor environmental conditions in public mining operations might come up in negotiations, or powerful California fruit growers might suddenly feel threatened by Chilean exports and press for more severe NTBs. In fact, the best prospects for export growth seem to lie in sectors that are not currently important but would benefit from tariff reductions on goods with higher value-added content.

Little attention has been given to the possible effects of increased imports from the United States on the Chilean economy. Because duties are already low and uniform, fears of being flooded by American goods and services have not yet surfaced. Traditional agriculture is the only sector with apprehensions about the possible elimination of variable duties on wheat, sugar, and oilseeds.

In sum, Chile's trade policy consists of a combination of unilateral liberalization, bilateral trade agreements, and multilateralism. A free trade agreement with the United States is seen as an important vehicle to brighten Chile's international image. Much more so than a further reduction in its already low tariffs, a FTA with the United States would be a clear signal to the international business community that Chile is well on its way to becoming a modern economy with stable and transparent trade and investment rules. Bilateral agreements with neighboring countries serve a different but related purpose within Chile's overall trade strategy. They provide preferential access to those markets for Chilean products and a shield against future restrictions if the Uruguay Round fails, or if the process of all-out trade liberalization in those countries cannot be sustained. Such agreements do not compromise in any way Chile's trade policy toward the rest of the world and may well help to crystalize the vision of a hemisphere-wide free trade area, in which Chile has a strong vested interest.

Notes

[1] However, in 1991, for the first time Chilean exports to Japan surpassed its exports to the United States.

[2] The North American Free Trade Agreement (NAFTA) includes the United States, Canada, and Mexico.

[3] See P. Meller, "La Apertura Comercial Chilena: Lecciones de Política" (BID Seminar, Santiago, Chile, December 1991).

[4] The Latin American Integration Association (ALADI in Spanish) includes Argentina, Bolivia, Brazil, Chile, Colombia, Ecuador, Mexico, Paraguay, Peru, Uruguay, and Venezuela.

[5] An agreement on health standards for trade in fresh produce has been signed.

[6] Between 1974-76 and 1981, the average real exchange rate shifted from 232 to only 149 Chilean pesos per U.S. dollar. This represents a real appreciation of the peso of nearly 56 percent over the five-year period.

[7] The weighted tariff that Chilean exports faced during 1990 was only 2.5 percent. Had Chile been included in GSP in 1990, the same structure of exports would have encountered an average tariff of only 2 percent, with over half of Chilean exports entering the United States duty-free.

[8] See Erzan and Yeats, Chapter 4 of this volume.

[9] For 1990, the average ad valorem equivalent rate during the high season was as follows: 0.6 percent for grapes, 3 percent for pears and quinces, 0.6 percent for peaches, and 1.5 percent for plums.

[10] See Allen R. Wastler, "Compromise Reached on Fruit Import Bill," *The Journal of Commerce*, (October 18, 1990). The compromise was strongly supported by the Port of Philadelphia, which handles 70 percent of U.S. fruit imports from Chile.

[11] The Southern Cone Common Market (Mercosur) is a newly created trade area (prospective common market), including Argentina, Brazil, Uruguay, and Paraguay. The Andean Pact includes Bolivia, Colombia, Ecuador, Peru, and Venezuela.

Chapter Seven

U.S.-Central America Free Trade

Sylvia Saborio

Like many others in Latin America, the countries of Central America greeted the idea of a hemisphere-wide free trade area with a mixture of excitement, skepticism, and trepidation. Excitement about the prospect of forming part of a larger and more prosperous region. Skepticism about the actual benefits that the region might derive from such an enterprise. And trepidation about the dramatic adjustments that the adventure would imply. Closer analysis suggests that all those sentiments are indeed justified.

The concept of a hemispheric union has an inherent appeal for countries that have long sought to overcome the disadvantages of small size through integration. Indeed, the Central American Common Market (CACM)[1] was created in 1960 exactly for that purpose. As it happened, the CACM flourished in the 1960s during the "easy" stage of import substitution, foundered in the 1970s under the combined weight of external shocks and the CACM's own structural deficiencies, and practically perished in the 1980s under the strain of the financial and political crises that enveloped the region in those years. Thus, these countries also know well the perils of trying to build strength by pooling weaknesses.

This chapter refers to Central America as a "region." Except in a purely geographic sense, this is probably an exaggeration. There have always been, and still are, significant differences—political, economic, social—among the countries of Central America. Today, as in the past, centrifugal as well as centripetal forces are at work in the region. To be sure, today's rhetoric is more integrationist than it has been in years, and indeed, concrete measures are being taken to reinvigorate regional cooperation. Yet at the same time, each country is taking steps on its own to transcend the confines of the isthmus.

This ambivalence is most evident in the Central American countries' response to the Enterprise for the Americas Initiative (EAI) and the myriad overtures for preferential trade agreements it has unleashed. The appearance of being no longer confined to a choice between going it alone or joining their immediate neighbors is weakening regional resolve: the prospect of hitching on to more glamorous partners is seductive. In the end, this opening may be only a mirage and in due time these countries will recognize the wisdom or the need to return to the regional fold, even if only to attain their ultimate goal of joining others. In the meantime, such ambivalence creates some ill will and much confusion about where these countries really want to go and how they intend to get there.

CENTRAL AMERICA'S TRADE PROFILE

The pattern of trade relations within the region and with the rest of the world provides a useful background for the analysis of the implications of trade liberalization for Central America (Tables 1–4).

Open Economies

The Central American economies are quite open: the ratio of merchandise trade (exports plus imports) to gross domestic product (GDP) currently ranges from a low of 40 percent in Guatemala to a high of 80 percent in Costa Rica, while the ratios for El Salvador, Honduras, and Nicaragua cluster around the regional average of 50 percent.

Trading Patterns

The United States is Central America's main trading partner. It is the dominant export market for all categories of exports from the region, with the exception of manufactures (other than textiles and apparel), which are directed primarily at other countries in the region (60 percent) and elsewhere in Latin America (20 percent). The United States is also Central America's dominant supplier of all categories of imports except fuels, where Venezuela (50 percent) and Mexico (20 percent) dominate, and motor vehicles, which come mainly from Japan (44 percent). Overall, the United States accounts for some 43 percent of the region's two-way trade.

TABLE 1. CENTRAL AMERICA'S EXPORTS BY REGION ($ millions and percent)

Country/Year	World ($ millions)	The Americas					Rest of World		
		United States	Canada	Mexico	Central America	Other Latin America and Caribbean	European Community	Japan	Other
Central America									
1980	4,465	35.7	0.4	0.6	25.4	3.4	23.0	3.1	8.4
1990	4,555	43.0	3.4	1.4	14.6	4.3	21.5	3.2	8.5
Costa Rica									
1980	1,032	34.9	0.4	0.6	26.7	7.8	22.6	0.8	6.2
1990	1,446	46.0	3.9	1.0	9.2	6.2	27.0	1.1	5.6
El Salvador									
1980	720	29.7	0.9	0.1	41.1	1.4	14.5	4.8	7.6
1990	594	39.0	2.5	0.8	28.3	3.6	22.7	1.1	2.1
Guatemala									
1980	1,486	28.7	0.5	1.2	27.2	2.0	24.6	3.3	12.5
1990	1,299	41.2	1.4	3.1	22.9	4.8	16.0	2.2	8.5
Honduras									
1980	813	53.1	0.1	0.1	10.3	3.1	23.8	4.2	5.4
1990	954	53.5	1.2	0.1	3.2	2.7	18.0	8.2	13.2
Nicaragua									
1980	414	38.7	0.4	0.0	18.2	1.5	31.3	3.1	6.8
1990	262	5.3	21.2	1.9	13.1	1.6	28.4	6.2	22.2

Source: United Nations Statistical Office, *U.N. COMTRADE Data Base*, New York.

TABLE 2. CENTRAL AMERICA'S IMPORTS BY REGION ($ millions and percent)

Country/Year	World ($ millions)	The Americas					Rest of World		
		United States	Canada	Mexico	Central America	Other Latin America and Caribbean	European Community	Japan	Other
Central America									
1980	6,022	33.0	1.6	3.7	18.3	20.0	10.7	7.8	4.92
1990	6,786	42.0	1.2	5.9	10.5	12.6	11.4	5.9	10.60
Costa Rica									
1980	1,596	34.5	2.2	6.1	13.8	16.2	10.5	10.8	5.97
1990	2,014	40.8	1.5	3.7	7.3	17.3	10.9	8.4	10.01
El Salvador									
1980	976	25.2	1.5	1.5	32.8	20.9	9.6	4.4	4.08
1990	1,350	45.3	1.0	7.9	18.2	7.4	10.8	3.4	5.95
Guatemala									
1980	1,559	33.7	1.2	4.4	10.0	24.1	13.0	8.3	5.35
1990	1,739	41.4	1.0	8.0	9.6	12.3	13.2	5.1	9.35
Honduras									
1980	1,009	42.2	1.8	2.2	10.3	17.9	10.8	9.9	4.94
1990	1,180	52.5	0.8	5.6	7.6	9.4	7.7	5.6	10.84
Nicaragua									
1980	882	27.5	1.2	2.0	33.9	21.0	7.9	3.2	3.19
1990	504	14.8	2.0	2.1	12.4	15.8	17.7	6.0	29.19

Source: United Nations Statistical Office, *U.N. COMTRADE Data Base*, New York.

TABLE 3. CENTRAL AMERICA'S EXPORTS BY COMMODITY AND REGION ($ millions and percent)

Commodity/Year	World ($ millions)	The Americas					Rest of World		
		United States	Canada	Mexico	Central America	Other Latin America and Caribbean	European Community	Japan	Other
Total									
1980	4,465	35.7	0.4	0.6	25.4	3.4	23.0	3.1	8.4
1987	3,670	42.1	1.6	0.4	14.1	4.6	23.7	3.6	9.9
1990	4,555	43.0	3.4	1.4	14.6	4.5	21.5	3.2	8.5
Coffee and Bananas									
1980	1,874	46.9	0.8	0.0	0.4	0.3	40.1	3.9	7.8
1987	1,947	47.9	1.8	0.0	0.2	0.2	33.9	4.2	11.8
Other Food Products									
1980	1,342	66.1	0.1	0.2	13.5	1.5	14.6	0.8	3.1
1987	1,354	57.8	1.4	0.1	7.9	2.0	20.1	0.5	10.1
Other Primary									
1980	575	7.9	0.4	1.2	5.9	2.9	37.9	9.5	34.2
1987	245	25.6	0.1	5.0	12.3	10.4	20.2	17.0	9.4
Clothing and Textiles									
1980	259	5.9	0.1	0.1	85.7	4.2	3.6	0.1	0.4
1987	146	55.0	1.8	0.2	36.5	3.2	3.1	0.0	0.3
Other Manufactures									
1980	867	8.3	0.1	1.8	77.1	10.1	2.0	0.1	0.5
1987	546	18.1	0.4	0.5	59.1	18.9	1.5	0.1	1.3

Sources: United Nations Statistical Office, *U.N. COMTRADE Data Base*, New York; 1987 and 1988 data are based on SITC, Rev. 2; and International Monetary Fund, *DOT: Direction of Trade Statistics* (Washington, DC: International Monetary Fund).

TABLE 4. CENTRAL AMERICA'S IMPORTS BY COMMODITY AND REGION ($ millions and percent)

Commodity/Year	World ($ millions)	The Americas					Rest of World		
		United States	Canada	Mexico	Central America	Other Latin America and Caribbean	European Community	Japan	Other
Total									
1980	6,022	33.0	1.6	3.7	18.3	20.0	10.7	7.8	4.9
1987	5,598	31.2	1.7	6.7	11.1	12.7	16.8	7.0	12.8
1990	6,786	42.0	1.2	5.9	10.5	12.6	11.4	5.9	10.6
Food									
1980	670	47.3	1.1	0.7	31.2	6.2	10.4	0.6	2.5
1987	601	48.3	1.6	2.1	17.9	6.7	16.6	0.2	6.6
Other Primary									
1980	182	43.6	9.2	5.6	16.6	6.6	7.2	4.8	6.3
1987	255	30.5	5.6	19.4	11.4	13.2	9.6	0.8	9.7
Mineral Fuels									
1980	1,133	4.1	0.0	6.4	2.0	86.8	0.3	0.1	0.3
1987	671	18.9	0.1	19.8	5.8	49.6	2.6	0.2	3.0
Machinery and Transport									
1980	1,292	40.9	1.1	2.6	4.8	4.2	15.5	23.3	7.8
1987	1,552	32.3	1.2	2.7	2.3	6.7	21.4	19.0	14.4
Other Manufactures									
1980	2,747	37.1	2.2	3.7	28.2	4.1	13.0	5.7	6.0
1987	2,520	29.8	2.1	5.5	16.3	7.8	18.6	3.7	16.1

Sources: United Nations Statistical Office, *U.N. COMTRADE Data Base*, New York; 1987 and 1988 data are based on SITC, Rev. 2; and International Monetary Fund, *DOT: Direction of Trade Statistics* (Washington, DC: International Monetary Fund).

The European Community (EC) absorbs some 20 percent of the region's exports (mainly coffee and bananas) and supplies around 11 percent of the region's import needs (mostly chemicals, machinery and transport equipment). Two-way trade with Japan and other industrial countries is relatively small: altogether, it only amounts to about 10 percent. Trade with the rest of Latin America, including Mexico, is quite asymmetrical, largely on account of fuel imports. Currently, Latin America absorbs about 6 percent of the region's exports and supplies around 19 percent of its imports.

Intraregional Trade Decline

Over the last decade, intraregional trade decreased dramatically. The severe payments crisis that rocked the region in the early 1980s, along with disruptions caused by civil unrest, led to a veritable implosion of trade among regional partners. Between 1980 and 1986 intraregional exports fell from 25 percent to only 10 percent of the total: this amounts to a drop of 63 percent in the dollar value of such exports. Since then, the share of intraregional exports has risen to around 15 percent of the total; but in value terms, they are still some 40 percent below their 1980 level. The ratio of intraregional to total imports also fell from about 18 percent in 1980 to around 10 percent. Unlike exports, however, the shift in procurement patterns (toward suppliers in the United States and Latin America) appears to be more permanent, as the share of intraregional imports has remained virtually unchanged since 1985. In 1990, the dollar value of intraregional imports was still 35 percent lower than in 1980.

Traditional Export Concentration

Despite efforts to promote and diversify exports, throughout the 1980s Central America's exports declined both in volume and in value and became increasingly concentrated along traditional lines. Several factors contributed to this outcome: the slump in primary commodity prices and recession-induced demand for those commodities; the collapse of the regional market, which wiped out a great deal of trade in manufactures; and supply constraints, partly related to the wars and partly to the lack of essential imports.

Country Differences

Important country differences color the regional picture. Costa Rica, for instance—less oriented to the regional market, with a more diversified export structure and a more aggressive export policy—increased the value of its exports by 40 percent during the 1980s. Honduras—whose exports consist basically of coffee and bananas to the United States and European markets and virtually does no trade with the rest of Central America—also managed to increase its exports marginally. Guatemala—despite a successful drive to increase its nontraditional exports to the U.S. market—was not able to compensate for the loss in regional sales and saw its exports decline by 13 percent. El Salvador's exports declined by 20 percent, owing to war and the collapse of the regional market, which used to take 40 percent of its exports. Finally, in Nicaragua, exports dropped by 40 percent as a result of war, the payments crisis, and the U.S. trade embargo.

This analysis reveals that the trade environment in the hemisphere is of utmost importance for the Central American countries: in the aggregate, the Americas constitute the market for over two-thirds of Central America's exports and the source of almost three-quarters of its imports. This generalization, of course, belies crucial differences in the relative importance of various trading partners in the hemisphere. Nevertheless, the idea of somehow consolidating and expanding the hemispheric market of over 700 million people and a combined GDP of $6.8 trillion boggles the mind. Before turning to the potential for trade expansion, trade liberalization—the premise on which this potential lies—is examined.

THE CHALLENGE OF TRADE LIBERALIZATION

Since the mid-1980s, most countries in Central America have been liberalizing their trade and payments regimes, not merely to excise the anti-export bias of their commercial policies but also to create a pro-export environment throughout the economy. This has entailed major changes in the management of the exchange rates—including the consolidation of multiple exchange markets and significant real depreciation of the currencies; considerable reductions in the degree of import protection via tariff cuts and removal of nontariff barriers (NTBs) (Table 5); and the establishment of several programs to promote nontraditional exports, ranging from tax exemptions and tax rebates to preferential credit allocations and reducing red tape surrounding export activities (Table 6).[2]

To be sure, not every country in the region undertook reforms with the same zeal or at the same time. Nevertheless, by the end of the decade a great deal of convergence in policies had occurred, as a result of their process of accession to the General Agreement on Tariffs and Trade (GATT), their structural adjustment programs with the World Bank, and reform programs sponsored by the United States Agency for International Development (USAID). The decline of political tensions in the region has also made possible joint actions in recent years. For instance, at their sum-

TABLE 5. FOREIGN TRADE AND EXCHANGE REGIMES IN CENTRAL AMERICA, 1991

	Costa Rica	El Salvador	Guatemala	Honduras	Nicaragua
Foreign Trade Regime					
Tariff range (percent)	10-50[a]	5-35	5-37[b]	4-35[c]	5-20[d]
Exchange Rate Regime	Managed float/ exchange controls	Independent float/ exchange controls	Independent float	Managed float/ exchange controls	Managed float/ exchange controls
Memorandum Items (1990)					
Gross domestic product	5,057	5,732	8208	4,522	1,954
($ millions, 1988 prices)					
Total external trade	4,072	2,583	3,300	2,158	1,071
($ millions, 1988 prices)					
External trade coefficient (percent)	80.5	45.1	40.2	47.7	54.8

Note: All countries have agreed to a tariff range of 5-20 percent by the end of 1994.

[a]Excludes a temporary surcharge of 2 percent and a levy of 1 percent on extra-regional imports.
[b]Excludes a surcharge of 3 percent on extra-regional imports.
[c]Excludes a general surcharge of 5 percent and an additional 10 percent on final products. The surcharges cover all imports, but Central America will be exempt as of 1992.
[d]Excludes a stamp tax of 3 percent and selective consumption taxes of up to 75 percent that act as import tariffs.

Sources: Economic and Social Progress in Latin America, 1991 Report (Washington, DC: Inter-American Development Bank, October 1991); and Exchange Arrangements and Exchange Restrictions, 1991 Report, (Washington, DC: International Monetary Fund, 1991).

TABLE 6. EXPORT PROMOTION MEASURES

Measure	Costa Rica	El Salvador	Guatemala	Honduras	Nicaragua
Free Trade Zones					None
Tax Exemptions					
Machinery and intermediate imports	100%[a]	100%	100%	100%	
Profits	100% (8 years) 50% (4 years)	100% (10 years extendable)	100% (12 years)	100%	
Local Market Sales	Up to 40% subject to approval	No limit subject to approval	Up to 20% subject to approval	No limit when no national production	
Drawback Industries					None
Tax Exemptions					
Machinery and intermediate imports	100%	100%	100%	100%	
Profits	100%[b]	100% (10 years)	100% (10 years)	100% (10 years)	
Local Market Sales	None	No limit subject to approval	No limit with payment of corresponding taxes	None	
Export Incentives	None	8% of value added	None	None	

TABLE 6. (Continued)

Measure	Costa Rica	El Salvador	Guatemala	Honduras	Nicaragua
Nontraditional Export Incentives[c]					
Tax Exemptions		None[d]			
Machinery and intermediate imports	100%		100%	100%	100%
Profits	100%[b]		100% (10 years)	100% (10 years)	80%
Tax Rebates	Up to 12% of FOB value[e]		None	None	15% of FOB value[f]
Requirements	35% minimum national value added		None	Generate at least 25 direct jobs	Export at least 25% of production

Notes: The figures for Nicaragua are from the proposed "Ley de Promocion de Exportaciones," which has not yet been approved. FOB indicates free on board.

[a]Normally there are no restrictions for imports to the zone, but raw materials or intermediate imports may be restricted if the Ministry of Industry determines that local products can meet the price, quality, and delivery conditions required by the import firms.

[b]In the case of registered foreign investments, a tax of 15 percent is charged when repatriating the profits.

[c]Guatemala and Honduras apply export taxes of 2 percent and 1 percent, respectively.

[d]The only nontraditional export incentive offered by El Salvador is a cash bonus of 8 percent of FOB value.

[e]Declines each year and disappears in 1997.

[f]Declines to 10 percent in 1993, 5 percent in 1995, and disappears in 1997.

Sources: ECLAC, "Politicas Industriales de Centroamerica y Panama," LC/MEX/R.310 (New York: United Nations, August 5, 1991); World Bank, *Trade Liberalization and Economic Integration in Central America*, Report No. 7625-CAM (Washington, DC: World Bank, 1990), pp. 29, 32; and the Ministry of Economy, Industry and Commerce, Costa Rica.

mit in El Salvador in July 1991, the presidents of Central America committed their countries to removing all obstacles to intraregional trade by 1992 and to reverting to a common external tariff schedule by the end of 1994 limiting tariffs on virtually all extra-regional imports to a maximum of 20 percent.[3]

Domestic Implications of Trade Reform

Presidential pronouncements notwithstanding, the trade liberalization process will be neither easy nor painless. Not only is there a well-entrenched clientele for protection and privilege among both old industrialists and new age entrepreneurs, but politicians and bureaucrats also will resent having to exercise more discipline in the management of economic affairs and having less leeway to dispense favors to their constituents.

Trade reform will have important domestic repercussions in three areas: import competition, export development, and macroeconomic management.

IMPORT COMPETITION. Improved resource allocation is, of course, a major goal of trade reform. In the industrial sector—where import protection has been the highest—rising competitive pressures will likely lead to the failure of inefficient firms. Considering the shocks the Central American economies experienced over the last decade, however, the most vulnerable firms have likely succumbed already, and most survivors of the debacle can probably withstand some additional competition in a more favorable economic environment. Many firms have not only withstood heightened domestic competition but have, in fact, become successful exporters to markets outside the CACM. Nevertheless, competitive pressures will mount as trade barriers continue to decline, and unemployment may rise, unless new job opportunities are created—presumably in export-oriented activities—to pick up the slack.

Much of the agricultural activity in these countries has been geared to export and stands to gain from trade reform. The main exception is grain production (rice, beans, maize) for domestic consumption. Resistance to competition in this area derives from three main sources: national security arguments about food self-sufficiency; the high social and political costs relative to the efficiency gain (grain production employs a large number of small farmers and peasants, but accounts for only a small share of agricultural value added); and finally, the fact that most other countries also protect their small farmers and do so for essentially the same reasons. Despite opposition, strides have been made to align domestic support prices to international prices, eliminate the wedge between producer and consumer prices, and remove quantitative restrictions on grain trade. The surge in nontraditional agricultural activities for export has presumably eased the transition in the countryside.

A third area where increased foreign competition is bound to raise thorny political questions is in the provision of essential services such as banking, insurance, electricity, and communications. For some time now, the Central American countries have been grappling with the issue of privatization of these services, many of which have been in the public domain. When the issue becomes no longer a matter of *private* ownership but *foreign* ownership of these essential services, political tensions can be expected to rise.

EXPORT DEVELOPMENT. Expansion of export activities will be crucial to generate job opportunities to absorb both the growth in the labor force and workers displaced by import competition and trimming in the public sector. Moreover, faced with continuing external financial constraints—due to lack of credit and limited capacity to assume further debts—these countries' access to imports will increasingly depend on their ability to generate export earnings. In turn, the expansion of their export capacity will depend largely on their ability to increase domestic savings (public and private) and to attract foreign direct investment in export-related activities.

Developing a viable export sector is not only a task for the private sector, however. Governments must help the process along, but in ways that are both effective and fiscally sound. Costa Rica's experience is instructive in this regard. A generous system of fiscal incentives was set up to promote nontraditional exports to markets outside the CACM. As a result, nontraditional exports have risen sharply at an average annual rate of nearly 28 percent over the last seven years. However, the incentive program is seriously flawed. First, it is not cost effective. A recent study by the International Monetary Fund (IMF) found that the direct cost of the export subsidy, not counting its administrative costs, amounted to $2.27 per $1.00 of additional net exports.[4] This is partly because the tax rebate is based on the gross value of exports, so that much of it ends up subsidizing imports instead. Second, export subsidies are not carefully calibrated. To the extent that they exceed the margin of support required to make an activity profitable and are not subject to a rapidly declining scale, they probably retard, rather than promote, industrial efficiency. Finally, as structured, incentives benefit particular exporters but do nothing to enhance the competitiveness of the export sector as a whole. The resistance to redressing such obvious flaws is an ominous sign that now as in the past, well-meaning, temporary arrangements, designed to serve some broad national purpose, threaten to become permanent transfer mechanisms to particular interest groups.

In light of these shortcomings and other countries' experience with export promotion,[5] export incentives should be overhauled. Export promotion should rely less on fiscal incentives and more on measures that enhance international competitiveness more directly such as improved physical infrastructure, more efficient transportation and communications services, better market information and quality control systems, streamlined customs administration, and adequate export finance. This would make sense not only from the standpoint of the sustainability of the export drive, allocative efficiency, and public finance, but also to reduce the susceptibility of exports to countervailing action in foreign markets.

MACROECONOMIC MANAGEMENT. Trade reform demands great discipline of governments. Trade liberalization implies that governments cannot deal with external imbalances by imposing direct import or exchange controls; they must adjust domestic activity and exchange rates instead. A compensatory devaluation of the currency is likely to be required to attenuate the import surge that might otherwise result from a reduction in import restraints. However, a faster pace of currency devaluation would result in severe inflationary pressures, unless the money supply were strictly controlled. Moreover, given the large external debt overhangs in these countries, currency devaluations would also exacerbate fiscal imbalances by increasing the local currency cost of debt service.

Indeed, grappling with the fiscal implications of trade reform will be one of Central America's most difficult issues. These countries have traditionally relied on trade taxes for a large share of their revenues, partly because taxing foreign transactions seemed less politically hazardous than taxing domestic activities and partly because trade taxes are easier to collect. Import duties currently represent between 20 percent and 40 percent of their total tax revenues. Deep tariff cuts could, therefore, have a potentially devastating impact on public finances. True, lower tariffs (if uncompensated by devaluation) would expand the import base, and potential contraband might come in legitimately instead. These effects are unlikely to prevent a sharp decline in import duty collections, however, because a large import expansion cannot be accommodated in the short term. Without a comprehensive tax reform that shifts the tax base to consumption or some other activity, trade liberalization could not be sustained in Central America.[6] For countries plagued by chronic fiscal deficits and a notoriously deficient capacity to set and collect taxes, this will be quite a challenge.

In sum, trade liberalization will require major changes in the domestic economy. At the microeconomic level, business incentives and attitudes must change. At the macroeconomic level, policies and institutions need overhauling. Transformations like these take time, but without them the liberalization process will ultimately fail.

Trade Liberalization and Regional Integration

Regional integration in the context of trade liberalization is not an unambiguous concept. It precludes the traditional notion of fostering industrial growth behind high tariff walls as the CACM attempted to do for years with only limited success. It is perfectly compatible, however, with the preferential elimination of barriers to intraregional trade, one of the region's most important tasks today. Indeed, efforts are under way to remove all trade and exchange restrictions on regional manufactures and, by the end of 1992, on agricultural trade as well, according to agreed price bands. Steps are also being taken to restore the region's payments clearing mechanism, the collapse of which in the 1980s helped to cut regional trade to a trickle.[7] Last, but not least, countries are now committed to preventing the kind of currency misalignments that played such havoc with regional trade and payments in the early 1980s. Such actions should go a long way toward restoring regional trade at least to its pre-crisis level.

Beyond liberalizing intraregional trade, Central American countries could usefully undertake joint actions to improve their competitiveness vis-à-vis the rest of the world, in areas where significant economies of scale would lower costs. For example, they could set up joint commercial offices, issue joint visas, and establish joint market information networks, distribution channels, inspection and quality control centers, and manpower training facilities. They could also seek to consolidate the region's financial markets to improve the quality and lower the cost of financial intermediation, establish a regional securities exchange, merge the national airlines into a regional carrier, and pool resources to strengthen the region's technological base to develop a competitive edge in areas other than low-wage, labor-intensive activities.[8]

In the process of liberalizing their trade regimes, countries will also need to undertake reforms in other areas such as taxation, investment, export promotion, and intellectual property protection. These reforms could be carried out independently, but harmonizing them would be far more efficient to prevent unnecessary (and unintended) distortions in the allocation of resources within the region.

A more pressing task for these countries will be to define the fundamental parameters of trade reform beyond 1994: its depth and pace, and whether it will be done individually or jointly, multilaterally or within particular preferential arrangements. Specifically, they will need to respond to the EAI and a host of other regional trade proposals.

A Grand Caribbean Basin?

First Mexico and Venezuela, then Colombia and the countries of the Caribbean Community (Caricom), have made overtures to Central

America for preferential trading arrangements.[9] Is it in the interest of Central America to pursue such arrangements? On purely economic grounds, the gains from signing separate agreements with those countries appear meager. The amount of trade involved is currently quite small, except for oil imports from Venezuela and Mexico. Because most of those countries have unilaterally liberalized their trade regimes, the potential margin of preference in those markets is also small. Thus, even though Mexico and Venezuela's proposals are cast in terms of "relative reciprocity"—whereby for a number of years Central America would receive greater market access than it extends in recognition of its lower level of development—such proposals on their own are unlikely to amount to much. They might even be counterproductive if they divert more trade than they create, or if tariffs are just swapped for intricate administrative mechanisms to handle "free trade" from different countries of origin.

From a broader perspective, this set of proposals outlines the contours of a "Grand Caribbean Basin" region. If trade among these countries were liberalized on a preferential but consistent basis, the region could become a building bloc for the larger hemispheric free trade area. As an intermediate step to that broader objective, regional integration could entail several advantages. First, it would expose countries to gradually rising levels of external competition until they become world class competitors. Second, it would help maintain the momentum for trade liberalization, especially if it will be a while before they (Mexico excepted) can aspire to enter into a full-fledged free trade agreement with the United States.[10] Finally, regional integration could expedite the negotiation of such an agreement by raising the stakes (and lowering the bureaucratic processing costs) of incorporating into a FTA an area that would be of only marginal economic interest to the United States even in the aggregate.

FREE TRADE WITH THE UNITED STATES?

It is probably fair to say that if Mexico and others were not trying to enter into free trade agreements with the United States, the Central American countries would have little interest in doing so. After all, they already have preferential access to the U.S. market for many products under the Generalized System of Preferences (GSP) and the Caribbean Basin Initiative (CBI). Moreover, these preferences are unilateral and, under the CBI, exclusive to a few small countries in the area.[11]

True, the CBI margin of preference (over the GSP) is small, and certain items of regional export interest are explicitly excluded from preferential treatment (notably textiles and clothing, footwear, leather goods, and canned tuna), while others are restricted under the arrangement (sugar, beef, veal, and ethanol). However, some items such as clothing assembled in the area receive certain preferences in terms of duty-assessment and guaranteed access levels to the U.S. market under production-sharing arrangements. These advantages—however small—appear to have been instrumental in attracting investment to the region when the economic and political climate was, to say the least, inhospitable.[12]

Unlike other countries in the Caribbean Basin, which receive preferences in the EC markets under the Lomé Convention and in the Canadian market through Caribcan, the attraction of Central America as an investment site rests almost exclusively on its preferential access to the U.S. market. Mexico's entry into the North American Free Trade Agreement (NAFTA) would erode such preferences. In addition, if Mexico obtained preferential access where Central America does not have it (e.g., for textiles and clothing), the region—and everyone else—would then face *negative* preferences on those products in the U.S. market.

With Mexico as a springboard for unrestricted entry into the U.S. and Canadian markets, Central America is rightly concerned lest whatever locational advantage it had to serve the North American market will disappear. Before the deal is even struck, anecdotal evidence is surfacing of prospective investors shelving plans to invest in Central America and going to Mexico instead, and of established investors reconsidering expansion plans or plant relocation. While a stampede is not likely, it is by no means out of the question, considering the footloose nature of many of these firms. But the greater worry is that new investment might not be forthcoming.

Because Central America already offers generous terms to investors in free trade zones and drawbacks and other export-related activities, these countries have little margin to make themselves more attractive.[13] They have all signed framework trade and investment agreements with the United States under the EAI. In addition, Costa Rica, sensing that it has much to lose from investment diversion, is about to sign a bilateral investment agreement with the United States to try to avert such losses.

In the trade arena, Mexico is a competitor for virtually every Central American export to the U.S. market. Preliminary estimates of the first-round effects of granting Mexico exclusive preferential access to the U.S. market suggest that, after Brazil, Central America would suffer the most trade diversion—nearly 20 percent of the total for the entire hemisphere (Erzan and Yeats, Chapter 4 of this volume). Although in absolute terms the diversion is not great, as trade follows investment, it would grow over time, if Mexico were *inside* and Central America remained *outside* the free trade area.

Aside from preventing trade diversion, what would Central America actually *gain* in terms of market access by entering into a free trade agreement with the United States? In the short run, apparently, not much. Currently, around 80 percent of U.S. imports from Central America enter the U.S. market duty free, either under most favored nation (MFN) preferences, GSP, or CBI. On the remaining 20 percent of dutiable imports, average tariffs are generally low, although particular items in such categories as apparel and footwear are protected by tariffs as high as 30 to 40 percent.

A summary of the main tariff and nontariff barriers to Central American exports in the U.S. market are presented in Table 7. As shown, the trade-weighted average tariff for the region as a whole is less than 2 percent, although this average conceals considerable differences between countries and among products. Nontariff barriers of various types affect some 15 percent of the region's exports to the United States. The incidence of such barriers is highest among food products (particularly in the form of health and safety regulations and flexible import fees), and textiles and apparel (mainly quotas and other quantitative restraints). As with tariffs, the incidence of NTBs varies considerably among countries and is far higher for Costa Rica, because of its more diversified export structure.[14]

These data show that access barriers to the U.S. market for Central American exports are low overall, except in highly sensitive areas—textiles and clothing, sugar, beef, and a few other agricultural products—where the United States may be extremely reluctant to grant additional market access. If such sectors were excluded, the FTA would not be a *free* trade agreement, and the benefits for Central America in terms of enhanced market access would be virtually nil. Even if such sectors were included, export expansion would be modest: the step increase in regional exports to the United States attributable to the removal of tariffs and the relaxation of NTBs (so that the full effect of the tariffs could be felt) has been estimated at only 7.6 percent (16.5 percent in the case of Costa Rica, which faces the highest barriers). (See Erzan and Yeats, Table 8, Chapter 4 of this volume.)

Considerations about assured *future* market access would also come into play in any free trade agreement with the United States. Indeed, one of the main reasons for a FTA with the United States is to preclude market closure, particularly through the arbitrary use of antidumping and countervailing actions by the United States. On the whole, the countries of Central America are probably too small and unimportant to invite such actions. Moreover, precisely to avoid harming these minuscule exporters when investigating such abuses by others, the 1989 amendment to the CBI legislation introduced separate cumulation rules for the determination of injury and the application of sanctions under U.S. trade remedy laws for these countries. Nevertheless, the concern about future access is genuine, particularly as these countries move into more "sensitive" exports. The question is whether a free trade agreement—or

TABLE 7. U.S. TRADE BARRIERS TO IMPORTS FROM CENTRAL AMERICA (percent)

	Costa Rica	El Salvador	Guatemala	Honduras	Nicaragua	Central America
Tariff Barriers[a]						
Foods and feeds	0.0	0.0	0.0	0.0	14.9	0.0
Agricultural materials	0.1	0.0	0.0	0.0	1.0	0.0
Coal and petroleum	0.4	0.0	0.7	0.4	0.0	0.6
Ores and metals	0.0	0.0	0.0	0.0	3.0	0.1
Manufactured goods	11.5	5.5	9.5	9.4	5.7	10.0
All goods	3.9	0.8	0.6	1.2	6.7	1.8
Nontariff Barriers[b]						
Fruits and nuts, fresh and dried	0.3	74.5	9.3	2.1	—	2.8
Other food products	78.2	67.5	64.9	59.8	—	69.2
Other primary, plus metals and minerals	23.8	0.0	0.0	0.0	—	11.3
Textiles and apparel	52.7	4.8	8.9	0.0	—	38.0
Other manufactures	6.6	5.7	3.6	0.7	—	5.0
All Goods	**26.2**	**7.0**	**11.4**	**11.6**	**—**	**15.0**
of which:						
Hard core nontariff barriers[c]	10.9	5.2	8.1	1.8	—	7.1

Note: NTB coverage figures for Nicaragua were not included because of distortions caused by the U.S. trade embargo. Data in Central America column are trade weighted.

[a]Average of 1989 tariff rates weighted by 1986 trade weights.
[b]NTB trade coverage ratio, using 1989 NTBs weighted by 1986 trade weights.
[c]Hard core NTBs consist of quantitative restrictions and flexible import fees.

Source: International Trade Division, World Bank, Washington, DC.

any other type of agreement, for that matter—can really protect weak countries from being harassed by far stronger trading partners.

Ultimately, the benefits to Central America from enhanced access to the U.S. market will depend critically on the region's ability to attract additional investment in export-oriented activities and to remove such obstacles to export growth as red tape and perverse incentives, inadequate financial and physical infrastructure, and defective quality control. Until such bottlenecks are removed, export expansion will continue to be constrained, regardless of market opportunities. In the end, the main benefits from a FTA are likely to be those derived from the improvement in these countries' own domestic policies; its main drawbacks are the considerable economic—and political—adjustment costs linked to the domestic reforms needed to gain admission to the FTA.[15]

CONCLUSIONS AND RECOMMENDATIONS

The countries of Central America might well have preferred the *status quo ante*, which offered them unilateral, though limited, preferences in the U.S. market. Now that Mexico and others are seeking preferential free trade agreements with the United States, they will also want to join for essentially defensive reasons, i.e., not so much for what they might gain, but for what they might lose by not joining. As nonmembers, Central Americans would not only face a competitive disadvantage in the U.S. market but would also suffer discrimination vis-à-vis the United States in other members' markets. The cost of exclusion from the FTA would be too high and would increase with every new entrant to the preferential trade area.

If Central America is to join the FTA, it would be to its advantage to do it sooner rather than later. This would minimize the cost of exclusion and prevent a temporary competitive disadvantage from becoming a permanent investment loss. The threat of investment diversion is imminent— indeed, it is already happening *in anticipation* of a successful NAFTA. Unfortunately, a full-fledged free trade agreement between the United States and Central America, which would avert such a threat, is not likely to happen any time soon. The United States has made it clear that it will not proceed with further agreements until the NAFTA has been completed and its effects evaluated. In any case, Central America is not yet ready to take on the rigors of full trade liberalization.

To bridge this gap, the United States should extend to the countries of Central America whatever preferential trade and trade-related benefits (beyond those provided by the CBI) it grants Mexico and others on an interim basis, say through 1995. During this period, Central American countries would not be required to undertake additional reciprocal obligations but would be expected to continue with domestic and trade reforms under agreements with the IMF, World Bank, Inter-American Development Bank (IDB), GATT, and USAID. Progress in the implementation of such reforms could be monitored in the context of the framework trade and investment agreements already in place with each of these countries. By 1995, both sides would agree to negotiate in good faith toward a full-fledged agreement to expand two-way trade.

Such a provision would temporarily protect these tiny economies from the unintended fallout of Mexico's entry into NAFTA, while providing a mechanism for transition from unilateralism to some type of reciprocity in U.S. commercial relations with these countries. This is no free ride, considering the obvious asymmetries involved and the enormity of the reforms these countries must undertake to become eligible for a FTA, relative to both the marginal adjustment required of the United States and their own limited capabilities. The cost to the United States would be virtually nil, because the Central American countries account for little more than 1 percent of total U.S. imports, and 80 percent of them are already duty free. Yet, it would give these countries both a strong incentive and a fighting chance to sustain the process of economic reform on which they have embarked.

Notes

[1] The Central American Common Market (CACM) includes Costa Rica, El Salvador, Guatemala, Honduras, and Nicaragua.

[2] For a more detailed account of these developments see Sylvia Saborio and Constantine Michalopoulos, "Central America at a Crossroads," World Bank Working Paper (forthcoming); also see Sylvia Saborio, "Central America," John Williamson, (ed.) *Latin American Adjustment: How Much Has Happened?* (Washington, DC: Institute for International Economics, April 1990).

[3] See *Declaración de San Salvador*, July 17, 1991.

[4] See Alexander Hoffmaister, "The Cost of Export Subsidies: Evidence from Costa Rica," IMF Working Paper, WP/91/94, Washington, DC, October 1991.

[5] See, for instance, Thomas Vinod and John Nash: "Reform of Trade Policy: Recent Evidence from Theory and Practice," *World Bank Research Observer*, Vol. 6, No.2 (July 1991), pp.219-40.

[6] The need for tax reform as a precondition to trade liberalization is not peculiar to Central America. See, for instance, Ziba Farhadian-Lorie and Menachem Katz: "Fiscal Dimensions of Trade Policy," IMF Working Paper WP/88/43, Washington, DC, May 18, 1988; and Mario I. Blejer and Adrienne Cheasty, "Fiscal Implications of Trade Liberalization," Vito Tanzi, ed., *Fiscal Policy in Open Developing Economies* (Washington, DC: International Monetary Fund, 1990).

[7] The regional payments arrangement required that any bilateral balance outstanding after the multilateral clearing in local currency be settled in dollars. Beginning in the late 1970s, Nicaragua ran up arrears with the clearing house. The mechanism faltered and finally collapsed in 1986. By then, trade in the region was limited to cash or barter terms.

[8] See Rudolf Buitelaar and Juan Alberto Fuentes, "The Competitiveness of the Small Economies of the Region," *CEPAL Review* No. 43 (April 1991), pp. 83-96.

[9] Framework agreements have been signed with Mexico and Venezuela and are being negotiated with Colombia and Caricom.

[10] See U.S. Trade Representative Carla Hills, "Toward a Dynamic New Era of Growth," Address before the Central American Conference on Trade and Investment, San José, Costa Rica, August 12, 1991.

[11] CBI-type preferences were extended to Bolivia, Colombia, Ecuador, and Peru through the Andean Trade and Preference Act, signed into law on December 4, 1991.

[12] Preferential access to the U.S. market appears to have been a critical factor in decisions by many textile producers in Asia, who had lost their GSP privileges and exhausted their textile quotas, to relocate their offshore assembly operations in Central America (and the Caribbean).

[13] For a fuller discussion of current investment and incentive measures in the region, see CEPAL, "Politicas Industriales de Centroamerica y Panama," LC/MEX/R. 310, August 5, 1991.

[14] The figures in Table 7 underestimate somewhat the current degree of U.S. market protection against Central American exports. They were calculated using 1986 trade weights; since then, Central America's "export bundle" has shifted quite considerably toward more highly protected items. Of course, had the protection been truly formidable, this could not have happened.

[15] The conditions for admission are spelled out in Carla Hills, Address, August 12, 1991, op. cit.

Chapter Eight

U.S.-Caricom Free Trade

DeLisle Worrell

Trade and international transactions remain the engines of growth for countries of the Caribbean Community (Caricom)[1] on the eve of the twenty-first century, as they have been for the last 500 years. Since World War II, these transactions have tended overwhelmingly toward a U.S.-Caribbean axis. This reflects the declining economic and political influence of the United Kingdom, which had been Caricom's most important source of imports and foreign exchange until the war.

Changes in Caricom production structures have reinforced economic ties to the United States. New products and activities such as oil, bauxite, tourism, and offshore services catering mainly to North America are displacing agricultural staples exported to the United Kingdom. The U.S. dollar has become the standard for external transactions of Caricom, and the United States is now the region's principal source of foreign direct investment.

The revolution in international transport and communications has brought the North American and Caribbean populations closer through tourism, migration, remittances, and capital transactions. The United States became the principal destination for Caricom migrants after the United Kingdom blocked free migration from the English-speaking Caribbean in the early 1960s. New financial techniques have drawn Caribbean money supplies into the U.S. dollar area by providing a means of avoiding exchange controls that were meant to insulate Caribbean monies.

Caricom's economic future is closely wedded to the economies of North America, however the institutional arrangements linking them may evolve. Changes from the current arrangements under the Caribbean Basin Initiative (CBI) and the Canada-Caribbean Agreements (Caribcan) to a free trade area are bound to affect the prospects for Caricom.

EXTERNAL ECONOMIC RELATIONS OF CARICOM

The United States dominates the external economic relations of Caricom. It is the largest source of tourists; the main market for oil, bauxite, manufacturing, and data services; the principal source of foreign direct investment; and the main source of remittances and other transfers. Most Caricom countries earn well over 50 percent of their foreign exchange from sales to the United States. The United States is, in turn, the main supplier of imports, as well as the main source of finance to the region.

The Caribbean derives most of its foreign exchange from tourism and other services such as international banking and data services (Table 1). Tourism and other services account for 48 percent compared to 44 percent for merchandise exports. The United States provides about 60 percent of tourists, buys nearly one-half of its exports, and supplies nearly two-thirds of its imports (Figure 1). Europe is a distant second, accounting for about 14 percent of tourists, accepting about 40 percent of merchandise exports, and supplying less than one-quarter of imports. Trade with Europe is on par with intra-Caricom transactions and tourist flows. Canada is the only other significant source of foreign exchange for Caricom countries.

The integration of Caricom into the U.S. market is even stronger than balance-of-payments data would indicate. The U.S. dollar is the principal transaction currency and the universal store of value in the Caribbean. Many non-U.S. transactions are denominated in U.S. dollars, and there is a preference for U.S. dollar-denominated financial and real assets. Economic links between the Caribbean community in the United States and the Caribbean population residing in the home islands are very strong—through migration, tourism, and the flow of remittances. Remittances account for more than 5 percent of foreign-exchange receipts, (see "transfers," Table 1). American multinational corporations (MNCs) have investments in Caricom countries in oil production and distribution, hotels, information services, shipping, export agriculture, and bauxite production.

The financial markets of Caricom countries are firmly linked to the United States because of the ease of travel and capital movements. Autonomous domestic monetary policy in the Caribbean is possible only for relatively short periods and within a fairly narrow compass. In gen-

TABLE 1. CARICOM COUNTRIES' SOURCES OF FOREIGN EXCHANGE, 1989 ($ millions)

Item	Merchandise Exports	Tourism	Other Services	Transfers[a]	Other	Total
Antigua and Barbuda[b]	28.5	188.4	0.0	18.7	−12.8	222.8
The Bahamas	259.2	1,214.3	212.6	1.0	15.1	1,702.2
Barbados	146.9	528.7	109.6	5.8	130.8	921.8
Belize	124.4	28.5	41.9	31.1	−5.9	220.0
Dominica	55.6	12.3	0.0	17.2	−16.0	69.1
Grenada[c]	32.8	47.5	1.5	21.6	−18.2	85.2
Jamaica	1,017.0	593.0	244.6	296.3	74.8	2,225.7
St. Kitts and Nevis	32.8	40.3	3.5	15.2	−9.8	82.0
St. Lucia	111.9	113.0	22.5	12.4	−12.1	247.7
St. Vincent	74.6	25.2	5.7	30.2	−22.4	113.3
Trinidad and Tobago[c]	1,453.3	91.9	165.2	−29.6	66.2	1,747.0
Total Exports[d]	**3,337.0**	**2,883.1**	**807.1**	**419.9**	**189.7**	**7,636.8**
Percent of Total Exports	43.7	37.8	10.6	5.5	2.5	100.0
Trinidad and Tobago Non-oil	508.2	—	—	—	—	—
Total Exports, excluding oil	**2,391.9**	**2,883.1**	**807.1**	**419.9**	**189.7**	**6,691.7**
Percent of Total Exports	35.7	43.1	12.1	6.3	2.8	100.0

[a]Tranfers are mainly remittances.
[b]1987.
[c]1988.
[d]Caricom except Guyana and Montserrat.

Sources: International Monetary Fund, *Balance of Payments Yearbook* (Washington, DC: International Monetary Fund, 1990); and International Monetary Fund, *International Financial Statistics* (Washington, DC: International Monetary Fund, 1989).

eral, the Caribbean cannot achieve inflation rates lower than those achieved by the United States. On the other hand, policies that inflate domestic prices cause capital flight and currency depreciation.

These economic links are reflected in trade arrangements and official ties. Caricom countries have preferential access to the U.S. market through the provisions of the Generalized System of Preferences (GSP). In the 1980s the United States introduced the Caribbean Basin Recovery Act which provided one-way free trade access to the United States for countries in the Caribbean Basin, along with investment promotion and related activities. The U.S. tariff codes (HTS 9802.00.60 and HTS 9802.00.80), which allow for low duties on goods made from U.S. materials, have been a major stimulus for the growth of export manufacturing in Caricom countries. Several Caribbean countries have double taxation treaties with the United States, intended to smooth the way for invest-

FIGURE 1. CARICOM COUNTRIES' DIRECTION OF TRADE, 1990 *(percent)*

EXPORTS TO

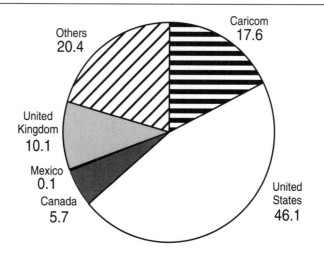

IMPORTS FROM

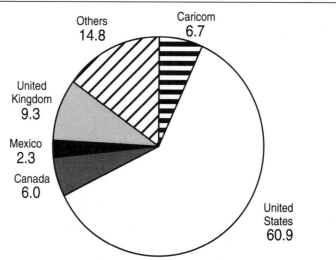

Note: Totals may not add due to rounding.

Source: International Monetary Fund, *Direction of Trade Statistics Yearbook,* various issues, Washington, DC.

ment in the region. Some countries have signed trade and information-exchange agreements to ease the establishment of financial services and tourism. On the debit side, the reduction in U.S. sugar quotas has been a significant blow to Caribbean sugar exporters.

The counterpart of the overarching rise in U.S. economic influence in the Caribbean has been the weakening of traditional links to the United Kingdom, although there remain important economic relationships with the United Kingdom and the European Community (EC) as a whole. Caricom countries are signatories to the Lomé Agreement, which provides official development assistance, loans, and one-way free trade access to the EC, to developing countries from Africa, the Caribbean, and the Pacific. The agreement includes quotas for the supply of sugar at remunerative prices. Europe has become an important source of tourists to the Caribbean, and a limited amount of European foreign direct investment reaches Caricom, much of it linked to tourism.

Caricom has strong economic links with Canada, though not on the scale and intensity of its ties with the United States. The main areas of Canada-Caribbean interaction are imports, selected exports to Canada (bauxite, molasses, rum, offshore services), migration to Canada and remittances of migrants, foreign direct investment (in particular banking, insurance, tourism, and public utilities), and official development finance (particularly for infrastructure).

These links derive from strong historical roots in trade, banking, and insurance, and shared traditions of British parliamentary influence. The ties have been cemented by official agreements. The Canada-West India Agreement, effective in 1926, provides access to Canadian markets for traditional commodities and makes a provision for official development assistance. The Caribcan arrangement, announced in February 1986, has widened the scope of one-way free trade from Caricom to Canada, although important commodities such as clothing are not included. Double taxation agreements have been concluded between Canada and several Caricom countries.

Direct economic links between Mexico and Caricom are limited to oil exports to the region, in large part financed by a special credit agreement between Mexico, Venezuela, and Caricom countries. Mexico is a rival with Caricom in tourism services, manufacturing, and data services for the North American market. Thus, whereas the accession of Canada to the North American Free Trade Agreement (NAFTA) consolidates markets to which Caricom has a large measure of free access, the accession of Mexico threatens Caribbean interests, particularly in clothing and textiles, for which Caricom does not have free access to North America.

Caribbean economic links with potential members of a western hemisphere free trade area, other than the United States and Canada, are few. Oil exported from Venezuela to Caricom countries is the only traded product of any significance, although Venezuela and Brazil also export a few consumer items to the Caribbean. There is a small tourist trade, in both directions, between Venezuela and the East Caribbean.

A FREE TRADE AREA AND CARIBBEAN ECONOMIC DEVELOPMENT

With some hesitancy and trepidation, Caricom has embraced the idea of a Caribbean-North American Free Trade Area in principle. Preliminary discussions have been held between representatives of the United States and the Caricom countries, and a framework agreement was signed between the two parties in July 1991. The initial focus has been on the non-trade aspects of the Enterprise for the Americas Initiative (EAI), particularly debt relief and investment. Serious discussions of the trade issues are yet to begin.

Caricom's economic objectives are to:

- increase its market share in tourism, export manufacturing, export agriculture, and traded services;
- attract direct investment in these areas to boost local knowledge of markets and up-to-date processes;
- accelerate investment that will improve competitiveness by reducing unit labor costs;
- achieve a balance of income and expenditure that eliminates excess demand for foreign exchange, stabilizes the exchange rate, and lowers inflation.

North America is the main area of interest because it offers what, for Caricom countries, is an infinitely large market for the products and services, in which the Caribbean has or can acquire a comparative advantage.

The main obstacle to faster export growth in the Caribbean is lack of knowledge of export markets, appropriate technologies, new processes, new products, changes in tastes, new and potential competitors, and so forth. International collaboration is the most effective way to ensure a constant flow of information that might address these issues. Many forms of international collaboration may be effective, depending on circumstances. Foreign direct investment gives the local producer a strong ally in the export market.

In terms of market access, nontariff barriers (NTBs) to entry into the North American market have been the most significant obstacles to the growth of nontraditional exports. Caribbean producers are often ensnared by regulations (especially with respect to agricultural products) that producers established in the North American market know well. Moreover, U.S. producers are not averse to manipulating regulations to their own advantage. This is often done at state and local levels in contradiction to policies being pursued by the federal government to liberalize access to the U.S. market. To make matters worse, technical assistance and fiscal incentives provided by Caribbean governments to improve their exporters' knowledge of the market are liable to invite charges of unfair competition and to be subject to countervailing duties in North America.

The Caribbean has had great difficulty in the 1970s, the 1980s, and now in the 1990s, in increasing labor productivity enough to allow for competitive production with rising real incomes. The demand for higher real incomes is especially strong in the Caribbean because of the demonstration effect of North American consumption patterns. If the demand for higher real incomes is not to result in overpricing, loss of market share, and economic stagnation, labor productivity must increase sufficiently so that firms can produce a better product or sell at a lower price.

The aspirations for a better quality of life have led, in the 1970s and 1980s, to severe imbalances between expenditure and income and between foreign-exchange spending and receipts. Governments resorted to the printing presses when national income could not accommodate insistent demands for improved lifestyles. As a result, the inflation virus affected one Caribbean nation after another as they exhausted foreign-exchange reserves and foreign credits and were left without resources to stabilize the exchange rate. A prerequisite for the new development strategy is a halt to the printing presses. Foreign debt relief is also essential for Jamaica and Guyana since no realistic scenario will permit the existing debt to be fully serviced.[2]

Contemporary economic policies of Caricom countries are based on the premise of openness to trade and receptiveness to foreign investment. The new foundation for Caricom economic integration is the sharing of human and material resources to improve the quality and competitiveness of Caricom's exports of goods and services. Policies have focused on institutional arrangements for sharing resources and widening access to markets for merchandise and services exports. On the import side, tariff levels have been reduced and relatively few nontariff barriers remain in place. In fact, despite the attention it received, import substitution never amounted to a significant proportion of Caricom output, even at the height of protective measures in the late 1970s. The countries that maintained strong trade barriers—Guyana, Jamaica, and Trinidad and Tobago—had dismantled most of their protective machinery by the end of 1991, as an element in the conditionality attached to their programs with the International Monetary Fund (IMF). The common external tariff, adopted by the majority of Caricom members, provides for tariffs in a range of 5 to 30 percent, except for a single category of final goods (where Caricom has the capacity to produce over 75 percent of domestic demand), where a 45 percent rate applies (Table 2). That category is not large because domestic production generally accounts for only a small proportion of domestic demand.

THE DESIRABILITY OF THE FREE TRADE AREA

The Caribbean market is already highly penetrated by U.S. exports and, in any case, the effective protection of Caricom production is low and falling. The investment climate has been favorable for more than a decade, with good infrastructure, an attractive human resource endowment, stable democracies, and liberal trade and investment regimes. The U.S. interest in a free trade area with Caricom seems motivated mainly by a philosophical commitment to free trade and political considerations. The potential gains for U.S. exporters and the additional opportunities for U.S. investors are not significant.

The Caribbean already enjoys relatively free access to two markets so large that Caricom's resources cannot hope to exploit them fully (i.e., North America and the European Community). However, there are weaknesses in both preferential agreements from the Caricom viewpoint: important potential exports from the region are excluded from the duty-free provisions and nontariff barriers are pervasive, particularly in nontraditional export areas. New trade agreements addressing these issues are highly desirable. Furthermore, the Caribbean wishes for access to North America on terms similar to those of such competitors as Mexico. In

---

TABLE 2. TARIFF RATES UNDER COMMON EXTERNAL TARIFF OF CARICOM, 1992 (percent)

Item	Noncompeting Imports	Competing Imports[a]
Inputs		
Primary	5	30
Intermediate	10	30
Capital	10	30
Final Goods		
Basic	10	30
Nonbasic	30	45

[a]Goods for which Caricom has the capacity to produce over 75 percent of domestic demand.

Source: Caricom Secretariat, *Common External Tariff of the Caribbean Common Market* (Georgetown, Guyana: Caricom, 1990).

---

a free trade area with the United States and Canada, Mexico may secure unrestricted access in items that are not eligible under the Caribbean Basin Initiative, and the Caribbean has a legitimate concern about possible changes in the rules of origin that might be to its disadvantage. Caricom does have an interest in gaining access to the Latin American market, but that cannot be a prime motivation when so much scope remains for increasing exports of goods and services to North America and the European Community.

ISSUES FOR NEGOTIATION

From a Caribbean perspective, five critical issues would need to be addressed in the context of a Caribbean-North American Free Trade Agreement.

Nontariff Barriers

The Canada-United States Free Trade Agreement (CAFTA) contains several provisions to counter nontariff barriers. Caricom negotiators will need to seek similar provisions in any Caricom-North American Free Trade Agreement. Enforcement remains a troubling issue. If NTBs are to be policed by joint councils set up under the Enterprise for the Americas Initiative, these councils must be provided with substantial powers to override the large variety of nontariff measures used to block exports, including quotas, safeguard and retaliatory duties, voluntary export restraints, health and safety regulations, technical standards, and arbitrary environmental requirements.

No Significant Exclusions

A major defect of the Caribbean Basin Initiative is the exclusion of textiles, apparel, and footwear from its provisions (Table 3). Caricom will need assurances that there will be no exclusions from any new free trade arrangement. Gains are expected from exports of clothing items with greater value added for Caricom than is permissible under U.S. Tariff Codes HTS 9802.00.60 and HTS 9802.00.80. Raw materials can be more widely sourced once the Caribbean is no longer confined to processing semifinished goods from the United States. This may attract investment from more diverse sources, including the Far East. If the Caribbean lacks free trade access, this investment may be diverted to Mexico and elsewhere.

Sugar is the other item of interest to Caricom. U.S. imports from Caricom countries are now under a temporary quota arrangement at

Source: World Bank, "Caribbean Exports: Preferential Markets and Performance" (Washington, DC: World Bank, 1988), p. 68.

TABLE 3. ITEMS EXEMPT FROM DUTY-FREE TREATMENT UNDER CARIBBEAN BASIN INITIATIVE, 1988 (percent)

Item	Tariff Range
Textiles and apparel subject to most-favored-nation status	5-40
Footwear, handbags, luggage, flat goods, work gloves, and leather wearing apparel	2-40
Canned tuna	6-35
Petroleum and products derived from petroleum	0.3-1.6
Watches and watch parts incorporating material originating in a communist country	5-20

prices linked to the U.S. government support price for U.S. sugar producers. This arrangement is satisfactory for Caricom producers for the time being. The quotas are sufficient to cover the sugar supplies available for sale to the United States. However, the quotas may be reduced at any time, and they are not expected to persist beyond the medium term. Free trade access is desirable for the long term, although it may involve reduced prices to Caricom sugar producers since the U.S. price support will presumably be eliminated.

No Undue Injury from Liberalization

Free access to the Caribbean market by U.S. producers must be phased in over a sufficient time period to allow Caribbean producers to gain needed knowledge for their full, active participation in the international market. Tourism and information services operate at international levels of efficiency, but the same is not yet true of most manufacturing and agricultural activities. The free trade agreements should contemplate a transitional period during which Caricom producers will be helped to acquire the knowledge and skills they now lack, and to effect organizational changes that will yield economies of scale and scope.

Reconciling Lomé Obligations

The provisions of the Lomé Convention require that the European Community be given at least as favorable trade treatment as any other international trading partner of the African, Caribbean, and Pacific signatories. Caricom would have to provide free trade access to the European Community if it provided similar access to North America. Since North America and the European Community account for practically all Caricom trade—the significant exceptions are cars, electrical equipment, some dairy items, and meat—a Caribbean-North American Free Trade Area would effectively mean total free trade for Caricom. That can be contemplated only after the long-term growth of a diversified Caribbean export sector is secure.

Rules of Origin

Caricom will wish to ensure that the rules of origin under a free trade agreement are not less favorable than those currently in force under the Caribbean Basin Initiative. That implies less stringent rules than for the CAFTA, where origin rules were set relatively tight to discourage firms from trying to gain access to a major market through their free trade partner. Caricom must also be wary lest the United States make the current rules of origin under CBI more exacting.

CARIBBEAN PROSPECTS INSIDE A NORTH AMERICAN FREE TRADE AREA

The potential gains for Caricom from a free trade area with the United States, Canada, and Mexico were estimated on the basis of comparative static analysis. The gains are deemed to derive from the growth in exports and the moderation of domestic inflation; transition costs and arrangements for phasing in reciprocity were disregarded in the analysis.

Trade Effects

The impact of a FTA on Caribbean exports will depend on two factors, the induced change in the real effective exchange rate and the elasticity of exports with respect to the exchange rate. The introduction of free trade will reduce the real effective exchange rate by the proportion of existing tariffs, weighted by the percentage of exports subject to tariffs, and modified by a similar weighted adjustment for tariffs removed from competing suppliers. This calculation, it turns out, leaves the real effective exchange rate changed little for these countries.[3]

To get a sense of what might be the impact at a lower level of aggregation, a short list of items that are not duty exempt under the CBI were analyzed: textiles and apparel that do not qualify under the HTS 9802.00.60 or HTS 9802.00.80 provisions, canned tuna, petroleum products, and watches and watch parts (Table 3). These items carry tariffs ranging from 5 to 40 percent for textiles and wearing apparel, 6 to 35 percent for canned tuna, 0.3 to 1.6 percent for petroleum products, and 5 to 20 percent for watches.[4]

Clothing exports have the greatest potential for expansion in response to free trade.[5] If exchange rates between North America and Caricom did not change during the transition to free trade, and if the rates of inflation of the two regions were comparable, the free trade area could boost exports of clothing and textiles now subject to tariffs by between 14 percent and 112 percent for Barbados, and between 10 percent and 84 percent for Jamaica.[6] From data provided by Erzan and Yeats (see Chapter 4 in this volume), and from data on exports of goods and services, the proportion of dutiable textiles to total exports of goods and services to North America was estimated to be in the vicinity of 1.5 percent. That translates into, at best, a one-time 3 percent increase in exports of goods and services. The gain would be considerably less if the new textile exports were not originally subject to the maximum tariff rate.

Caricom oil exports are subject to a maximum tariff of 1.6 percent and comprise about 30 percent of the Caribbean's exports to the United States. The weighted effect of removing tariffs on petroleum products on the overall real effective exchange rate for the Caribbean is therefore approximately 0.5 percent and the effect on total receipts from export of goods and services is negligible.

Price Effect

The effect of the free trade area on inflation can be inferred from the interrelations between the price of imports and domestic prices. Imports from North America and the European Community amount to 80 percent of the total for the Caribbean. Each 10 percent reduction in tariffs on imports from these sources should, therefore, reduce the price of imports by approximately 8 percent. Tariffs currently range from 5 to 30 percent under the Caricom common external tariff. Given domestic price elasticities with respect to imports in the range of 0.2 to 0.9,[7] the potential deflationary impact associated with import liberalization would be 1 to 22 percent. However, it is doubtful that these deflationary gains would be realized. Government revenues surrendered by the abolition of the customs tariff would have to be made up by other sources of taxation such as general consumption taxes. If the replacement taxes are to yield sufficient revenue, their effects on prices are likely to counteract the deflationary effect of the tariff removal.

On the whole, a free trade area with North America would have little effect on the Caribbean because of the preponderance of tourism and services, the low levels of tariffs currently in place, and the limited range of import substitutes still under protection. Two important caveats apply, however. One is the danger of trade and, especially, investment diversion on account of Mexico's entry into the NAFTA. The other is the potential benefits that would ensue from the removal of nontariff barriers in the U.S. market, particularly on items currently excluded from the CBI.

CONCLUSIONS AND RECOMMENDATIONS

The challenges and opportunities facing Caricom countries will not be significantly altered by the existence of a free trade area with North America. Historically, Caricom economies have been very open (Table 4), and that is the region's continuing destiny. A brief protectionist phase in Caricom economic policy was short-lived and involved only a minority of countries. It never had much effect on growth or on the balance of payments, although it created significant domestic distortions in Jamaica, Guyana, and Trinidad and Tobago. That phase ended when

TABLE 4. FOREIGN TRADE AND EXCHANGE RATE REGIMES IN CARICOM COUNTRIES, 1991

Foreign Trade Regime	
Tariff rates (percent)	
Range	0-45
Modal	10
Quantitative restrictions	Very limited
GATT Codes	
Antidumping	Nonsignatory
Subsidies	Nonsignatory
Customs valuation	Implemented
Exchange Rate Regime	
Jamaica, Guyana	Free float/full convertibility
Trinidad and Tobago	Fixed exchange rate/exchange controls
Others	Fixed exchange rate/no controls on current transactions
Memorandum Items (1989)	
Gross national product ($ millions)	13,265
Total external trade ($ millions)	12,137
External trade coefficient[a] (percent)	91.5

[a]Includes tourism and other services.

Source: World Bank, "Caribbean Common Market: Trade Policies and Economic Integration in the 1990s" (Washington, DC: World Bank, 1990), Table 4.

external imbalances forced those three countries to embrace IMF-World Bank orthodoxy in the 1980s.

Nevertheless, the Caribbean faces major challenges in managing the transition to economic maturity. Few companies in Caricom countries can compete as equals in international markets. The countries must embark on a process of learning, organizational reform, regional consolidation, and mergers to bring firms to a size that permits them to compete effectively in international markets. This means that the process of openness to the international economy must be gradual. During the transition period, financial and human resources should be provided to promote export capability and strengthen the competitive ability of firms. Careful research into the experience of successful exporters such as South Korea, Japan, and Singapore has uncovered the important role of institution building and export support in providing a competitive platform for export firms. The Caribbean needs assistance to mount a similar program to overcome defects of information, organization, and exporting techniques, and to cover the diseconomies of learning, the costs of information, and other externalities. If the process of integration into world markets is not to depress living standards in the Caribbean, resources must be concentrated on remedying these deficiencies during the transition period to free trade.

Naturally, Caricom must participate in discussions on trade liberalization wherever they might occur, including the NAFTA. To do so is no more than fulfilling the region's continuing destiny as open economies par excellence. In these negotiations Caribbean countries should make sure that:

■ Finance and technical assistance are included in the package to provide the institutional support needed to make Caricom firms more competitive in international markets and to overcome the costs and externalities of reaching that standard.

■ Effective mechanisms are put in place to control the use of nontariff barriers and other administrative impediments to free trade in goods and services. Such mechanisms must be transparent and provide built-in compensation for vast inequalities in size and political influence between the United States and the Caribbean.

■ The timing is appropriate for the implementation of the many provisions that will make up the free trade package. A long gestation period is necessary to ensure that Caribbean firms acquire the maturity that will enable them to be truly competitive and not be totally overwhelmed by North American giants.

Finally, Caribbean countries should insist that transitional measures be adopted to ensure that countries that accede to the free trade area at an early stage—in particular Mexico—do not unduly jeopardize their economic interests since their full participation in a free trade agreement with North America can only be expected to happen a few years hence.

Notes

[1] This analysis is based on the members of the Caribbean Community, which includes Antigua and Barbuda, The Bahamas, Barbados, Belize, Dominica, Grenada, Guyana, Jamaica, Montserrat, St. Kitts and Nevis, St. Lucia, St. Vincent and the Grenandines, and Trinidad and Tobago. Because the interests of the non-Caricom Caribbean are not dissimilar, the conclusions would also have validity for the independent countries of the non-English Caribbean.

[2] As a result of forgiveness and renegotiation, official and commercial debt-to-export ratios for Jamaica and Guyana have been reduced from 171 percent and 656 percent in 1989, respectively, to a projected 157 percent and 485 percent in 1992.

[3] Elasticities of exports of goods and services from the Caribbean with respect to a real effective exchange rate were calculated by Arnold McIntyre, "Determinants of the Caribbean's Export Performance," Caribbean Development Bank, mimeograph, January 1991. The elasticities are not significantly different from zero for Barbados, Jamaica, and Trinidad and Tobago, at the 5 percent level of significance. The elasticity was significant for Guyana but its value was only 0.1.

[4] Occasionally, the Caribbean has also been subject to quota limits on clothing—for Barbados in 1984, for Trinidad and Tobago in 1986, and for Jamaica in 1987.

[5] McIntyre, op. cit., finds a significant elasticity with respect to real effective exchange rates, for Barbados 2.8 and for Jamaica 2.1. The real effective exchange rates in this case were adjusted for inflation in competing producer countries.

[6] The rates of increase are calculated by multiplying the tariffs by the elasticities on the assumption that prices would fall by the full extent of the removal of tariffs.

[7] Elasticities of response to import prices are available for Trinidad and Tobago, see A. J. Bynoe, "Inflation in a Small Open Economy: A Case Study of Trinidad and Tobago," Ph.D. Thesis, New York University, May 1981; for Barbados see Andrew Downes, "Inflation in Barbados: An Econometric Investigation," *Economic Development and Cultural Change*, Vol. 33, No. 3 (April 1985).

Chapter Nine

U.S.-Andean Pact Free Trade

Alberto Pascó-Font and Sylvia Saborio

The economic alliance between the members of the Andean Pact[1] (AP) has teetered between survival and oblivion for years. The idea of forming a hemisphere-wide free trade area as articulated in the Enterprise for the Americas Initiative (EAI) has rekindled the spirit of regional cooperation, possibly giving the AP a new lease on life. Although the premise for collaboration is different today than in the past, some of the divisive issues that have plagued the alliance persist and may once again doom it to failure. This paper examines the recent evolution of the Andean Pact and explores the feasibility and implications for the AP of entering into a free trade agreement with the United States.

RECENT DEVELOPMENTS AND OUTLOOK

The AP dates back to 1969, when Bolivia, Colombia, Chile, Ecuador, and Peru subscribed to the Cartagena Agreement. Subsequently, Venezuela joined the pact in 1973, and Chile withdrew in 1976. The AP was formed to promote balanced and equitable development among its members through market integration and economic cooperation. This objective was to be reached by eliminating barriers to intraregional trade and forming a customs union, developing joint industrial programs, and harmonizing macroeconomic policies. After considerable progress during the early stage of import substitution, the regional integration process slowed down in the 1970s and stagnated in the 1980s, as member countries were beset by macroeconomic instability.

The AP was conceived as a way of expanding domestic markets to potentiate the import-substitution industrialization strategies that each country had been pursuing separately. By the end of the 1970s the failure of the industrialization strategy became increasingly evident, but not until the debt crisis of the early 1980s forced these economies to slash spending did the import-substitution model finally fall apart. Since then, with varying degrees of enthusiasm and success, Andean countries have undertaken structural adjustment programs. Among other reforms, their efforts entailed liberalization of trade and foreign-exchange regimes, drastic privatization programs, and a shift toward reliance on market forces and away from government intervention (Tables 1 and 2).

These developments called into question the original concept of the AP. As a result of this "identity crisis," the AP has redefined its goals and methods. In a departure from the past, the future Andean Common Market will be outward oriented and open to international competition.

The consolidation of the Andean Common Market aims to strengthen the capacity of member countries to compete internationally. The "Strategic Design for the Andean Pact's Orientation," approved by the Andean presidents at their Galápagos meeting in December 1989, reflects this new approach. It postulates two major objectives for the 1990s:

■ Consolidating the Andean economic area as an integrated market, including: harmonization of trade, monetary, and foreign-exchange policies; improving transportation and communication infrastructure and services; promoting integration and cooperation in productive sectors and in scientific and technological development; promoting free movement of capital, goods, services, and individuals within the region; and encouraging cross-border integration and tourism.

TABLE 1. ANDEAN PACT COUNTRIES' AVERAGE TARIFF RATES, 1986–1991 (percent)

Year	Bolivia	Colombia	Ecuador	Peru	Venezuela
1986	19.99	46.80	38.54	63.53	31.44
1987	19.99	48.04	39.23	67.46	33.59
1988	18.85	48.20	39.22	70.36	33.59
1989	16.65	44.53	42.50	72.13	27.77
1990	9.80	39.30	32.80	26.30	17.80
1991[a]	9.80	14.29	18.50	17.60	15.60

[a]Tariffs, November 1991.

Source: Junta del Acuerdo de Cartagena (JUNAC), Lima, Peru.

**TABLE 2. TARIFF DISPERSION IN ANDEAN PACT COUNTRIES'
SCHEDULES** (percent share of tariff lines per range)

Tariff Range	Bolivia	Colombia[a]	Ecuador[b]	Peru	Venezuela
>0 to 5	5.4	59.3	30.6	0.5	—
>5 to 10	94.6	17.3	17.5	—	19.6
>10 to 15	—	21.5	10.9	73.0	1.5
>15 to 20	—	0.5	14.9	—	29.8
>20 to 30	—	0.4	20.8	26.5	5.9
over 30	—	1.0	5.4	—	10.4
Total	**100**	**100**	**100**	**100**	**67**

Note: Numbers may not add because of rounding. Data as of November 1991.

[a]Does not include an additional variable tax of 5 to 10 percent.
[b]Does not include an additional 3 percent tax.

Source: Legal dispositions of member countries.

■ Improving the group's external relations, with an emphasis on promoting Latin American integration.

In the "Acta de la Paz" (November 1990) and the "Acta de Caracas" (May 1991), the Andean presidents agreed to expedite implementation of the strategic design agreements by advancing to 1992 the deadline for creating the Andean Free Trade Area and adopting the common external tariff (CET) to consolidate the Andean Common Market by 1995.[2] The presidents also emphasized the need for closer ties with other Latin American nations and renewed their commitment to forming a Latin America Common Market.

Yet, at their summit meeting in Cartagena, Colombia, in December 1991, AP presidents failed to reach full agreement on either the Andean Free Trade Area or the CET. The compromise foundered under the combined weight of political tensions within and between AP members. Internally, pressures are rising because of increasing unemployment and industrial dislocation brought about by domestic and trade reforms. Differences in the depth and speed of economic reforms and problems arising from large disparities in economic size and level of development among AP members have added to the pressures. For example, the two largest members of the AP—Colombia and Venezuela—account for two-thirds of the combined Andean gross domestic product (GDP) and three-fourths of its total trade. The two smallest members—Bolivia and Ecuador—together make up only 10 percent of the group's GDP and 12 percent of its trade. Average income of the richest member (Venezuela) is four times that of the poorest member (Bolivia).

The creation of the free trade area (FTA) ran into difficulties when both Ecuador and Peru threatened to withdraw from the AP. Ecuador balked at the proposed pace of liberalization as too abrupt. Meanwhile, Peru, which had drastically cut its tariffs but was suffering competitive losses on account of a severe real appreciation of its currency, insisted on being granted "special concessions" previously reserved for the less developed partners (Ecuador and Bolivia). In addition, Peru demanded the right to countervail against export subsidies by Colombia and Venezuela. To keep the process from stalling altogether, it was agreed to proceed with the creation of a free trade area among Colombia, Venezuela, and Bolivia on January 1, 1992, and to grant Peru and Ecuador a six-month extension to join the FTA. It is questionable whether AP members will be able to resolve their differences to everyone's satisfaction by then, especially since Colombia and Venezuela have suspended the negotiations with Peru following the April coup d'etat by President Alberto K. Fujimori.[3]

The adoption of the CET—a critical issue for the process of regional integration—proved even more controversial. According to the "Acta de Barahona" (December 1991), the CET would start out at five levels: 0, 5, 10, 15, and 20 percent to be reduced to three levels—5, 10, and 15 percent—by January 1994. Bolivia, however, would be allowed to maintain its two-tier structure of 5 and 10 percent. In addition, certain time-bound exceptions would apply in the agricultural and automotive sectors. Disagreements over the level and structure of the CET prevented its adoption. Colombia and Venezuela supported the proposal because the CET closely resembled their own tariff schedules. However, Ecuador rejected the proposed tariff levels as too low. In contrast, Peru criticized them as too high and dispersed, claiming that, as proposed, the CET would increase effective rates of protection, encourage rent-seeking behavior, and delay its trade liberalization program. As a result of the impasse, Colombia and Venezuela went ahead with the CET, thus forming a bloc within the AP, while the others maintained their own external tariff structures. Negotiations are scheduled to resume before mid-year, but this issue is unlikely to be entirely resolved in the intervening months.

These conflicts reveal the chasm in some of these countries between the political will at the highest levels to move forward and the ability to steer competing domestic constituencies toward change. Colombia and Venezuela clearly feel hampered by the "convoy problem"[4] and insist that others should comply with what was agreed in the "Acta de Barahona." Otherwise, they may well ignore the AP and follow on their own. Indeed, Colombia and Venezuela have been conducting trade negotiations with Mexico within the "Group of Three," to the consternation of other AP members. To placate their concerns, it was agreed to invite Mexico to negotiate a trade agreement with the AP as a whole, based on the understandings reached so far with Colombia and Venezuela.

These problems are to some extent unavoidable. Given the record of the last two decades, however, it is unclear whether the AP will be able to sort through these problems without delaying—or derailing altogether—the regional integration process. This year will be a critical period during which the readiness of member countries to form a common market by 1995 will be tested.

Despite these challenges, the Andean Pact is unlikely to dissolve formally. Member countries are under pressure to resolve their differences or to reduce them enough to proceed with the full FTA and the CET by the mid-1992 deadline. In the worst scenario, Peru will threaten to (but will probably not) leave the AP[5]; Bolivia and Ecuador will invoke their special status to postpone or neutralize any agreement deemed harmful to their interests; and Venezuela and Colombia will concur, because their trade links with both countries are marginal. In the most likely outcome, the facade of a united AP will be maintained as long as Colombia and Venezuela can continue to steer the process to their own advantage.

For purposes of analysis, it is assumed that the AP as a bloc will remain a valid regional entity. Accordingly, it is in the context of the ongoing process of regional integration that the opportunities and challenges of a potential free trade agreement with the United States will be examined in this chapter.

U.S.-ANDEAN PACT TRADE RELATIONS

Andean Pact Trade Profile

Andean Pact countries are relatively open economies: total trade accounts for around 30 percent of the Andean GDP. After increasing substantially in the 1970s, trade declined in the 1980s in all AP countries except Colombia. Between 1980 and 1989, Colombian exports expanded by 45 percent, as oil exports rose from $100 million to $1.4 billion and manufactured exports grew by 68 percent. Although Venezuela's nontraditional exports nearly tripled between 1980 and 1987 (from $980 million to $2.8 billion), its total exports declined by 35 percent because of a drop of over $8 billion in its oil exports. Ecuador's exports also fell, by 5 percent, mainly because of the drop in oil prices. Bolivian exports declined 21 percent from 1980 to 1989 owing to the fall in international tin prices and the domestic economic crisis. Domestic factors were also instrumental in the decline of Peruvian exports in the 1980s. Paralleling the decline in exports, total AP imports dropped by 25 percent between 1980 and 1989.[6]

The United States is the main AP trading partner: in 1989 it supplied 38 percent of total AP imports and absorbed 44 percent of its exports. Trade with the European Community (EC), represented some 23 percent of AP imports and 16 percent of its exports. Two-way trade with the rest of Latin America and Canada amounted to around 18 percent of the total. Finally, intra-AP trade itself constituted only about 5 percent of these countries' total trade, and most of it was commerce between Colombia and Venezuela (Table 3).

Over the last decade, the importance of the United States as a market for Andean products increased, while its role as a supplier declined. Between 1980 and 1989 AP exports to the United States rose over 25 percent, while its imports from the United States declined by a third. As a result of these divergent trends—induced in a large measure by the debt crisis and the recession that engulfed these economies throughout much of the 1980s—the balance of trade between the United States and the AP changed dramatically during the decade. Thus, while in 1980-82 the AP had a $2 billion trade deficit vis-à-vis the United States, by 1988-1989 the AP was running a trade surplus of $5 billion with the United States.

TABLE 3. ANDEAN PACT TRADE 1970–1989 ($ millions)

	Value		
	1970	1980	1989
Imports by Origin			
United States	1,844.7	9,772.2	6,499.0
European Community	1,012.6	4,355.7	3,996.0
Japan	319.8	1,986.0	1,076.0
Andean Pact	110.7	993.0	812.0
Other America[a]	393.5	2,979.1	2,901.0
Other Asia	41.0	519.1	261.0
Other World	377.1	1,963.5	1,527.0
Total	**4,099.4**	**22,568.6**	**17,072.0**
Exports by Destination			
United States	1,909.9	8357.5	11,219.0
European Community	1,086.8	4,324.9	4,084.0
Japan	242.1	1,431.9	1,065.0
Andean Pact	113.0	1,168.9	987.0
Other America[a]	1,630.1	10,636.8	4,813.0
Other Asia	10.8	292.2	265.0
Other World	387.4	3,009.9	2,719.0
Total	**5,380.0**	**29,222.0**	**25,152.0**

[a]Includes Canada and Latin America minus the Andean Pact.

Source: Junta del Acuerdo de Cartagena (JUNAC), Lima, Peru.

In terms of product composition, Andean exports to the United States are highly concentrated in a few items and consist basically of energy products (70 percent), agricultural and food products (18 percent), and minerals (8 percent). The main Andean imports from the United States are currently industrial inputs (47 percent), capital goods (27 percent), and transport equipment (9 percent). As a result of the persistent foreign-exchange crunch experienced in the 1980s, the share of consumer goods in total AP imports from the United States dropped from around 15 percent to 6 percent in the course of the decade (Table 4).

TABLE 4. ANDEAN PACT TRADE WITH THE UNITED STATES BY PRODUCT GROUP 1980–89 ($ millions)

Andean Pact Imports From United States

Product Group	1980	1985	1989
Nondurable consumer goods	588.3	287.4	274.0
Durable consumer goods	762.9	304.1	159.9
Fuel, lubricants, and related	63.4	110.9	140.6
Raw materials and inputs for agriculture	213.2	260.4	296.0
Raw materials and inputs for industry	4,040.7	3,073.8	3,096.0
Construction materials	230.0	83.6	121.6
Capital goods for agriculture	131.3	85.6	63.5
Capital goods for industry	2,411.3	1,556.1	1,779.6
Transport equipment	1,226.8	550.5	555.7
Others	18.3	28.8	11.9
Total	**9,686.3**	**6,341.3**	**6,498.9**

Andean Pact Exports To United States

Product Group	1980	1985	1989
Nondurable consumer goods	396.1	814.4	1,446.7
Durable consumer goods	44.9	79.1	169.1
Fuel, lubricants, and related	6,279.7	7,860.2	7,680.8
Raw materials and inputs for agriculture	6.7	14.4	60.9
Raw materials and inputs for industry	2,005.0	1,547.7	1,725.9
Construction materials	47.7	128.9	109.2
Capital goods for agriculture	1.3	1.0	5.1
Capital goods for industry	9.3	12.8	59.9
Transport equipment	20.5	6.8	39.0
Others	37.3	38.6	22.8
Total	**8,848.5**	**10,503.7**	**11,319.3**

Note: Numbers may not add due to rounding.

Source: Junta del Acuerdo de Cartagena (JUNAC), Lima, Peru.

U.S.-Andean Pact Accords

The breadth and depth of U.S.-AP relations over the years is reflected in a large number of agreements covering a wide range of topics. A recent survey tallied 220 treaties or bilateral agreements between AP countries and the United States concerning such topics as agriculture (17 percent), defense and military aid (13 percent), and trade and finance (11 percent).[7]

Two developments of recent vintage are noteworthy in the trade field. One is that all AP member countries have signed individual bilateral trade and investment agreements with the United States, under the Enterprise for the Americas Initiative.[8]

The ultimate objective of these agreements is the gradual elimination of trade and investment barriers. To that end, they constitute a monitoring framework for detecting problems and opportunities in trade and investment, and a consultative mechanism for solving problems in these areas. As mere consultative agreements, however, they do not generate contractual obligations between the parties. Given the Andean countries intent to forge a relationship with the United States as a regional entity,[9] these individual accords may need to be superseded by a regional one, or certain Andean-wide guidelines would need to be developed to multilateralize the negotiating process with the United States.

The second development is the recently enacted Andean Trade Preference Act (ATPA), which highlights the special relationship that has evolved between most AP member countries and the United States, in the effort to combat drug trafficking.[10] Modeled on the Caribbean Basin Initiative[11] (CBI), the ATPA would provide, over a 10-year period, duty-free access to the U.S. market to specified exports from Bolivia, Colombia, Ecuador, and Peru. As in the CBI, sensitive products are excluded from duty-free treatment—notably textiles, clothing, canned tuna, sugar, footwear, and petroleum and its derivatives. The ATPA contains no special provisions regarding nontariff barriers (NTBs) or the application of U.S. trade remedies and has no contractual basis. This means that the United States can unilaterally change at will the countries and products that qualify for benefits under the program. As it stands, eligibility for ATPA benefits is conditioned on the protection of intellectual property rights (IPR) and assured access on equitable terms for U.S. firms to markets and natural resources in beneficiary countries.

To the extent that the ATPA lowers some tariff barriers against Andean exports in the U.S. market, it will reduce the incentives for AP countries to enter into a reciprocal free trade agreement with the United States under the EAI.

U.S.-ANDEAN FREE TRADE: A PRELIMINARY ASSESSMENT

The notion of a free trade agreement between the United States and AP member countries has been enthusiastically endorsed by AP presidents. But in economic terms, what would the AP actually stand to gain from a FTA with the United States?

To explore this question, U.S. trade barriers to Andean exports were reviewed. Tables 5 and 6 show the level of tariffs and NTBs imposed by the United States on the main Andean export products. The tables reveal several interesting features of U.S.-AP trade. First, Andean exports are highly concentrated in a few products. In 1988-89, the number of tariff items with U.S. sales of more than $1 million was minute: 12 for Bolivia, 27 for Ecuador, 50 for Peru, and 82 in both Colombia and Venezuela. In Venezuela, exports of crude petroleum and nonpetroleum oils accounted for more than 80 percent of total exports to the United States. Second, the bulk of AP exports to the United States consists of raw materials. Third, most items exported to the United States (except textiles and a few other manufactures) face very low or no tariffs under most-favored-nation (MFN) treatment or are included in the Generalized System of Preferences (GSP). Indeed, the average trade-weighted tariff on Andean exports to the United States is only about 2 percent, and this is likely to drop further under the additional preferences provided by ATPA.

As far as NTBs are concerned, Erzan and Yeats (Chapter 4, Table 7) show that the share of Andean exports subject to U.S. NTBs ranges from a high of 85 percent in Venezuela to a low of 4 percent in Bolivia, with intermediate values in the 34 to 40 percent range for other AP members. "Hard core" NTBs are far less pervasive, affecting only 1 to 2 percent of total exports to the United States for Venezuela, Ecuador, and Bolivia; 5 percent for Colombia; and 9 percent for Peru. Nevertheless, these NTBs are most prevalent on manufactures, where the greatest potential for non-traditional exports lies. Indeed, Erzan and Yeats indicate that failure to relax NTBs in a prospective FTA with the United States would curtail the potential expansion of AP exports by as much as 40 percent, compared to a case in which tariffs were removed and NTBs were relaxed. But in neither case would AP exports expand significantly, because existing trade barriers are not very high.

On the other hand, despite the recent wave of trade liberalization in several Andean countries, U.S. exports still face a considerably higher average tariff in AP markets than Andean exports face in the U.S. market (Table 7). Moreover, even the adoption of the CET would not reduce these levels appreciably.

TABLE 5. U.S. TARIFFS AND NTBs TO MAIN ANDEAN EXPORTS

Country and Item	Value, 1989		Tariff (percent)	GSP	NTBs
	($ millions)	(share of all exports to U.S.)			
Bolivia					
Nuts	6.8	4.33	Free-17.5	Some	No
Mineral tin	13.5	8.58	Free	Yes	No
Wood	21.0	13.36	Free	No	No
Silver jewelry	24.0	15.25	Free	Yes	No
Refined tin	70.0	44.56	Free	Yes	No
Subtotal	**135.3**	**86.07**			
Total exported to U.S.	**157.2**	**100.00**			
Colombia					
Flowers	182.7	7.38	Free-8	Some	No[a]
Bananas	137.1	5.53	Free	Yes	No
Coffee	284.9	11.50	Free	Yes	No
Sugar	92.4	3.73	Free	Yes	Yes
Crude petroleum oils	935.3	37.76	5.25c/bbl	No	No
Noncrude petroleum oils	245.3	9.90	7	No	No
Clothing	70.0	2.82	3-30.4	No	No
Subtotal	**1,947.7**	**78.63**			
Total exported to U.S.	**2,476.8**	**100.00**			
Ecuador					
Shrimps	282.9	19.85	Free	No	No
Bananas	206.9	14.52	Free	No	No
Coffee	93.3	6.55	Free	Yes	No
Cocoa and by-products	68.0	4.77	Free-20	Some	Some
Crude petroleum oils	612.2	42.94	5.25c/bbl	No	No
Noncrude petroleum oils	66.4	4.66	10.5c/bbl	No	No
Subtotal	**1,329.7**	**93.27**			
Total exported to U.S.	**1,425.5**	**100.00**			
Peru					
Coffee	71.7	9.29	Free	Yes	No
Fish meal	41.6	5.39	Free	No	No
Nonprecious metals	48.1	6.23	Free	Yes	No
Crude petroleum oils	0.0	0.00	5.25c/bbl	No	No
Noncrude petroleum oils	115.1	14.92	7	No	No
Silver jewelry	74.6	9.66	Free	Some	No
Cotton products	58.5	7.59	Free-33	No	No
Copper products	83.0	10.05	Free-4.9	Some	No
Refined zinc	63.5	8.23	Free-19	Some	No
Subtotal	**556.2**	**72.05**			
Total exported to U.S.	**772.0**	**100.00**			
Venezuela					
Crude petroleum oils	5,610.5	86.48	5.25c/bbl	No	No
Noncrude petroleum oils	0.0	0.00	10.5c/bbl	No	No
Metal products	310.0	4.78	Free-20	Some	No
Subtotal	**5,920.5**	**91.25**			
Total exported to U.S.	**6,487.9**	**100.00**			

Note: Numbers may not add due to rounding.

Source: *U.S. Custom House Guide,* (Washington, DC: McGraw-Hill, 1991).

Thus, a FTA that resulted in reciprocal elimination of mutual trade barriers could be expected to lead to a much higher expansion of U.S. exports to AP countries than vice versa, at least in the short term. In all likelihood, U.S. products would end up displacing both Andean products and those previously supplied by other countries. The product composition of trade among AP members and the United States reveals clear potential for conflict in this regard. For example, most Colombian imports from the AP come from Venezuela (fertilizer, industrial alcohols, and some iron and steel products), and to a lesser extent from Peru (synthetic fibers and copper manufactures). The United States, however, also supplies Colombia with limited amounts of all those products. Since American firms are typically larger, more mature, and better funded than their AP competitors, without some import protection, Venezuelan and Peruvian exports to Colombia would likely be displaced by U.S. products. Similarly, Colombian exports to Peru and Venezuela, would likely succumb to U.S. competition. A rapid and complete process of import liberalization vis-à-vis the United States could wipe out a large portion of intra-Andean trade because virtually all of it is in manufactures. It could also destroy local industries that, given enough time to adjust, could become competitive enterprises. This is not an argument for protection but for gradual import liberalization.

In sum, the potential static benefits for the AP from a FTA with the United States are probably only marginal in the short run and could

TABLE 6. ANDEAN EXPORTS' ACCESS TO THE UNITED STATES (percent)

Item	Bolivia	Colombia	Ecuador	Peru	Venezuela
Weighted Tariff Rates[a]	0.44	2.14	0.50	3.43	0.48
Foods and feeds	8.75	0.00	1.01	0.00	1.39
Agricultural materials	0.00	4.00	—	0.00	—
Coal and petroleum[b]	—	1.39	0.00	7.00	0.01
Ores and metals	0.00	0.00	—	2.86	5.80
Manufactures	0.00	12.53	—	5.44	0.00
Nonclassified	—	0.00	—	—	0.00
NTB Coverage Ratio[a]	4	39	40	34	85

Note: Items without data are not traded in important amounts with the United States.

[a]1986, trade weights.
[b]This rate could change because it is calculated in cents per barrel and depends on the price of the barrel.

Sources: *U.S. Custom House Guide* (Washington, DC: McGraw-Hill, 1991; JUNAC, UNCTAD data taken from Refik Erzan and Alexander Yeats, International Trade Division, World Bank.

TABLE 7. FOREIGN TRADE AND EXCHANGE RATE REGIMES IN ANDEAN PACT COUNTRIES, 1991

Item	Bolivia	Colombia	Ecuador	Peru	Venezuela
Foreign Trade Regime					
Tariff Rates (percent)					
Average	9.8	14.29	18.5	17.6	15.6
Range	5 and 10	0-75	0-50	5-25	0-50
GATT Codes					
Antidumping	Nonsignatory	Observer	Nonsignatory	Observer	Nonsignatory
Subsidies	Nonsignatory	Observer	Nonsignatory	Observer	Observer
Customs valuation	Nonsignatory	Nonsignatory	Nonsignatory	Nonsignatory	Nonsignatory
Exchange Rate Regime	Fixed exchange (crawling peg)	Multiple exchange (free and fixed)	Float	Float	Float
Memorandum Items (1989)					
Gross domestic product ($ millions)	4,352.0	40,306.8	8,505.0	28,659.3	34,563.6
Total external trade ($ millions)	1,244.0	10,958.0	3,028.0	4,038.0	16,598.0
External trade coefficient (percent)	28.6	27.2	35.6	14.1	48.0

Source: Junta del Acuerdo de Cartagena (JUNAC), Lima, Peru.

be negative due to trade diversion, if sensitive sectors and nontariff barriers in the United States were excluded from negotiations. In the longer run, positive dynamic effects linked to the exploitation of scale economies and industrial modernization and expansion through new investment could outstrip initial adjustment costs, provided the additional investment did, in fact, materialize. For that to happen, the indirect effects of the FTA—in terms of locking in domestic reforms and enhancing the credibility of local governments—would have to be substantial. Even with a FTA, the AP would continue to face competitive disadvantages in the U.S. market vis-à-vis Mexico, given the latter's size and location.

An important reason for the Andean countries to seek a free trade arrangement with the United States is defensive—i.e., to secure unrestricted access to the U.S. market in the future. Mexico's entry into the North America Free Trade Agreement (NAFTA) is unlikely to have much of a negative impact on current Andean exports to the United States, because they consist largely of raw materials. However, it could severely constrain the potential growth of nontraditional Andean exports—textiles, leather apparel, flowers, tropical fruits—which have begun to make inroads in the U.S. market. It could also make it more difficult to attract foreign direct investment, especially if the pace of economic reform and the consolidation of the regional market are slowed down by continuing dissent among AP members.

Although AP countries should do everything they can to avoid future exclusion from the U.S. market, they must also take decisive action to improve their capacity to respond to enhanced market opportunities. Accordingly, they will need to act on the supply side to remove constraints to export growth. Indeed, the Andean countries' top priority in the short to medium term should be to stabilize and modernize their economies to become world class competitors. For that, outward-looking regional integration could be a valuable, if painful, intermediate step.

CONCLUSIONS AND RECOMMENDATIONS

Despite the evident political will to strengthen relations with the United States, a FTA between the United States and the AP is not a foregone conclusion. Naturally, much will depend on the speed with which the United States proceeds with free trade agreements beyond the NAFTA. Whether the United States limits FTAs to subregional groups to individual countries (with the possible exception of Chile) will also be a factor. The latter might well be a decisive factor in influencing the AP to firm up or break up.

The Andean countries have no alternative but to become better integrated into the world economy, but rushing into a FTA with the

United States, separately or together, might not be in their best interests. Ideally, they should first consolidate the Andean Common Market. The regional integration process would smooth their transition into a more competitive environment by letting local firms develop the scale economies of the extended regional market before exposing them to fierce competition from abroad. Obviously, this process would have to take place with a reasonably low level of external protection. This is why a low and simple CET is important. A separate but related reason for consolidating the AP first would be to forestall an exchange of bilateral preferences between individual AP members and the United States (or other partners). Such bilateral agreements would tend to displace a fair amount of intra-AP trade and might also result in a complex (and potentially trade-distorting) set of rules and procedures to administer trade flows by origin or destination.

In the meantime, Andean countries should concentrate on stabilizing their economies, modernizing their industries, and coping with their social problems. As a corollary, they should undertake gradual, unilateral trade liberalization, as Bolivia has done. These measures are a prerequisite for a well-functioning Andean Common Market, as much as for any trade arrangement with the United States.

The prospect of finding their industrial exports at a competitive disadvantage in the U.S. market will put pressure on AP members to accelerate the pace of reform so they can join the FTA as soon as possible. This pressure will become stronger over time, because the cost of exclusion from the FTA rises with each new entrant.

To expedite this process, existing bilateral agreements between individual AP members and the United States might be conveniently replaced or folded into a joint framework trade and investment agreement between the Andean Pact and the United States. Such an agreement might be based on the Memorandum of Understanding of 1979, in which most of its principles and guidelines are still valid.[12] The long dormant special committees provided for under that accord could be reactivated and reassigned to deal not only with trade policy issues but also with institutional and procedural matters, and to facilitate the flow of information regarding business opportunities. At the same time, the AP should develop adequate coordinating mechanisms among its members to allow for joint negotiations with the United States.

From the AP perspective, the overarching objective of the negotiations should be to obtain enhanced and assured access for Andean products to the U.S. market under stable and contractually bound conditions. In deference to the vast differences in the level of development of the parties involved, the principle of "relative reciprocity" should prevail, particularly in two areas: 1) intellectual property protection, where a balance must be struck between protection of foreign patents, trademarks, and copyrights and the legitimate need for technology transfer under reasonable conditions; and 2) the timetable for phasing out tariff and nontariff barriers. In principle, negotiations should be as comprehensive as possible, covering all tradables (services as well as goods); all types of restrictions (tariffs, NTBs, and other trade restraints, including trade remedies, i.e., antidumping, countervailing, and Section 301 actions); and provisions for the settlement of disputes.

Finally, for the Andean countries to reap the benefits from enhanced access to the U.S. market, they will need large additional investments both to expand their export capacity in particular sectors and to remove general supply bottlenecks that may block the export drive. Improvements in the region's economic climate should help to induce additional private investment, both domestic and foreign. The EAI investment and debt relief provisions would also help in this regard. In addition, these countries' efforts on the drug front should be recognized and supported. Without outside assistance, it is most unlikely that they could succeed at simultaneously waging war on drugs and poverty and becoming world class competitors.

Notes

[1] The Andean Pact includes Bolivia, Colombia, Ecuador, Peru, and Venezuela.

[2] Under the new directives, significant progress was made in the area of foreign investment. For example, the common regime for the treatment of developing-country capital (Decision 220 of 1987) was revised to promote foreign investment. The Cartagena Agreement Commission (JUNAC) approved Decisión 291 (March 21, 1991), giving foreign investors essentially the same rights and obligations as local investors and eliminating restrictions on foreign ownership throughout the AP.

[3] At a meeting in Quito in June 1992 it proved impossible to resolve remaining differences among AP members regarding the FTA and the CET.

[4] This refers to the idea that the least willing participant determines the pace of negotiations. See Ronald J. Wonnacott and Mark Lutz, "Is There a Case for Free Trade Areas?" in Jeffrey J. Schott (ed.), *Free Trade Areas and U.S. Trade Policy* (Washington, DC: Institute for International Economics, 1989), p. 60.

[5] This alternative is most unlikely because it has little popular support. Besides, it would be unrealistic to expect Peru to be more successful negotiating external trade relations on its own than in the context of the AP.

[6] *Compendio Estadístico del Grupo Andino: 1980-1990*, edited by the Information Unit of Junta del Acuerdo de Cartagena (JUNAC), Lima, Peru, 1990.

[7] See Sebastian Alegrett, "La Política Internacional de los Estados Unidos en el Continente Americano y las Posibilidades de Cooperacion del Grupo Andino," JUN/di 1309, internal document (Lima: Junta del Acuerdo de Cartagena (JUNAC), May 30, 1990).

[8] Bolivia's agreement (May 1990) preceded President Bush's announcement of the Enterprise for the Americas Initiative. Colombia signed on July 17, 1990; Ecuador, July 23, 1990; Peru, May 16, 1991; and Venezuela, April 8, 1991.

[9] In their "Andean Declaration for the Americas Initiative" (August 1990), the Andean presidents directed JUNAC to formulate proposals in the immediate future for the imple-

mentation of a hemispheric free trade area. Subsequently, a meeting was held in Lima (October 17-18, 1991) to define the main elements of the joint agenda for a meeting between the U.S. and the Andean presidents.

[10] The Andean Trade Preferences Act was signed into law by President Bush on December 4, 1991, as part of a larger trade bill.

[11] The Caribbean Basin Economic Recovery Act of 1983 provided duty-free customs entry to the United States for a range of products from Central American and Caribbean countries for 12 years. An amendment introduced to the bill in 1989 (CBI II) made the program permanent.

[12] Two Memoranda of Understanding were subscribed to by the U.S. government and the JUNAC in September 1979. The first related to scientific and technical cooperation. The second ("Memorandum of Understanding Between the Andean Pact and USA") was conceived as a preliminary step for the signature of an Economic Cooperation Agreement in four specific areas: trade, finance, science and technology, and industrial, agricultural, and infrastructural development (including transportation), with a special committee set up in each area. These were followed by the signature of a trade agreement between the United States and the AP on December 15, 1979, (Decisión 150).

Chapter Ten

U.S.-Mercosur Free Trade

Roberto Bouzas

This chapter discusses the likelihood and implications of a U.S.-Mercosur Free Trade Area (FTA), within the broader context of subregional economic integration. The first section reviews the process of economic integration in the Southern Cone, emphasizing the Southern Cone Common Market (Mercosur) future challenges and prospects. The second section provides a cursory overview of main U.S.-Mercosur trade and trade-policy issues. The third section makes a preliminary assessment of the incentives and implications of a U.S.-Mercosur FTA. Finally, the fourth section provides a summary and recommendations.

ECONOMIC INTEGRATION IN THE SOUTHERN CONE: RECORD, CHALLENGES, AND PROSPECTS

Movement toward closer economic cooperation between Argentina and Brazil has been an outstanding feature of intra-Latin American relations since the mid-1980s. Although achievements have generally fallen short of commitments, a clear-cut trend toward increasing economic interaction has emerged. In March 1991, Argentina and Brazil were joined by Paraguay and Uruguay to create the Mercosur by January 1, 1995. Mercosur's potential is suggested by an aggregate gross domestic product (GDP) of $420 billion, a population of 190 million, and $70 billion in foreign trade.

Argentine-Brazilian Economic Cooperation In The 1980s: The Record

In June 1986 Argentina and Brazil launched a Program of Economic Cooperation and Integration which aimed, in the short run, to reduce bilateral trade imbalances and to restore bilateral trade flows to their pre-debt crisis levels. In the long run, the program sought to foster closer economic ties between the two largest South American economies.[1]

In response to the negative political implications of the trend toward interindustry specialization and Argentine chronic deficits prevalent since the late 1970s, the program emphasized a balanced expansion of bilateral trade and intra-industry flows. In the first three years, 24 protocols for expanding trade, encouraging investment, fostering technological cooperation, and facilitating transportation were concluded.[2] Typically, they were flexible, selective, gradual, lacked detailed objectives, and favored a sectoral approach.

By 1989 the value of bilateral trade exceeded its pre-crisis levels, but bilateral economic cooperation was clearly losing momentum. The addition of products to the common list of capital goods benefiting from duty-free treatment had slowed markedly, and negotiations in other areas (especially automobile and agro-industries) were stagnant. The lack of progress on other issues was even more noticeable: in particular, the Investment Fund, the statute for binational enterprises, and the common currency had not evolved beyond preliminary sketches.

This modest outcome can be explained by a number of reasons. The protocols lacked precise objectives and enforcement mechanisms that might have given the process a rhythm of its own. As a result, every agreement was dependent upon detailed bilateral negotiations that became ever more difficult as nonconflicting issues were settled. Severe macroeconomic instability and policy volatility in both countries also created an unfriendly climate for economic integration. In particular, large fluctuations in bilateral real exchange rates produced wide shifts in competitiveness and provided a poor basis for expanding trade and investment in an enlarged market. Similarly, frequent trade policy changes (particularly in Argentina) resulted in uncertain preference margins. More generally, the lack of coordination between the content of the protocols and overall economic policy usually resulted in mutually conflicting objectives.

In an attempt to overcome the loss of momentum, in 1988 Argentina and Brazil signed a bilateral treaty binding them to create a common market by the end of 1998. In a 180-degree turn from the previous loose arrangement, Article 4 committed the countries to "harmonize customs policies; external and domestic trade policies; agricultural, industrial, transportation, communication, scientific and technological policies; and all other policies which they may agree. [They would also] gradually coordinate monetary, fiscal and exchange-rate policies as well as those affecting capital movements."

In mid-1990, even before the treaty was fully in force, the two new administrations signed the Buenos Aires Charter and agreed to:

- create the common market in five years instead of 10, by the end of 1994;
- replace product-by-product negotiations for automatic, across-the-board tariff cuts; and
- enforce the statute on binational firms.

Specifically, they agreed to grant bilateral trade a minimum preference margin of 40 percent on January 1, 1991, and increase it semiannually until tariffs levied upon bilateral trade flows are eliminated by the end of 1994. They also committed themselves to removing all nontariff barriers (NTBs) and reducing the number of products included in the exceptions lists by 20 percent a year.

By 1990 bilateral trade had grown to a total of $2.5 billion (150 percent above the 1985 value and more than 60 percent above the 1980-1990 average). Argentine exports had diversified toward manufactures from 22 percent of total sales in 1985 to about 44 percent in 1989. Though partly a result of overall economic conditions (real appreciation of the cruzeiro/austral exchange rate, liberalization of trade regimes both in Argentina and Brazil, and recession in Argentina), this shift was also a response to program incentives.[3] More importantly, economic cooperation has started to mobilize private interests: in fact, the automatic reduction of tariffs, the removal of NTBs and other restrictions on bilateral trade, and the political decision to maintain the pace of economic integration have all influenced private sector attitudes. The impetus toward subregional integration—joined in by Paraguay and Uruguay—has also gained strength from the announcement of the Enterprise for the Americas Initiative (EAI) and the launching of tripartite negotiations between Mexico, Canada, and the United States for a North American Free Trade Agreement (NAFTA).

Mercosur: Challenges and Prospects

In March 1991 Paraguay and Uruguay joined Argentina and Brazil in the project to create a common market by December 31, 1994, along the lines agreed to by the bilateral treaty of 1988 and ratified by the Buenos Aires Charter in 1990. Although Mercosur may be regarded as another example of the ideological escalation[4] typical of Latin American policymaking in the postwar period,[5] some new developments suggest that the outcome need not be as frustrating as in the past. First, trade regimes in the subregion have shifted away from the strong inward-orientation typical of import-substitution industrialization (ISI), which in the past had limited the scope for (even preferential) trade liberalization. Second, prevailing trends in the international trading system have strengthened the appeal of subregional economic integration. Third, the replacement of a conflict-prone approach characteristic of past Argentine-Brazilian relations with a collaborative attitude has nurtured common interests and has given the process a major political thrust.

Although full analysis of the incentives and obstacles to subregional economic integration is beyond the scope of this chapter, it is useful to review briefly the main issues to be addressed if Mercosur is to move toward a common market.[6] In the prevailing environment, reducing macroeconomic imbalances and promoting policy coordination are top priorities.[7]

MACROECONOMIC INSTABILITY. Macroeconomic stability is a necessary—though insufficient—condition for economic integration. Macroeconomic imbalances militate against economic integration because they usually result in large fluctuations in the level and composition of aggregate demand as well as in large shifts in relative prices (in particular real exchange rates). Large swings in real exchange rates breed uncertainty and high "risk premiums," increasing the relative cost of international transactions, and producing wide swings in competitiveness. The lower the tariffs and NTBs to trade are, the larger the effect on trade flows will be. Therefore, stable bilateral real exchange rates are essential for integration to progress smoothly.[8]

Various econometric studies show that in the 1980s the effect of exchange-rate volatility upon trade flows was not as large as might be expected as a result of the existence of high tariff and nontariff barriers, export promotion schemes, and economic recession or slow growth in both countries.[9] However, as trade barriers are lowered, real exchange-rate volatility will hinder economic integration and strengthen domestic resistance to closer economic ties. But macroeconomic instability takes not only the form of real exchange-rate volatility but also large fluctuations in aggregate demand. Because shifts in demand change trade flows and balances, persistent macroeconomic instability militates against a balanced expansion of trade.[10]

The main sources of aggregate demand and real exchange-rate instability in Argentina and Brazil have been large fiscal and external imbalances. If uncontrolled, they will impede progress toward a free trade area, customs union, or common market. However, mounting conflict between subregional integration and macroeconomic instability may create new incentives to come to grips with the most disturbing imbalances.[11]

POLICY COORDINATION. Even if macroeconomic instability is brought under control, subregional economic integration will demand closer coordination of trade and exchange-rate policies as well as credit, fiscal, and other macroeconomic and sectoral policies. Table 1 summarizes the main characteristics of national Mercosur trade regimes. Despite their shift away from inward-orientation in the 1980s, member countries still maintain significantly different levels of protection.[12] Their trade regimes also differ in other respects such as participation in General Agreement on Tariffs and Trade (GATT) codes, export incentives, and regulations regarding temporary admission, drawbacks, and export processing zones.[13]

Economic integration will also demand closer coordination of exchange-rate management. So central are exchange-rate policies to macroeconomic management (at least in the two largest countries), that closer cooperation is hard to imagine without convergent macroeconomic conditions. If disparate performances prevail, even the most flexible approach to exchange-rate coordination (instituting similar foreign-exchange regimes) may become impracticable. Unlike other monetary and exchange-rate cooperation pacts, Mercosur lacks any motor for propelling policy alignment.

Finally, to promote convergent competitive conditions in each national market and prevent investment diversion, policy coordination will gradually have to extend to foreign investment, credit, and fiscal policies. Again, although macroeconomic constraints point in a similar direction in all Mercosur countries, harmonization of disparate credit and fiscal policies is likely to prove slow and problematic. In contrast, more compatible foreign investment regimes might be relatively easier to achieve.

Because the challenges to Mercosur are monumental, its future evolution is uncertain. However, although a common market is unlikely to emerge in 1994, sustained progress toward a free trade area seems within reach. To succeed, member countries will have to keep the momentum of the last couple of years. In this context, although ideological escalation may be a reminder of the past, it may also provide—given the new domestic and international environment—the driving force to break free of the status quo.

U.S.-MERCOSUR TRADE AND TRADE-POLICY ISSUES: AN OVERVIEW

Globally, U.S.-Mercosur bilateral trade is marginal, but it contributed to about a third of total intra-hemispheric trade flows (and a much higher proportion of non-oil hemispheric trade flows). The relative importance of reciprocal trade for the United States and Mercosur is very dis-

TABLE 1. FOREIGN TRADE AND EXCHANGE RATE REGIMES IN MERCOSUR COUNTRIES, 1991

	Argentina	Brazil 1991	Brazil 1994[a]	Paraguay	Uruguay
Foreign Trade Regime					
Tariff Rates (percent)					
Average	11.77	32	14.2	16.1	26.8[b]
Range	5-35	0-85	0-40	3-56.5	10-30
Modal	5	40	20	n.a	30
Quantitative restrictions	very limited	limited		limited	limited
GATT Codes					
Antidumping	nonsignatory	implemented		nonsignatory	nonsignatory
Subsidies	nonsignatory	implemented		nonsignatory	implemented
Customs valuation	implemented	implemented		nonsignatory	nonsignatory
Exchange Rate Regime	fixed exchange rate/full convertibility	managed float/ exchange controls		managed float/ exchange controls	managed float/ free exchange market
Memorandum Items (1989)					
Gross domestic product ($ billions, 1980 prices)	75.2	297.7		5.4	6.9
Total external trade ($ billions, 1980 prices)	13.8	57.5		2.1	2.8
External trade coefficient (percent)	18.4	19.3		38.9	40.1

[a]1994 target.
[b]Prior to November 1990 reform.

Source: Based on *Statistical Yearbook for Latin America and the Caribbean* (Santiago, Chile: CEPAL, 1990); Instituto de Economia Internacional, *Boletín de Conjuntura Industrial*, Vol. 11, No. 1, Rio de Janeiro (April 1991); and J. B. M. Machado, "Integración Economica y Arancel Aduanero Común en el Cono Sur," *Integración Económica*, Vol. 167, 1991.

parate: Mercosur accounts for less than 2 percent of U.S. foreign trade, but for Mercosur, the United States is a far more important export outlet than even the subregion. The United States absorbs 20 percent of Mercosur exports versus 9 percent in intra-regional sales (Table 2). In the 1980s, aggregate U.S.-Mercosur trade was heavily influenced by macroeconomic conditions, particularly rapid U.S. import growth, and the Latin American debt crisis. As a result, Mercosur imports from the United States declined, while its exports to North America burgeoned.[14]

U.S.-Brazilian Trade Relations

In 1989 U.S.-Brazilian trade contributed to more than two-thirds of total U.S.-Mercosur exchanges. Although Brazil has a highly diversified trade pattern, the United States is its single most important partner (in 1989 it supplied one-fifth of Brazilian imports and provided an outlet for about one-quarter of its exports) and its share has been expanding markedly in the 1980s. Though much less important to U.S. trade, Brazil ranks as the second largest partner in Latin America and the fourth largest source of imports from the developing world. Large bilateral trade imbalances, widespread protectionism and export-promotion policies in Brazil, and increasing U.S. recourse to "procedural protectionism" and aggressive unilateralism have been at the root of mounting bilateral trade friction in the last decade.[15] As discussed below, many of these differences have disappeared since the late 1980s as a result of changing Brazilian trade policies.

Most U.S. imports from Brazil are manufactures (Table 3) and its share has grown markedly in the 1980s. The largest contributors are machinery and transport equipment, light manufactures (especially footwear and iron and steel products), and food products. The bulk of U.S. exports to Brazil are chemicals, machinery, and transport equipment.

In 1989 one-quarter of U.S. imports from Brazil entered duty-free under the GATT most favored nation (MFN) clause; an additional 16 percent received the benefits of the Generalized System of Preferences (GSP), and the remaining 59 percent faced generally low tariffs (Table 3).[16] The average tariff on U.S. imports from Brazil (using 1986 trade weights) was 5.8 percent—not unduly high, but still 60 percent above the average for U.S.-world imports. However, several Brazilian exports (particularly processed food products and light manufactures) faced much higher rates in the 20-50 percent range.[17] In addition, many processed primary products from Brazil faced extensive tariff escalation in the U.S. market (Table 4).

U.S. NTBs are also significant. According to United Nations Conference on Trade and Development (UNCTAD) data, more than one-

TABLE 2. MERCOSUR EXPORTS BY REGION 1990 ($ millions and percent)

Exporter	Total Exports	Mercosur	Chile	Andean Pact	CACM	Mexico	Canada	United States	Other Western Hemisphere	Rest of World
					($ millions)					
Argentina	12,352.6	1,832.7	462.3	511.7	41.2	321.4	81.2	1,699.2	79.2	7,323.7
Brazil	32,266.0	1,249.0	713.0	921.0	131.0	416.0	733.0	7,551.0	309.0	20,243.0
Paraguay	958.7	379.3	—	—	—	—	—	39.4	—	540.0
Uruguay	1,693.7	599.3	16.4	16.4	1.1	32.0	13.1	165.2	2.9	847.3
Mercosur	47,271.0	4,060.3	1,191.7	1,449.1	173.3	769.4	827.3	9,454.8	391.1	28,954.0
					(percent)					
Argentina	100.0	14.8	3.7	4.1	0.3	2.6	0.7	13.8	0.6	59.3
Brazil	100.0	3.9	2.2	2.9	0.4	1.3	2.3	23.4	1.0	62.7
Paraguay	100.0	39.6	—	—	—	—	—	4.1	—	56.3
Uruguay	100.0	35.4	1.0	1.0	0.1	1.9	0.8	9.8	0.2	50.0
Mercosur	100.0	8.6	2.5	3.1	0.4	1.6	1.8	20.0	0.8	61.3

Note: Numbers may not add due to rounding.

Source: International Monetary Fund, *Direction of Trade Statistics* (Washington, DC: IMF, 1991).

quarter of U.S. imports from Brazil were subject to NTBs in 1986 (Table 3).[18] The most important NTBs were excise taxes, antidumping and countervailing duties and actions, and voluntary export restraints agreements. Brazil has also been the Latin American country most severely hit by U.S. antidumping and countervailing duties and undertakings.[19]

TABLE 3. U.S. IMPORTS FROM MERCOSUR AND CONDITIONS OF ACCESS TO U.S. MARKET 1989 (percent)

	Argentina	Brazil	Paraguay	Uruguay[a]	World
U.S. Import Structure					
Foods and feeds	31.9	19.4	21.9	14.4	5.7
Agricultural materials	1.0	3.3	2.3	5.4	2.2
Coal and petroleum	13.2	8.5	0.0	0.0	11.4
Ores and metals	4.2	6.0	0.0	4.6	3.4
Manufactures	49.1	61.7	75.0	70.8	74.5
Nonclassified	0.6	1.1	0.8	4.8	2.8
Total	**100.0**	**100.0**	**100.0**	**100.0**	**100.0**
Conditions of Access to U.S. Market					
MFN duty-free imports	18.0	25.0	33.0	18.0	—
GSP duty-free imports	26.9	15.8	22.7	31.8	—
Tariff-paying imports	55.1	59.2	44.3	50.2	—
Total	**100.0**	**100.0**	**100.0**	**100.0**	**—**
Weighted Tariff Rates[b]					
Foods and feeds	4.1	11.1	3.3	0.8	3.0
Agricultural materials	1.2	0.0	0.0	2.8	0.7
Coal and petroleum	0.4	0.6	0.0	0.0	0.6
Ores and metals	0.0	0.3	0.0	0.0	0.6
Manufactures	3.3	4.7	4.5	11.3	4.5
All goods	2.9	5.8	3.3	2.5	3.6
Imports with trade of at least $50,000 paying tariffs equal to or higher than 5%[b]	22.5	27.9	27.2	43.1	—
Nontariff Barrier Coverage Ratio[b]	28.6	26.1	14.0	6.8	—

[a]Because exports of nonmonetary gold contracted markedly between 1986 and 1989, comparison of trade (1989) and tariff data (1986) for Uruguay is misleading.
[b]1986 trade weights.

Sources: Based on *Commodity Trade Statistics 1989* (New York: United Nations, 1991); International Trade Division, World Bank; and *Boletín Comercial* (Washington, DC: OAS-CECON, 1990).

TABLE 4. EXAMPLES OF POST-TOKYO ROUND U.S. TARIFF ESCALATION (percent)

Item	Nominal Tariff
Meat	
Fresh, chilled, or frozen	1.6
Prepared or preserved	2.3
Fish	
Fresh, chilled, or frozen	0.5
Prepared or preserved	1.1
Fruits	
Fruits and nuts, fresh or dried	1.1
Preserved and fruit preparations	20.3
Sugar	
Beet and cane, raw	0.6
Refined sugars	9.9
Leather	
Hides and skins	0.8
Leather	3.7
Leather products	9.2
Paper	
Pulp and waste paper	0.0
Paper and paperboard	0.3
Paper manufactures	3.8
Wool	
Sheep's or lamb's wool, not carded or combed	5.2
Sheep's or lamb's wool, carded or combed	11.1
Yarn of wool	12.9
Fabrics of carded wool	37.3
Cotton	
Not carded or combed	0.5
Carded or combed	5.0
Yarn	8.7
Fabrics	10.4
Iron and steel	
Ingots and other primary forms	1.6
Plates and sheets	5.3
Aluminium	
Aluminium and aluminium alloys, unwrought	0.6
Aluminium and aluminium alloys, worked	3.2

Source: Alexander Yeats, "La Progresividad de las Barreras Comerciales," J. M. Finger and A. Olechowski, (eds.) *La Ronda Uruguay, Manual para las Negociaciones Comerciales Multilaterales* (Washington, DC: World Bank, 1987).

Aggressive U.S. unilateralism has also been a major source of bilateral trade conflicts. Since mid-1970 Brazil has been subject to five Section 301 investigations and was the first and only Latin American country to incur retaliation due to U.S. demands on pharmaceutical patent protection. In 1989, after passage of the U.S. Omnibus Trade and Competitiveness Act, Brazil was designated a priority country under Section Super 301 for restrictive import practices. Similarly, it was put on the Special 301 "watch list" for allegedly inadequate protection of U.S. intellectual property rights and, in particular, pharmaceutical patents.

Conflicts regarding "unfair trade" practices have receded as the Brazilian trade regime has undergone a major overhaul.[20] In March 1990 most quantitative restrictions were eliminated and a four-year calendar (starting in 1991) was established for gradual reduction of nominal tariffs. In 1990 elimination of the import license system led the United States Trade Representative (USTR) to remove Brazil from the "priority country" list of Section Super 301, and another major Section 301 case was terminated when restrictions affecting software imports were eased. Similarly, Brazil's commitment to improve patent protection led to a suspension of U.S. sanctions on exports of paper, pharmaceutical, and electronic products.[21]

U.S.-Argentine Trade Relations

As in the case of Brazil, the United States is Argentina's main trade partner and its importance grew in the 1980s. Although by the end of the decade the United States had become the principal supplier (jointly with Brazil) and customer of Argentina, its share in total Argentine trade was comparatively low—around 15 percent (Table 2). For the United States, trade with Argentina is clearly marginal.

In contrast to the commodity composition of total exports, Argentine sales to the United States include a relatively large share of manufactures (49 percent, mostly iron and steel products, processed primary commodities, and processed food products).[22] Some of these exports have risen rapidly since the mid-1980s as the fall in domestic demand led to excess capacity in intermediate goods sectors (especially iron and steel products). As in the case of Brazil, U.S. exports to Argentina are mostly manufactures, especially machinery, transport equipment, and chemicals.

In 1989 less than one-fifth of Argentine exports to the United States entered duty-free under the MFN clause, whereas an additional quarter was granted GSP duty-free access (Table 3). Duties on the remaining half were comparatively low: the trade-weighted average tariff was just 2.9 percent. Several products, though, faced nominal tariffs, ranging from 20 to 42 percent.[23] Similar to Brazil, the relatively high share in exports of processed primary products and light manufactures suggests that the effects of tariff escalation may be non-negligible (Table 4).

U.S. NTBs are more important obstacles to bilateral trade than nominal tariffs and tariff escalation. In 1989 about 28.6 percent of total Argentine exports were subject to some kind of NTB, especially specific excise taxes, countervailing duties, quotas, and flexible import fees[24] (Table 3). Traditionally, high protection in Argentina has also been a source of trade friction with the United States. However, starting in the mid-1980s Argentine trade liberalizing initiatives have greatly diminished tariff and nontariff barriers.[25]

Argentina has also come under pressure from the United States for "unfair trade" practices, including five Section 301 investigations since the late 1970s. Following the enactment of the Omnibus Trade and Competitiveness Act, Argentina was included in Section 301 "watch list" on the grounds of alleged inadequate protection of U.S. intellectual property rights. However, none of these conflicts led to U.S. sanctions and most either lost substance or receded as a result of changing Argentine policies.

Finally, both countries are major cereal grain and oilseed producers and exporters. Although bilateral trade in these sectors is negligible, U.S. export promotion programs and subsidies have created friction in third-country markets. The support provided by the Export Enhancement Program (EEP) and the export credit and credit guarantee programs of the Commodity Credit Corporation have priced Argentine exports out of many third-country markets, leading to recurrent bilateral conflicts.[26]

Uruguay and Paraguay Trade Relations with the United States

Paraguay and Uruguay are much more open economies than either Argentina or Brazil (Table 1). However, since their external trade patterns are geographically diversified, the U.S. share of these small countries' foreign trade flows is modest. In any case, the United States remains an important supplier to Paraguay and an important market for Uruguay's exports (Table 2).

By the late 1980s, light manufactures (textile and apparel products, leather and footwear) were the bulk of U.S. imports from Uruguay. Of total imports, 18 percent entered duty-free under MFN, and an additional 32 percent paid no duties under the GSP. Disaggregated data for 1986 show that the weighted-average tariff rate was just 2.5 percent, although some products were subject to relatively high nominal tariffs.[27] Conversely, NTBs, mainly quotas and flexible import fees, affected a comparatively low share (6.8 percent) of total exports.

Main U.S. imports from Paraguay include light manufactures (textiles and apparel, wood products, and leather) and food products. In

1989, 33 percent of Paraguay's exports to the United States entered duty-free under MFN and an additional quarter benefited from GSP. The average tariff on U.S. imports from Paraguay was just 3.3 percent, but 28.1 percent of total exports worth at least $50,000 were subject to duties higher than 5 percent. The NTBs coverage ratio was 14 percent, basically in the form of quotas and flexible import fees on sugar exports.

INCENTIVES AND IMPLICATIONS OF A U.S.-MERCOSUR FTA: A PRELIMINARY ASSESSMENT

Many key parameters of a U.S.-Mercosur FTA remain unknown, including whether there will be a negotiation. Any discussion of incentives and implications must thus be qualitative and highly speculative. In this section, the conventional distinction between net static and dynamic gains from economic integration is used. However, attention is also given to the role of defensive reasons and other broader policy issues that are likely to arise in a FTA negotiation.

Net Static Gains and Resource Allocation

According to conventional theory, Jacob Viner's distinction between trade creation and trade diversion effects is still the benchmark for measuring the desirability of preferential trading arrangements.[28] The removal of trade barriers results in trade creation and welfare gains insofar as it improves the allocation of resources and increases productive efficiency. Welfare losses linked to trade diversion occur to the extent that imports from less efficient FTA members displace low-cost foreign suppliers. Consequently, the overall desirability of a FTA depends on the net welfare effects of the competing forces of trade creation and trade diversion.[29]

Temporarily assuming away terms-of-trade changes, some characteristics of participating countries enhance the potential for trade creation and reduce the scope for trade diversion, namely: 1) their degree of mutual competitiveness[30]; 2) the height of preexisting barriers to bilateral trade; 3) the degree to which they are natural trading partners (i.e., the extent of their trade before the agreement); and 4) the height of their trade barriers against the rest of the world.

Theoretically, the scope for trade diversion in a U.S.-Mercosur FTA seems to be large. A cursory examination of the structure of bilateral trade suggests that the bulk of U.S.-Mercosur flows is complementary rather than competitive (see previous section). The U.S. exports technology and capital-intensive goods (chemicals, machinery, and transport equipment), while Mercosur sales to the United States are tilted toward natural resource and labor-intensive products.[31] Yet the United States and Mercosur are not natural trade partners: even the smaller Mercosur countries have a (geographically) diversified trade pattern. Furthermore, Brazil is still a relatively protected economy, although the trends toward liberalization are clear.[32]

Relatively high protection in Brazil—and eventually in Mercosur—suggests that efficiency gains from trade liberalization might be considerable. However, within the restricted analytical framework of trade-creation and trade-diversion effects, it is unclear why preferential liberalization would be better for Mercosur than unilateral liberalization. In fact, a FTA with the United States (a potential supplier of most Mercosur imports) would be tantamount to unilateral liberalization with the additional welfare cost of trade diversion.[33] Furthermore, given the disparate size of the economies, adjustment costs would most likely fall disproportionately upon Mercosur. If those countries (particularly Brazil) are not prepared to bear the high adjustment costs that would accompany substantial unilateral trade liberalization, a FTA with the United States would face similar difficulties.

In terms of market access, since U.S. tariff rates are generally low, the prospects for an expansion of Mercosur exports are generally limited. To be sure, this does not exclude substantial export growth for selected products facing high nominal tariffs. However, a large part of Mercosur exports to the United States also face important NTBs (see previous section). Because NTBs have been largely used to replace tariff protection lost in multilateral trade negotiations (MTNs) and to complement tariff protection in industries that already have relatively high tariffs,[34] it is doubtful whether the United States would dismantle (even preferentially) its most restrictive NTBs. Therefore, U.S. readiness to remove NTBs would be critical in determining the extent to which market access conditions improve. However, some NTBs may not be susceptible to bilateral treatment.[35]

One estimate suggests that the expansion of Mercosur exports due to U.S. preferential tariff removal may be modest, about 13 percent of total exports.[36] On the other hand, given the higher level of protection in Mercosur, the preferential removal of barriers to U.S. products would almost certainly lead to a far larger expansion of U.S. exports to those countries.

Dynamic Effects of a FTA

Though difficult to quantify, the dynamic effects of economic integration are generally considered to be more relevant than the net welfare gains stemming from trade liberalization.[37] W. Fritsch argued that for most developing countries the benefits from scale economies would be purely notional because of the preeminence of labor-intensive industries and uncertainty about the stability of the preferential agreement.[38] However, for Brazil—and probably Argentina—the potential benefits may be relevant. On the one hand, the United States is a very large market compared to Mercosur. On the other hand, sectors in which scale economies prevail (i.e., intermediate goods, machinery, and transport equipment) will most certainly benefit from having—presumably—more secure and unimpeded access to the U.S. market. The latter may also contribute to the overcoming of supply constraints by stirring "animal spirits" and fostering new investments.

A FTA with the United States could also enhance foreign investment inflows. The relevance of this effect is underlined by new analytical perspectives and empirical findings that emphasize trade and investment linkages in determining patterns of specialization, particularly in semi-industrialized economies.[39] However, it is highly likely that at least some of the potential benefits to Mercosur will be preempted by those accrued to the first countries to join a FTA with the United States, particularly if they enjoy other locational advantages, as is the case with Mexico.

More generally, a FTA with the United States may stimulate capital inflows (and reflows) and help finance prospective current account deficits. Although this may allow higher rates of economic growth for some time (by relieving external constraints), it may also serve to sustain overvalued domestic currencies and ultimately affect competitiveness and resource allocation. However, the risk of capital market "speculative bubbles" in countries that still display relatively fragile macroeconomic environments should not be dismissed.

Finally, a FTA with the United States could also improve expectations and the general business climate by providing more certainty to the future course of domestic economic policies. This effect would be considerable in the Southern Cone economies plagued by policy volatility in the 1980s. Similarly, by binding policy reforms to an international agreement, it may also make policy reversal more costly in the future.

Defensive Reasons and FTA Negotiations

Economist Jeffrey Schott has argued that one of the strongest reasons to enter into FTAs with the United States may be defensive.[40] Certainly, for any country for which the United States is a relevant export market, maintaining access and avoiding discrimination can provide a strong incentive. The U.S. market absorbs about a quarter of Mercosur total exports and a much higher share of manufactured exports. Furthermore, this share has grown rapidly in the 1980s. Available estimates indicate that of all Latin America, Mercosur countries (especially Brazil) would bear the largest cost of displaced exports to the United States as a result of preferential access granted to Mexico within NAFTA.[41]

Moreover, a FTA with the United States would also discriminate against third-country exports to participating Latin American countries. This effect would not weigh high in the case of Mexico (its trade relations with the region are modest), but if other countries join the agreement or negotiate separate deals with the United States, its impact might be important. For Mercosur countries (particularly Brazil and Argentina), exports to other Latin American markets remain considerable, even after the abrupt shrinkage of the early 1980s, and there is a large potential for expansion. Because the United States can export most of the products traded intraregionally (particularly manufactures), U.S. preferential access to Latin American markets is likely to displace competing Latin American exports to those markets. As a result, defensive incentives to enter into FTA negotiations with the United States would largely depend upon how far the latter goes in negotiating FTAs in the hemisphere. For sure, defensive reasons for an agreement might have to be weighed against the potential costs of retaliation from third parties. Considering the Mercosur countries' high market diversification, this contingency cannot be taken lightly.

Some Broader Policy Issues

Negotiations for a U.S.-Mercosur FTA would involve broader policy issues than those reviewed so far. Putting aside temporarily the welfare loss of trade diversion, one major issue is whether a preferential arrangement tantamount to free trade would be a reasonable policy for large, semi-industrialized developing countries.[42] In fact, despite the intellectual and political consensus that inward-orientation makes unsound policy and that efficiency, specialization, and tradeability must be fostered, there are still powerful arguments in favor of active trade and industrial policies.[43] It seems reasonable to argue that a FTA with the United States would seriously limit the scope for activism, although—if appropriately designed—could provide known time limits for competitiveness to be enhanced and rationalization to proceed.

This caveat extends to the "new issues" that are likely to rank high among U.S. negotiating priorities. A FTA with the United States (vis-à-vis a multilateral agreement) will likely imply a fuller acceptance of U.S. negotiating objectives in areas such as services trade, intellectual property protection, and trade-related investment measures.[44] A crucial issue would then be whether participating countries would follow the U.S. lead on these sensitive issues.

Differences in the potential partners' size and level of development are also likely to become an issue, insofar as they influence the cost-benefit distribution and may eventually lead to polarization and increased "dependence" rather than "interdependence." Whether or not a superior alternative exists, this perception might make negotiations politically unfeasible.

The payments and exchange-rate implications of a U.S.-Mercosur FTA agreement might also be problematic. In particular, if a FTA is accompanied by a policy of aligning Mercosur domestic currencies to the U.S. dollar, a large part of Mercosur external trade might be subject to the vagaries of the U.S. dollar exchange rate.

The prospect of negotiations between Mercosur and the United States will play a role in the process of subregional economic integration. If subregional negotiations go awry, especially for the major members, the existence of an alternative option—however unclear—may alter the dynamics of intra-Mercosur negotiations. This might be the case, for example, if national preferences for trade liberalization remain sharply divergent and, therefore, the issue of a common external tariff becomes increasingly intractable.

Finally, it might be worthwhile to raise a voice of caution to the use of policies with long-run and major structural implications (such as entering into a FTA with the United States) in response to short-run pressures and events. Expectations that a FTA with the United States may induce large capital inflows (or reflows) and contribute to financing current account deficits may prove not only exaggerated (particularly for countries that do not enjoy the locational advantages of Mexico) but misplaced. Although the need to induce capital inflows (or reflows) is beyond question, adequate consideration needs to be given to the broader implication of the policies designed to bring it about.

SUMMARY AND RECOMMENDATIONS

Major uncertainties persist about the parameters of prospective NAFTA/Mercosur FTA negotiations. No details have yet been defined for either NAFTA or Mercosur. In particular, will NAFTA include an accession clause and, if so, what will it be? Will Mercosur evolve toward a common market or, rather, settle as a FTA? In the former case, will the common external tariffs be low or high? And equally important, how will the global trading system evolve in the next decade?

A FTA between the United States and Mercosur may be problematic in various respects. A major issue relates to the partners' differences in size and level of development, which will affect the distribution of costs and benefits and might eventually make a negotiation politically unfeasible.

For Mercosur, efficiency gains from trade creation under a FTA with the United States would have to be weighed against potentially large welfare losses from trade diversion. In fact, because the United States and Mercosur are not natural trading partners and protection within Mercosur may be considerable, the potential for trade diversion could be large. Similarly, the reallocation of resources stemming from the elimination of trade barriers will be accompanied by high adjustment costs, which given the disparities in size, might pose obstacles to a FTA.

The dynamic gains from a FTA are likely to be more attractive than net static welfare gains. In fact, enhanced investment flows and competition, scale economies, and reduced uncertainty can all boost economic growth in Mercosur. However, potential benefits in terms of export expansion would depend on the treatment of NTBs. Since many exports of interest to Mercosur face NTBs in the United States and their removal is uncertain, potential benefits would have to be correspondingly qualified. Furthermore, there are cases (such as agricultural trade) in which NTBs are not even amenable to bilateral treatment. Insofar as national regulatory regimes remain different, the scope for continued procedural protectionism in the United States may be wide, therefore limiting effective market access.

The positive effects of a FTA on capital inflows should not be exaggerated, particularly in the case of Mercosur countries, which do not enjoy the locational advantages of Mexico. Furthermore, some of the potential benefits might be preempted by those accrued by the first countries to join a FTA with the United States.

Because for Mercosur countries a FTA with the United States would be tantamount to unilateral liberalization (except for trade diversion), whether or not this is an appropriate policy course is debatable. The caveats are both political and economic and relate to the broader issue of whether a FTA with the United States would be the best course for large, semi-industrialized economies, such as Brazil. Some Mercosur countries might be more eager than others for a FTA with the United States. Consequently, the option of negotiating such a FTA will likely play a role in intra-Mercosur negotiations. One or more Mercosur members might find an incentive to break away if progress is too slow or is in an undesired direction.

For Mercosur defensive considerations are likely to carry a good deal of weight in deciding whether to negotiate a FTA with the United States. Developments in the international trade system will therefore be the benchmark for assessing costs and benefits of preferential trade liberalization. Further antagonism between trade blocs and a more aggressive and bilateralist U.S. trade policy would strengthen the incentives to "buy insurance" against mounting protectionism and marginalization in the world economy. In a scenario of fragmentation, even economies with highly diversified markets would probably do better as members of an "unnatural" trade bloc than as independent participants in a conflictive trade environment. Similarly, the larger the number of Latin American countries that enter into FTAs with the United States, the higher the incentives for Mercosur countries to follow the same course. Because the potential of the regional market for Mercosur exports is high, the costs of discrimination may be considerable. As economies with diversified markets, Mercosur countries will have to weigh carefully whether or not other trade partners are likely to retaliate against a FTA with the United States, since retaliation could counteract the benefits of larger exports to the latter.

Finally, FTA negotiations should not be launched under the pressure of short-run policy considerations (such as strengthening finance availability), without paying attention to their long-run and structural implications. In this respect, the present excitement over FTAs with the United States may be premature. It is fair to say, however, that the prospective materialization of NAFTA has fostered defensive incentives that cannot be neglected. The chain reaction this might create in Latin America may eventually become a decisive factor for Mercosur. These considerations underline the need for a more accurate assessment of the incentives to create a Western Hemisphere Free Trade Area and, eventually, the design of appropriate mechanisms to reach that objective.

In the short to medium term, Mercosur countries should focus on advancing the subregional integration process and promoting a transparent accession mechanism as part of NAFTA. Progress toward subregional integration could strengthen Mercosur's eventual bargaining stance vis-à-vis the larger and more powerful U.S.-NAFTA partners and, indeed, the rest of the world. In the meantime, trade issues of common interest can be addressed in the context of the U.S.-Mercosur framework trade and investment agreement.

Notes

[1] J. T. Araujo Jr., "A Ata de Buenos Aires e as Perspectivos de Interpração no Cone Sul," Texto para Discussao Interna No. 33 (Rio de Janeiro: FUNCEX, September 1990).

[2] Outstanding examples were the protocols on capital goods, wheat, agro-industries, binational firms, and those creating an Investment Fund and a common currency. For a review, see: M. Hirst, "Continuidad y Cambio del Programa de Integración Argentina-Brasil," Serie de Documentos e Informes de Investigación, No. 108 (Buenos Aires: FLACSO, 1990); and D. Chudnovsky and F. Porta, "Las Dos Etapas del Programa Argentino-Brasileño de Integración. Evaluación de lo Actuado e Incertidumbres Futuras," *Investigación Económica*, Vol. L, No. 196 (1991).

[3] Hirst, "Continuidad y Cambio," op. cit., and D. Chudnovsky and F. Porta, "Las Dos Etapas," op. cit.

[4] "Ideological escalation" refers to the well-established tradition of "resolving" great policy dilemmas by having them superseded by even more ambitious goals.

[5] A. Hirschmann, "The Turn to Authoritarianism in Latin America and the Search for its Economic Determinants," in D. Collier, (ed.), *The New Authoritarianism in Latin America* (Princeton, NJ: Princeton University Press, 1979).

[6] The economic rationale for economic integration in the subregion is discussed in R. Dornbusch, "Los Costos y Beneficios de la Integración Económica Regional," *Integración Latinoamericana*, No. 113 (1986); J. T. Araujo Jr., "Os Fundamentos Economicos do Programa de Integracao Argentina-Brasil," *Revista de Economía Política*, Vol. 8, No. 3 (1988); and D. Chudnovsky and F. Porta, "En Torno a la Integración Argentino-Brasileña," *Revista de la CEPAL*, No. 39 (1989). A useful review of new theoretical developments that strengthen the case for preferential trade liberalization is provided by R. Pomfret, "The Theory of Preferential Trading Arrangements," *Weltwirtschaftliches Archivs*, Vol. 122 (1986).

[7] The remainder of this section focuses on the two largest Mercosur partners.

[8] Real exchange-rate uncertainty also discourages investment for an enlarged market and hinders rational economic calculations of costs and benefits of alternative approaches to economic integration. In such a context, the very notion of a common external tariff may become irrelevant. See J. T. Araujo Jr., "A Opcao por Soberanias Compartidas Na América Latina: O Papel da Economía Brasileira," P. da Motta Veiga, (ed.), *Cone Sul: A Economía Política da Integracao* (Rio de Janeiro: FUNCEX, 1991).

[9] CEPAL, "La Coordinación de las Políticas Macroeconómicas en el Contexto de la Integración Latinoamericana" (Santiago, Chile: CEPAL, 1991); and R. M. Iglesias, "A Política Cambial de Argentina e o Brasil no Periodo 1970/89," Motta Veiga, (ed.) *Cone Sul*, op. cit.

[10] Available estimates suggest that the evolution of aggregate demand was a key determinant of bilateral trade flows in the 1980s. Ibid.

[11] Supranational agreements can help to make policymaking more transparent and predictable. As the Argentine and Brazilian experiences of the late 1980s suggest, "demonstration effects" might also play a role.

[12] Therefore, negotiating common external tariffs will be complex. In particular, trade liberalization has proceeded more rapidly in Argentina than in Brazil, and these different approaches are likely to persist in the future. Slower trade liberalization in Brazil illustrates the complexity of improving efficiency in a large, semi-industrialized developing country that has followed an ISI strategy for several decades. See W. Fritsch and G. Franco, "The Quest for Efficient Industrialization in a Technologically Dependent Economy: The Current Brazilian Debate," Texto para Discussao, No. 229 (Rio de Janeiro: Departamento de Economía PUC-RJ, 1989); and J. T. Araujo Jr., "Uma Estrategia Nao Liberal para a Abertura da Economía Brasileira," Textos para Discussao, No. 255 (Rio de Janeiro: IEI-FEA/UFRJ, 1991).

[13] See J. B. M. Machado, "Integración Económica y Arancel Aduanero Común en el Cono Sur," *Integración Económica*, No. 167 (1991); E. Baldinelli, "Armonización de Politícas

Crediticias, Fiscales y de Promoción de Exportaciones," *Integración Económica*, No. 167 (1991).

[14] This section focuses on trade relations between the most relevant trade partners, namely: the United States, Argentina, and Brazil.

[15] These conflicts have gone beyond the bilateral arena, as shown by the divergent positions maintained in the Uruguay Round of multilateral trade negotiations (MTNs). In particular, besides long-standing differences on issues like the structure of protection, graduation, NTBs and technology transfer, Brazil and the United States sharply diverged on the so-called "new issues" of services trade, intellectual property rights, and trade-related investment measures.

[16] Brazil has been one of the developing countries most affected by competitive need exclusions from GSP. In 1989 almost half of all GSP-eligible items were precluded from obtaining benefits. Organización de Estados Americanos/CECON, *Boletín Comercial* (Washington, DC: OEA, 1991).

[17] Nominal tariff rates were as high as 49.8 percent for concentrated orange juice, 41.6 percent for wool woven fabrics, 37.5 percent for other citrus fruit juices, 31.0 percent for grape juice, and higher than 20 percent for selected apparel and textile products and scrap tobacco. On aggregate, more than 30 percent of Brazilian exports to the U.S. with trade of at least $50,000 paid duties of 5 percent or higher. See Refik Erzan and Alexander Yeats, "Prospects for United States-Latin America Free Trade Areas: Empirical Evidence Concerning the View from the South" (Washington, DC: World Bank, 1991).

[18] This estimate fails to account for the full effect of the most restrictive trade barriers because the lower the value of trade (i.e., the more effective the trade barrier) the lower the weight that enters into the calculation.

[19] For a discussion, see L. V. Pereira, "O Protecionismo dos Paises Desenvolvidos e o Acesso de Produtos Brasileiros aos Mercados Externos," *Epico*, No. 18 (Rio de Janeiro: IPEA-INPES, 1990). Also see, M. P. Abreu and W. Fritsch, "Obstacles to Brazilian Export Growth and the Present Multilateral Trade Negotiations," Texto para Discussao No. 187 (Rio de Janeiro: PUC/RJ, 1988).

[20] For a summary presentation of recent changes in Brazil's trade regime, see IEI, *Boletín de Conjuntura Industrial*, Vol. 11, No. 1 (April 1991).

[21] New legislation is pending before Congress.

[22] The share of manufactures in total Argentine exports in 1989 was just over one-third.

[23] Outstanding cases were 41.6 percent for woven wool fabrics, 37.5 percent for some citrus fruit juices, 24.6 percent for scrap tobacco, 19 percent for ceramic floor and wall tiles, and 25 percent for selected types of cheese. In all, one-quarter of Argentine exports valued at $50,000 or more faced duties of 5 percent or higher. See Erzan and Yeats, op. cit.

[24] Again, this measure underestimates the effects of NTBs like sanitary regulations which inhibit U.S. imports of Argentine meat. According to the UNCTAD inventory, products affected by specific excise taxes in 1986 were crude petroleum, some kinds of fruit or vegetable juices, and alcoholic beverages. Countervailing duties were charged upon nonrubber footwear, wool, selected textiles and apparel products, certain steel products, and leather wearing apparel. Finally, quotas and flexible import fees were levied against cheese and other dairy products, fish, sugar beets and cane, and some textile and apparel products. After 1986 two leading export sectors (steel products and hides) were hit hard by countervailing duties.

[25] This process has not been linear. Foreign-exchange constraints and fiscal urgencies have been two reasons behind policy volatility. However, by the early 1990s Argentina was one of the more open economies in Latin America. For an overview of Argentine trade policies in the 1980s, see J. Berlinski, "Trade Policies in Argentina: 1964-1988" (Buenos Aires: Instituto Di Tella, 1988) mimeo.

[26] In mid-1991 Argentina complained forcefully when it was made public that Brazilian importers were negotiating the purchase of 700,000 tons of wheat from the United States under the incentives of the Export Enhancement Program (EEP).

[27] The 1986 trade-weighted average tariff is not representative because of large exports of nonmonetary gold. In 1986, U.S. imports of manufactures from Uruguay paid a trade-

weighted average tariff of 11.3 percent, almost triple the world average. In any case, Erzan and Yeats, op. cit., estimate that in 1986 about 14.3 percent of exports with at least $50,000 in trade were subject to tariffs of 5 percent or higher.

[28] Jacob Viner, *The Customs Union Issue* (New York: Carnegie Endowment for International Peace, 1950).

[29] Recent developments in the theory of preferential trading arrangements suggest that a FTA may be desirable even if trade diversion effects dominate due to: 1) less distorted consumption patterns and higher consumer welfare; 2) lower priced intermediate inputs and increased productive efficiency; 3) enhanced efficiency due to scale economies; and 4) extensive nontariff barriers. See Ronald J. Wonnacott and Mark Lutz, "Is There a Case for Free Trade Areas?" in Jeffrey Schott, (ed.), *Free Trade Areas and U.S. Trade Policy* (Washington DC: Institute for International Economics, 1989).

[30] If the participating countries are highly efficient by world standards, complementarity might not be a burden because the gains per unit of trade creation will be large. Ibid.

[31] It is worth questioning whether the United States is the most efficient producer of technology and capital-intensive goods imported by Mercosur. Conversely, Mercosur countries might be less efficient producers of labor-intensive products than some Asian economies.

[32] Mercosur's low common external tariffs would reduce the scope for trade diversion, but this issue is unresolved, as pointed out earlier in this chapter.

[33] W. Fritsch, "The New Minilateralism and Developing Countries," op. cit.

[34] E. J. Ray, *U.S. Protectionism and the World Debt Crisis* (Westport, CT: Quorum Books, 1989).

[35] This is clearly the case for NTBs to agricultural trade, especially subsidies, an extremely relevant issue for Mercosur.

[36] Erzan and Yeats, op. cit.

[37] El-Agraa's list of dynamic effects include: 1) scale economies; 2) external economies; 3) polarization effects; 4) effects upon investment flows; and 5) enhanced economic efficiency. See A. M. El-Agraa, "The Theory of Economic Integration," *International Economic Integration* (London: Macmillan, 1982). Empirical estimates on the effects of the Canada-U.S. FTA suggest that most Canadian gains would accrue from the exploitation of scale economies stimulated by an enlarged market. See R. G. Harris, "Summary of a Project on the General Equilibrium Evaluation of Canadian Trade Policy," *Canada-United States Free Trade*, J. Whalley and R. Hill (eds.), (Toronto: University of Toronto Press, 1985). Similarly, in the case of Mexico, many observers have emphasized the potential benefits of diminished uncertainty and enhanced direct investment flows. See CIDAC, *El Acuerdo de Libre Comercio Mexico-Estados Unidos* (Mexico City: Diana, 1991).

[38] Fritsch, "The New Minilateralism," op. cit.

[39] W. Fritsch and G. Franco, "Trade Policy, MNCs and the Evolving Pattern of Brazilian Trade, 1970-85," Texto para Discussao, No. 230 (Rio de Janeiro: Departamento de Economía PUC-RJ, 1989).

[40] Schott, "More Free Trade Areas?" op. cit.

[41] Mercosur exports would account for an estimated 55 percent of total Latin American exports displaced from the U.S. market (the share for manufactures is 65 percent). In any case, the absolute values involved are small (an estimate of about $20 million using 1986 data). See Erzan and Yeats, Box 1, in this volume.

[42] This issue is distinct from the caveats previously raised in regards to the huge transition costs which might be involved in rapid trade liberalization in large semi-industrialized economies.

[43] Fritsch and Franco, op. cit.

[44] Of course, a scenario of mounting U.S. aggressive unilateralism would preempt some of the flexibility accorded by more lax multilateral agreements.

■

Appendix
Membership of Selected
Regional Trade Agreements

Membership of Selected Regional Trade Agreements

RECIPROCAL TRADE ARRANGEMENTS

AP or Andean Pact: Andean Subregional Integration Agreement
The five members include Bolivia, Colombia, Ecuador, Peru, and Venezuela. Chile withdrew in 1976.

CACM: Central American Common Market
The five members include Costa Rica, El Salvador, Guatemala, Honduras, and Nicaragua.

CAFTA: Canada-United States Free Trade Agreement
The two members include Canada and the United States.

Caricom: Caribbean Community
The thirteen members include Antigua and Barbuda, The Bahamas, Barbados, Belize, Dominica, Grenada, Guyana, Jamaica, Montserrat, St. Kitts and Nevis, St. Lucia, St. Vincent and the Grenadines, and Trinidad and Tobago.

LAIA: Latin American Integration Association
The eleven members include Argentina, Bolivia, Brazil, Chile, Colombia, Ecuador, Mexico, Paraguay, Peru, Uruguay, and Venezuela.

Mercosur: Southern Cone Common Market
The four members include Argentina, Brazil, Paraguay, and Uruguay.

NAFTA: North American Free Trade Agreement
The three prospective members are Canada, Mexico, and the United States.

WHFTA: Western Hemisphere Free Trade Area
The potential membership would include all countries in the Western Hemisphere.

UNILATERAL TRADE ARRANGEMENTS

Caribcan: Canadian-Caribbean Agreements
Effective since 1986, Caribcan provides duty-free access to the Canadian market for certain imports from the Commonwealth Caribbean countries. The beneficiaries include Angilla, Antigua and Barbuda, The Bahamas, Bermuda, Belize, British Virgin Islands, Cayman Islands, Dominica, Grenada, Guyana, Jamaica, Montserrat, St. Christopher and Nevis, St. Lucia, St. Vincent and the Grenadines, Trinidad and Tobago, and Turks and Caicos Islands.

CBI: Caribbean Basin Initiative
Established by the Caribbean Basin Recovery Act of 1983 and amended in 1989 (CBI-II), the CBI provides duty-free access to the U.S. market for certain imports from Central America and the Caribbean. The beneficiaries include Antigua and Barbuda, Aruba, The Bahamas, Barbados, Belize, British Virgin Islands, Costa Rica, Dominica, the Dominican Republic, El Salvador, Grenada, Guatemala, Guyana, Haiti, Honduras, Jamaica, Montserrat, the Netherlands Antilles, Nicaragua, Panama, St. Kitts and Nevis, St. Lucia, St. Vincent and the Grenadines, and Trinidad and Tobago.

About the Overseas Development Council

The Overseas Development Council's programs focus on U.S. relations with developing countries in five broad policy areas: U.S. foreign policy and developing countries in a post-Cold War era; international finance and easing the debt crisis; international trade beyond the Uruguay Round; development strategies and development cooperation; and environment and development.

Within these major policy themes, ODC seeks to increase American understanding of the economic and social problems confronting the developing countries and to promote awareness of the importance of these countries to the United States in an increasingly interdependent international system. In pursuit of these goals, ODC functions as:

■ A center for policy analysis. Bridging the worlds of ideas and actions, ODC translates the best academic research and analysis on selected issues of policy importance into information and recommendations for policymakers in the public and private sectors.

■ A forum for the exchange of ideas. ODC's conferences, seminars, workshops, and briefings brings together legislators, business executives, scholars, and representatives of international financial institutions and nongovernmental groups.

■ A resource for public education. Through its publications, meetings, testimony, lectures, and formal and informal networking, ODC makes timely, objective, nonpartisan information available to an audience that includes but reaches far beyond the Washington policymaking community.

Stephen J. Friedman is the Chairman of the Overseas Development Council, and John W. Sewell is the Council's President.

O | D | C

Overseas Development Council
1875 Connecticut Ave., NW
Washington, DC 20009
Tel. (202) 234-8701

Overseas Development Council
Program Advisory Committee

279

About the Authors

ROBERTO BOUZAS is a senior fellow/researcher at the Department of International Relations of the Latin American Faculty of Social Sciences (FLACSO) in Argentina and a research associate at the Argentine National Council for Scientific and Technical Research (CONICET). He has edited five books and has written numerous journal, magazine, and newspaper articles. He has been deputy director of the Institute of U.S. Studies at CIDE in Mexico and held visiting professorships at Brazilian, Mexican, and U.S. universities.

ANDREA BUTELMANN is a researcher at the Center for Latin American Economic Research (CIEPLAN) in Santiago, Chile. She has taught at the economics departments of Universidad Católica de Chile, Universidad Adolfo Ibañez, and Universidad de Chile. She has been a consultant for the World Bank and USAID.

REFIK ERZAN is a senior economist in the International Trade Division at the World Bank. He previously worked at the U.N. Conference on Trade and Development and the Institute for International Economic Studies at the University of Stockholm. He has consulted for the Swedish Export Credit Corporation, the U.N. Industrial Development Organization, and the International Labor Office. He has written extensively on North-South trade issues.

ALICIA FROHMANN is a researcher on international relations at the Latin American Faculty of Social Sciences (FLACSO) in Chile. She is editor of the journal *Cono Sur* and her book *Puentes sobre la Turbulencia, La Concertación Política Latinoamericana en los 80* was published in 1990.

RICHARD G. LIPSEY is a professor of economics at Simon Fraser University and a fellow at the Canadian Institute for Advanced Research. He has held a chair in economics at the London School of Economics and was chairman of the Department of Economics and dean of the Faculty of Social Sciences at the new University of Essex in England. From 1970 to 1986, he was Sir Edward Peacock professor of economics at Queens University in Ontario. From 1983 to 1989 he was senior economic advisor for the C.D. Howe Institute. He has authored several textbooks in economics and over 80 articles in learned journals on various aspects of theoretical and applied economics. Among his monographs on economic policy is *Evaluating the Free Trade Deal: A Guided Tour Through the Canada-U.S. Agreement* (with Robert York). He is also a frequent commentator on economic policy issues in Canada.

EDUARDO LIZANO was Governor of the Central Bank of Costa Rica and President of the Central American Monetary Council from 1984 to 1990. He also serves as an advisor to many international organizations including the World Bank, the U.N. Development Programme, the Inter-American Development Bank, the U.N. Economic Commission for Latin America and the Caribbean (ECLAC), and the U.N. Conference on Trade and Development. He is a professor of economics at the Universidad de Costa Rica and is the author of numerous books, articles, and reports.

PETER MORICI is a professor of economics and Director of the Canadian-American Center at the University of Maine. He is also an adjunct senior fellow at the National Planning Association and the Iacocca Institute. He is the author of numerous articles and books, including *Trade Talks with Mexico: A Time for Realism* (National Planning Association, 1991); *Making Free Trade Work: The Canada-U.S. Agreement* (Council of Foreign Relations Press, 1990); *Reassessing American Competitiveness* (National Planning Association, 1988); and *A New Special Relationship: Free Trade and Canada-U.S. Relations* (Institute of Research on Public Policy and Carleton University, 1991).

ALBERTO PASCÓ-FONT is a researcher for the Development Analysis Group (GRADE) in Lima, Peru. He has been a lecturer at the Universidad del Pacífico since 1990.

SYLVIA SABORIO is a senior fellow at the Overseas Development Council and director of ODC's program on international trade. Before joining ODC, she held a number of senior positions in the Government of Costa Rica, most recently as Minister-Counselor for Finance at the Costa Rican Embassy in Washington and member of Costa Rica's debt negotiating team. From 1980 to 1986, she worked at the Department of International Economic and Social Affairs of the United Nations. She is associate professor (on leave) at the University of Costa Rica. She has written extensively on trade, development, and finance.

JOSÉ MANUEL SALAZAR-XIRINACHS is the program director of Economic Programs and chief economist at the Federation of Private Enterprise of Central America and Panama (FEDEPRICAP). From 1988 to 1990 he was Executive President of the Costa Rican Development Corporation (CODESA). He has been a consultant for the World Bank, CEPAL, ONUDI, and PNUD. In addition, he has been a professor of international economics at the Universidad de Costa Rica, Cambridge University, and the National University (Costa Rica).

CRAIG VANGRASSTEK serves as a consultant to Latin American regional institutions, governments, and United Nations agencies. He was the Bogota correspondent for *The Journal of Commerce* (New York), is a regular contributor to *El Financiero* (Mexico City), and edits the *Washington Trade Report*. His publications include *The Trade and Tariff Act of 1984: Trade Policy in the Reagan Administration* (with Stephen Lande, Lexington Books, 1986) and the revised edition of the *Scholars' Guide to Washington, D.C. For Latin American and Caribbean Studies* (Smithsonian Institution Press, 1992).

GUSTAVO VEGA is associate professor and academic coordinator of the Program on United States and Canadian Studies at the Center for International Studies at El Colegio de Mexico. He has been a visiting professor and fellow at the University of California at San Diego, Duke University, and Georgetown University, as well as the Institute for International Studies and Training in Japan. He has published extensively on Mexican-U.S. economic relations, Mexican economic foreign relations, and North American free trade issues. Among his most recent publications is *México ante el Libre Comercio con America del Norte* (El Colegio de Mexico y la Universidad Tecnológica de México, 1991).

DELISLE WORRELL has been the Deputy Governor at the Central Bank of Barbados since 1990 and has been with the Bank since 1973. He has held fellowships at the Institute for International Economics, Princeton University, and Yale University and has been a consultant for USAID, the World Bank, and the Inter-American Development Bank. He is the editor and author of several books and numerous articles, including *Economic Adjustment Policies for Small Nations: Theory and Experience in the English-Speaking Caribbean* (with Compton Bourne, Praeger Publishers, 1987).

ALEXANDER J. YEATS is a principal economist in the International Trade Division at the World Bank. From 1973 to 1987 he served as Senior Economic Affairs Officer at the U.N. Conference on Trade and Development. He has also worked for the Board of Governors of the Federal Reserve and The Ford Foundation. He has authored numerous books and has been published extensively in journals and magazines. Among his recent publications is *Quantitative Methods for Trade Barrier Analysis* (Macmillan Press, 1990).

POVERTY, NATURAL RESOURCES, AND PUBLIC POLICY IN CENTRAL AMERICA

Sheldon Annis and contributors

Rural poverty and environmental degradation are steadily worsening in Central America, undercutting the prospects for regional peace and economic recovery. This volume analyzes strategies that aim to reduce poverty and protect the environment in the region. It lays out a policy agenda for both Central Americans and donor nations.

Poverty, Natural Resources, and Public Policy in Central America presents the latest thinking on five key challenges in the region. These include the equity and ecological consequences of traditional and nontraditional agricultural export strategies; procedures for nongovernmental organizations and international agencies to promote sustainable development; the potential role of taxation for generating much-needed revenue and addressing the region's inequitable land distribution; the surge of cross-border environmental problems and their related political tensions; and finally the need to reconcile resource conservation with multiple human uses of tropical lands.

CONTENTS:

Sheldon Annis:	Overview
Oscar Arias and James D. Nations:	A Call for Central American Peace Parks
Stephen B. Cox:	Citizen Participation and the Reform of Development Assistance in Central America
Alvaro Umaña and Katrina Brandon:	Inventing Institutions for Conservation: Lessons from Costa Rica
Stuart K. Tucker:	Equity and the Environment in the Promotion of Nontraditional Agricultural Exports
John Strasma and Rafael Celis:	Land Taxation, the Poor, and Sustainable Development

Sheldon Annis is associate professor of geography and environmental studies at Boston University. He is the author of *God and Production in a Guatemalan Town* and co-editor of *Direct to the Poor: Grassroots Development in Latin America.*

U.S.-Third World Policy Perspectives, No. 17 Fall 1992, 280 pp.

ISBN: 1-56000-015-5 (cloth) $24.95
ISBN: 1-56000-577-7 (paper) $15.95

O | D | C

AFTER THE WARS:

Reconstruction in Afghanistan, Indochina, Central America, Southern Africa, and the Horn of Africa

Anthony Lake and contributors

After a decade or more of fighting and destruction in various regions of the world, new policies in Washington and Moscow as well as the fatigue on the ground are producing openings, at least, for peace. Negotiations are at different stages regarding Afghanistan, Indochina, Central America, Southern Africa, and the Horn of Africa—but all share new possibilities for peace.

This volume analyzes the prospects for post-war reconstruction and development in these regions, tackling the difficult quandaries they face individually and collectively: Among realistic potential alternatives, what kind of new political structures can best manage post-war reconstruction/development? Which economic policies would be most effective in maintaining peace and political coalitions? Should the focus be on the reconstruction of pre-war economic life or on creating new patterns of development? What are the prospects for democracy and human rights?

The authors thus consider the relationship of economic planning and likely political realities: For example, might diplomats seeking to stitch together a fragile coalition to end the fighting also be creating a government that cannot make the hard economic choices necessary for sustained peace? Might economists calling for post-war economic programs that are theoretically sound but politically unsustainable threaten a tenuous peace?

CONTENTS:

Anthony Lake:	Overview: After the Wars—What *Kind* of Peace?
Selig S. Harrison:	Afghanistan
Nayan Chanda:	Indochina
Benjamin L. Crosby:	Central America
Mark C. Chona and Jeffrey I. Herbst:	Southern Africa
Carol J. Lancaster:	The Horn of Africa

Anthony Lake is Five College Professor of International Relations at Mount Holyoke College. He was Director of Policy Planning from 1977 to 1981 at the U.S. Department of State, and before that a member of the National Security Council staff. He has also been director of the International Voluntary Services and of various projects at the Carnegie Endowment for International Peace and The Ford Foundation. Between 1963 and 1965, he served on the U.S. embassy staff in Hue and Saigon, Vietnam. His most recent book is *Samoza Falling*.

U.S.-Third World Policy Perspectives, No. 16 1990, 224 pp.

ISBN: 0-88738-880-9 (paper) $15.95

ISBN: 0-88738-392-0 (cloth) $24.95

O | D | C

Overseas Development Council

SPECIAL PUBLICATIONS SUBSCRIPTION OFFER

U.S.-Third World Policy Perspectives

Policy Essays • Policy Focus

As a subscriber to the ODC's three publications series, you will have access to an invaluable source of independent analyses of U.S.-Third World issues—economic, political, and social—at a savings of 30 percent off the regular price.

■ Brief and easy-to-read, each **Policy Focus** briefing paper provides background information and anaylsis on a current topic on the policy agenda. In 1992, 6-8 papers will cover aspects of U.S. trade, aid, finance, and security policy toward the developing countries.

■ **Policy Essays** explore critical issues on the U.S.-Third World agenda in 60-80 succinct pages, offering concrete recommendations for action. In 1992, a special five-part "conditionality series" will explore the potential utility and the limits of attaching conditions to aid, trade, and technology transfers to encourage sustained changes in certain policies and behavior of other governments. A separate essay explores the North-South environmental strategies, costs, and bargains to be raised at the U.N. Conference on Environment and Development.

■ **U.S.-Third World Policy Perspectives,** ODC's policy book series, brings a wide range of expertise to bear on current issues facing American policymakers. Each volume presents creative new policy options or insights into the implications of existing policy. *Natural Resources, and Public Policy in Central America* will be released in late 1992.

SUBSCRIPTION OPTIONS

Special Publications Subscription Offer*	$65.00
(All U.S.-Third World Policy Perspectives (1), Policy Essays (5-6), and Policy Focus briefing papers (8-10) issued in 1992.)	
1992 Policy Focus Subscription Offer*	$20.00
(Foreign)	$19.00
Individual Titles	
U.S.-Third World Policy Perspectives	$15.95
Policy Essay	$9.95

* Subscribers will receive all 1992 publications issued to date upon receipt of payment; other publications will be sent upon release. Book-rate postage is included in price.

All orders require prepayment. For individual titles, add $1.00 per item for shipping and handling. Please send check or money order to:

Publication Orders
Overseas Development Council
1875 Connecticut Avenue, NW
Suite 1012
Washington, DC 20009

O | D | C

ECONOMIC REFORM IN THREE GIANTS:

U.S. Foreign Policy and the USSR, China, and India

Richard E. Feinberg, John Echeverri-Gent, Friedemann Müller, and contributors

Three of the largest and strategically most important nations in the world—the Soviet Union, China, and India—are currently in the throes of historic change. The reforms of the giants are transforming global economic and geopolitical relations. The United States must reexamine central tenents of its foreign policy if it is to seize the opportunities presented by these changes.

This pathbreaking study analyzes economic reform in the giants and its implications for U.S. foreign policy. Each of the giants is opening up its economy to foreign trade and investment. What consequences will this new outward orientation have for international trade, and how should U.S. policy respond to these developments? Each giant is attempting to catch up to global technological frontiers by absorbing foreign technologies; in what areas might cooperation enhance American interests, and in what areas must the U.S. protect its competitive and strategic assets? What role can key international economic institutions like the GATT, the IMF, and the World Bank play to help integrate the giants into the international economy?

CONTENTS:

Richard E. Feinberg, John Echeverri-Gent, and Friedemann Müller:	Overview: Economic Reform in the Giants and U.S. Policy
Friedemann Müller:	Economic Reform in the USSR
Rensselaer W. Lee III:	Economic Reform in China
John Echeverri-Gent:	Economic Regorm in India
John Echeverri-Gent, Friedemann Müller, and Rensselaer W. Lee III:	The Politics of Economic Reform in the Giants
Richard P. Suttmeier:	Technology Transfer to the Giants: Opportunities and Challenges
Elena Borisova Arefieva:	The Geopolitical Consequences of Reform

Richard E. Feinberg is vice president of the Overseas Development Council and co-editor of the U.S.-Third World Policy Perspectives series. From 1977 to 1979, Feinberg was Latin American specialist on the policy planning staff of the U.S. Department of State.

John Echeverri-Gent is a visiting fellow at the Overseas Development Council and an assistant professor at the University of Virginia. His publications are in the fields of comparative public policy and the political economy of the development of India.

Friedemann Müller is a visiting fellow at the Overseas Development Council and a senior research associate at Stiftung Wissenschaft und Politik, Ebenhausen, West Germany. His publications on the Soviet and Eastern European economies have focused on economic reform, energy policy, and East-West trade.

U.S.-Third World Policy Perspectives, No. 14 1990, 256 pp.

ISBN: 0-88738-316-5 (cloth) $24.95

ISBN: 0-88738-820-5 (paper) $15.95

O | D | C

PULLING TOGETHER:

The International Monetary Fund in a Multipolar World

Catherine Gwin, Richard E. Feinberg, and contributors

Side-stepped by the developed countries, entangled in unsuccessful programs in many Latin American and African nations, whipsawed by heavy but inconsistent pressure from commercial banks and creditor countries, and without effective leadership from its major shareholders, the IMF is losing its bearings. It needs a sharp course correction and a strong mandate from its member countries to adjust its policies on each of five critical issues: global macroeconomic management, Third World debt, the resuscitation of development in the poorest countries, the integration of socialist nations into the global economy, and relations with its sister institution, the World Bank. In addition, the IMF needs to bolster its own bureaucratic, intellectual, and financial capacities.

In an economically interdependent but politically centrifugal world, a strong central institution is needed to help countries arrive at collective responses to complex global economic problems. But only if its member states are willing to delegate more authority to the IMF can it help pull together a multipolar world.

CONTENTS:

Richard E. Feinberg and Catherine Gwin:	Overview: Reforming the Fund
Jacques J. Polak:	Strengthening the Role of the IMF in the International Monetary System
Peter B. Kenen:	The Use of IMF Credit
Jeffrey D. Sachs:	Strengthening IMF Programs in Highly Indebted Countries
Guillermo Ortiz:	The IMF and the Debt Strategy
Louis M. Goreux:	The Fund and the Low-Income Countries

Catherine Gwin, guest co-editor of this volume, is currently the Special Program Advisor at the Rockefeller Foundation. In recent years, she has worked as a consultant on international economic and political affairs for The Ford Foundation, The Rockefeller Foundation, The Asia Society, and the United Nations.

Richard E. Feinberg was Executive Vice-President and Director of Studies of the Overseas Development Council and is currently President of the Inter-American Dialogue.

U.S.-Third World Policy Perspectives, No. 13 1989, 188 pp.

ISBN: 0-88738-313-0 (cloth) $24.95

ISBN: 0-88738-819-1 (paper) $15.95

O | D | C

FRAGILE COALITIONS:

The Politics of Economic Adjustment

Joan M. Nelson and contributors

The global economic crisis of the 1980s forced most developing nations into a simultaneous quest for short-run economic stabilization and longer-run structural reforms. Effective adjustment is at least as much a political as an economic challenge. But political dimensions of adjustment have been much less carefully analyzed than have the economic issues.

Governments in developing countries must balance pressures from external agencies seeking more rapid adjustment in return for financial support, and the demands of domestic political groups often opposing such reforms. How do internal pressures shape external bargaining? and conversely, how does external influence shape domestic political maneuvering? Growing emphasis on "adjustment with a human face" poses additional questions: Do increased equity and political acceptability go hand-in-hand? or do more pro-poor measures add to the political difficulties of adjustment? The capacity of the state itself to implement measures varies widely among nations. How can external agencies take such differences more fully into account? The hopeful trend toward democratic openings in many countries raises further, crucial issues: What special political risks and opportunities confront governments struggling simultaneously with adjustment and democratization? The contributors to this volume explore these issues and their policy implications for the United States and for the international organizations that seek to promote adjustment efforts.

CONTENTS:

Joan M. Nelson:	The Politics of Long-Haul Economic Adjustment
John Waterbury:	The Political Management of Economic Adjustment and Reform
Stephen Haggard and Robert R. Kaufman:	Economic Adjustment in New Democracies
Laurence Whitehead:	Democratization and Disinflation: A Comparative Approach
Joan M. Nelson:	The Politics of Pro-Poor Adjustment
Thomas M. Callaghy:	Toward State Capability and Embedded Liberalism in the Third World: Lessons for Adjustment
Miles Kahler:	International Financial Institutions and the Politics of Adjustment

Joan M. Nelson has been a visiting fellow at the Overseas Development Council since 1982; since mid-1986, she has directed a collegial research program on the politics of economic adjustment. She has been a consultant for the World Bank, USAID, and the IMF, as well as a staff member of USAID. She has taught at the Massachusetts Institute of Technology, the Johns Hopkins University School of Advanced International Studies, and Princeton University's Woodrow Wilson School.

0 | D | C

U.S.-Third World Policy Perspectives, No. 12 1989, 186 pp.

ISBN: 0-88738-283-5 (cloth) $24.95

ISBN: 0-88738-787-X (paper) $15.95

ENVIRONMENT AND THE POOR: Development Strategies For A Common Agenda

H. Jeffrey Leonard and contributors

Few aspects of development are as complex and urgent as the need to reconcile antipoverty and pro-environmental goals. Do both of these important goals—poverty alleviation and environmental sustainability—come in the same package? Or are there necessary trade-offs and must painful choices be made?

A basic premise of this volume is that environmental degradation and intractable poverty are often especially pronounced in particular ecological and social settings across the developing world. These twin crises of development and the environment can and must be addressed jointly. But they require differentiated strategies for the kinds of physical environments in which poor people live. This study explores these concerns in relation to irrigated areas, arid zones, moist tropical forests, hillside areas, urban centers, and unique ecological settings.

The overview chapter highlights recent efforts to advance land and natural resource management, and some of the real and perceived conflicts between alleviating poverty and protecting the environment in the design and implementation of developing policy. The chapters that follow offer economic investment and natural resource management options for reducing poverty and maintaining ecological balance for six different areas of the developing world.

CONTENTS:

H. Jeffrey Leonard:	Overview
Montague Yudelman:	Sustainable and Equitable Development in Irrigated Environments
J. Dirck Stryker:	Technology, Human Pressure, and Ecology in the Arid and Semi-Arid Tropics
John O. Browder:	Developmental Alternatives for Tropical Rain Forests
A. John De Boer:	Sustainable Approaches to Hillside Agricultural Development
Tim Campbell:	Urban Development in the Third World: Environmental Dilemmas and the Urban Poor
Alison Jolly:	The Madagascar Challange: Human Needs and Fragile Ecosystems

H. Jeffrey Leonard, guest editor of this volume, is the vice president of World Wildlife Fund and The Conservation Foundation and Director of the Fairfield Osborn Center for Economic Development.

O | D | C

U.S.-Third World Policy Perspectives, No. 11 1989, 256 pp.

ISBN: 0-88738-282-7 (cloth) $24.95

ISBN: 0-88738-786-1 (paper) $15.95